THE BOOK OF DAYS

For comments or questions about this book, visit our website:
The Lost Stories Channel, at loststorieschannel.com.

© 2024 by W. Kent Smith – All Rights Reserved
Published in the United States by
Lodestar Cinema Creations,
in association with Staten House
West Covina, California
Smith, W. Kent (1959-)

It should be noted that this book contains much of the same material from a larger work entitled *Tales of Forever: The Unfolding Drama of God's Hidden Hand in History*, published in 2016, and as such differs in that this version presents edited excerpts from Act One and Act Three.

Also, this is the companion text to *The Book of Tales: Stories That Confirm the 5,500-year Prophecy Given to Adam About the Coming of Christ*.

Front Cover and Title Page Painting: *The Expulsion of Adam and Eve from Paradise*, Benjamin West, 1791

Book Exterior and Interior Designed and Executed by W. Kent Smith

ISBN: 979-8-89379-515-8

Manufactured in the U.S.A.
May 2024

THE BOOK OF DAYS

*In Search of the 5,500-year Prophecy Given
to Adam About the Coming of Christ*

by

W. Kent Smith

in association with

Staten House

Books by W. Kent Smith

For Ted,

Best Friend and Dad

CONTENTS

A Case for The Book

I HAVE STUDIED in four seminaries and before that, a leading Christian college, yet never was I introduced to any of the material W. Kent Smith has brought forth here in *The Book of Days,* a work that sheds light on long-lost truths that the majority of modern Christians know nothing about. God has preserved many things concerning His purposes as well as His indelible fingerprints on history. This book sets out to tell the story of those purposes and of those fingerprints.

My initial interest in *The Book* was due to my research into a 5,500-year messianic prophecy that I became aware of while studying the Early Church and *The Septuagint Bible,* the Greek translation of *The Old Testament* used by 2nd Temple Judaism and the Early Church. Known as "the prophecy of the Great Five and a Half Days," this messianic prophecy is certainly the greatest promise that God ever gave to mankind. According to this prophecy, given to Adam and Eve when they were expelled from Eden, the Messiah would come to Earth to rescue humanity after 5,500 years.

In addition to my interest concerning this prophecy, I was struck by several questions about 2nd Temple Judaism: What motivated the rabbis in the late first and early second century when they "canonized" *The Hebrew Bible*? Why did *The Septuagint* version of *The Old Testament* have different books from the *Masoretic* Text? And why were so many previously accepted texts, such as *The First Book of Enoch,* completely ignored and excluded? I knew that earlier Jews had had a broader canon of Scripture than the one that the rabbis settled upon at Jamnia, but in many cases, I didn't realize how important these "excluded" books were to understanding so many of our best-known *Bible* stories. Kent's book picks up these themes and digs even deeper, with particular focus upon the 5,500-year prophecy.

According to the 5,500-year chronology of *The Septuagint,* the coming of Jesus perfectly fit the timing of this prophecy and was one of the reasons so many Jews came to believe He was the Messiah. At which time the rabbis proceeded to "tamper" with *The Hebrew Bible* at the end of the first century AD, rejecting *The Septuagint,* and then translating their "doctored" *Old Testament* into three new Greek versions for future Jewish use. Why? One of the main reasons was to obscure the 5,500-year prophecy in order to stop Jews from coming to Jesus as their Messiah.

The Book of Days traces several other ways that God supernaturally preserved the record of this prophetic word for humanity. But sadly, due to the ongoing influence of Rabbinic Talmudic Judaism and the unfortunate influence of the likes of Jerome, many Christians not only remain in the dark about this 5,500-year prophecy but also end up dismissing the best extant sources of evidence for its veracity. When one removes such blinders and trusts the testimony of Early Church writers like Justin Martyr and Tertullian, we see, as *The Book of Days* reveals, that God Himself protected arguably the most significant messianic prophecy of all time. You may not agree with all of the author's conclusions, but I assure you that your "traditions" will be challenged if you allow the evidence he presents to inspire you and your faith in the God of *The Bible*.

As I told the author when we met, I believe that new evidence is forthcoming that will shed even more light on these issues and convince countless people that the things he contends are in fact true. Of course, only time will tell. But, until then, read *The Book of Days* for yourself, and your fascination with God will grow, as will your trust in His promises.

For such a time as this...

Rev. David J. Hess
Rock OC Church
Dana Point, California

A thousand years in Your sight, Lord, are like a day that has just gone by, or like a watch in the night.

Psalm 90:4

But of this one thing don't be ignorant, my beloved, that one day with the Lord is as a thousand years, and a thousand years as one day.

Second Peter 3:8

God said to Adam, "When I will send the Word Who created you, against Whom you have transgressed, the Word will save you when the five and a half days are fulfilled." But when Adam heard about the Great Five and a Half Days, he thought there'd only be five and a half days until the end of the world. Then God explained to him, that after 5,500 years One would come to rescue him and his descendants.

The First Book of Adam and Eve 3:1-6

BOOK ONE

*The important fact is ... that for 700 years after
the commencement of the Christian Era ... the
average estimation of the period from Adam to
Christ was some 5,500 years.*

Nathan Rouse, *A Dissertation on Sacred Chronology*

In Our Darkest Hour

IT IS SAID *The Bible* contains more than three thousand promises that God has made to humanity. Many are conditional and require a response from the recipients before God keeps those promises, while many are kept unconditionally, regardless of whether the recipients cooperate in their fulfillment.

This is the story of one of those promises that God kept unconditionally, a promise made to Adam and his descendants that was to be the key to unlocking every other promise God would ever make to humanity. As it turns out, it is also a promise of God that involves some of the most overlooked aspects of biblical history. Why?

Because unbeknownst to most modern-day Christians in the West, the men who recorded the events surrounding this fulfilled promise were quoting from the Greek translation of *The Old Testament* called *The Septuagint*. As a result, their understanding of biblical history was far different from ours today.

Case in point, the writers of *The New Testament* believed that the time from Adam to Christ represented a 5,500-year timeline, as opposed to the one inspired by the *King James* Version of *The Bible*, which depicts this time period as being some 4,000 years. Why does that matter?

It matters because this lesser-known timeline of 5,500 years, found in *The Septuagint*, does everything to confirm God's control over history and faithfulness to His word while the traditional 4,000-year time frame does nothing but obscure and nullify another vitally important aspect concerning the most pivotal promise ever made and kept by God in history.

It is the story of this forgotten chapter of biblical history, then, that this work, *The Book of Days*, will seek to uncover and illuminate. In the telling of this tale of God's primordial promise, known as the prophecy of the Great Five and a Half Days, the reader will rediscover a long-lost truth regarding the Lord's plan to send humanity a Savior, when in our darkest hour, God provided the most clear-cut proof of His control and faithfulness the world would ever know.

About Time

Timing is Everything

ONE OF THE MOST overlooked aspects of *The Bible* is how certain promises of God are not just fired off like so much buckshot — promises here and promises there — and maybe they are fulfilled, and maybe they are not. Instead, some promises can be evaluated in time-specific terms, in order to determine whether or not they were fulfilled.

For example, the prophet Daniel was given a prophecy of the Coming of Christ that was a very specific promise involving time, as in the well-known Seventy Weeks of Daniel, where the Messiah would come after sixty-nine weeks of "years," and then He would be "cut off." As such, we can determine that from the time that the Persian king, Cyrus, ordered the rebuilding of the Temple of Jerusalem, to the time of Christ being crucified, was four hundred and eighty-three years.[1]

To those who look to the facts of history, then, the Advent of Christ was never something that God intended to catch humanity by surprise but, rather, was to be a clearly defined historical event that could be anticipated with a great deal of certainty.

Not Yet His Time

THEN, THERE ARE other biblical events that are less well known to contain a time-specific component, but upon closer examination, the importance of the element of time is unmistakable. In this case, we are talking about the Feast Days of Israel, or, more specifically, the feasts of Passover, Unleavened Bread, and First Fruits. At first glance, these feast days simply commemorate pivotal events in the emancipation of the Israelite nation from the bondage of Egypt. Concerning these festivals, *The Bible* tells us: "Speak to the children of Israel, and say to them, 'The Feasts of the Lord, which you shall proclaim as holy convocations — these are My appointed times.'"[2]

As for how these feast days function as "appointed times" of the Lord, most biblical scholars agree that not until the death and resurrection of Jesus were we finally able to grasp the true meaning and purpose of these feasts, as conveyed by the following facts of history.

Once, when Jesus was urged by His brothers to go to Jerusalem to confront the Pharisees, in a showdown He knew would cost Him His life, He

---

1 *Daniel* 9:25-26
2 *Leviticus* 23:2

refused to go, telling them, "Although your time is always at hand, My time hasn't come yet."[3] We see the same thing in the events of the wedding of Cana, when Mary told Jesus that they had run out of wine, which set the stage for His first miracle in turning water into wine. Again, Jesus' cryptic response alluded to the unique nature of divine timing: "Woman, why do you involve Me? My hour hasn't yet come."[4] Naturally, statements like this in *The Bible* are typically glossed over because their true meaning is not made obvious when reading them apart from their prophetic context. However, when we closely examine the Feast Days of the Lord, an often-overlooked aspect of these festivals begins to make itself known. Just like Daniel's prophecy of "weeks," these "days" of the Lord contain a time-specific element that is critical to understanding why God instituted them in the first place.

The first thing to take note of is that the Passover always takes place on the 14th day of the first month on the Hebrew calendar, followed the next day by the Feast of Unleavened Bread. To students of prophecy, the feasts of Passover and Unleavened Bread were not only events that God's people could look back to in commemoration of their emancipation from slavery in Egypt by the hand of Moses, but they also foreshadowed future events that spoke of humanity's emancipation from sin through the work of Jesus Christ. As such, the Passover lamb anticipated Jesus as the ultimate sacrifice for the sins of all mankind; the unleavened bread spoke of Jesus as the sinless One given for the sustenance of all humanity.

In the Fullness of Time

AS FOR THE time-specific element of these feast days—these appointed times of the Lord—consider this. While Passover can occur on any day of the week and Unleavened Bread starts on the following day, the Feast of First Fruits always begins on the first day of the following week. That means that the time from the beginning of Unleavened Bread, to that of First Fruits, varies from year to year. Depending on when Passover begins, then, the time from Unleavened Bread to First Fruits may last one day, two days, three days, or more. Why is that important?

To answer that, let us return our attention to that fateful day when Jesus' brothers tried to get Him to go to Jerusalem, but Jesus refused to go because it was not His time yet. Because had Jesus obliged His brothers and gone to Jerusalem that year, or had He gone the year after next, for that matter, He could not have fulfilled the meaning of the Feast of Unleavened Bread. Why? Because as it turns out, the year that Jesus steadfastly set His

---

3 *John* 7:6
4 Ibid. 2:1-4

face to go to Jerusalem — to die as the true Lamb of God — the time from the beginning of the Feast of Unleavened Bread, to that of First Fruits just happened to be three days and three nights. Thus, had Jesus not died the year that He did, these feast days would have failed to convey their ultimate meaning, which God intended to demonstrate to an onlooking world. But Jesus did die, "in the fullness of time,"[5] just as the Scriptures tell us concerning the Advent of Christ. That means that not only did His death occur as the Pascal lambs were being slain, but His sinless body also lay hidden in the tomb for the same three-day period that Jesus predicted the Son of Man would remain in the heart of the Earth.[6]

And so, to anyone who looks to this marvelous correspondence between events, one cannot fail to recognize that when Jesus rose from the grave in the exact year that He did — not the year before, and not the year after — He perfectly illustrated the true meaning of both the Feast of Unleavened Bread and the Feast of First Fruits. As such, not only did Christ rise as the first fruits of the dead after three days and three nights, but we, too, can look to that first resurrection as proof of God's promise that He will someday raise each and every one of us to newness of life.

A Long-Lost Chapter

THAT SAID, there is another time-specific promise of God, which is even more misunderstood than the preceding examples. That is because, unlike those promises found in the traditional *Bible*, this promise concerns a long-lost chapter of biblical history, one in which God made a primordial promise to Adam and Eve. And just like those promises concerning Daniel's Seventy Weeks and the Feast Days of the Lord, this little-known promise has everything to do with time.

In 1882, a British biblical scholar and linguist of Oriental languages, by the name of S.C. Malan, translated an ancient text and so gave the West its first glimpse of *The First Book of Adam and Eve*. In it we find what is certainly the first promise ever uttered by God, in which He told our first parents that after *five and a half* days — or 5,500 years, actually — He would send One Who would come in the flesh to rescue Adam and his descendants. Now, to those who are familiar with *The King James Bible*, this promise clearly recalls the most foundational promise in *Genesis*, where it is said a descendant of Eve would one day destroy the works of the devil and restore all creation.

Of course many reading this are understandably tempted to dismiss a book like *First Adam and Eve* as a complete fraud. But before you do, because you insist it is not in our modern version of *The Bible*, first consider this. The

---

5 *Galatians* 4:4
6 *Matthew* 12:40

promise in question may not be found word-for-word in the *King James* Version of *The Bible*, but there is undeniable evidence for it in *The Bible* quoted by the authors of *The New Testament*.

That is right; to those who look to the facts of biblical history, evidence for this promise is in *The Septuagint Bible*, which all scholars will tell you is the Greek Version of *The Old Testament*. Strange as it might seem to most Christians in today's Protestant-dominated world, *The Septuagint* actually contains a 5,500-year genealogy from Adam to Christ, which clearly echoes the Great Five and a Half Day prophecy found in *The First Book of Adam and Eve*.

How tragic, then, that when *First Adam and Eve* should have been held in supreme reverence because of this special correspondence between it and *The Septuagint*, this marvelous book was relegated to the dustbin of apocryphal history. That is, it was until more and more scholars, in the wake of the discovery of *The Dead Sea Scrolls*, began to connect it with other sacred texts like *The First Book of Enoch*, eventually paving the way to restoring this ancient prophecy of "days" to its rightful place in biblical history.

Some Foreword Thinking

Stranger than Fiction

THIS IS A TALE beyond imagination yet true, a tale stranger than any fiction ever conceived by the mind of mankind, because to tell the ultimate tale of God's faithfulness to humanity, one must weave together all the elements of the greatest tales ever told.

An ancient prophecy, a promise of "days," which precisely foretold the Advent of Christ, given to the primordial parents of our race and recorded in the oldest story contained in the biblical record—a prophecy that bears a striking similarity to the messianic chronology found in *The Septuagint Bible*, the book most often quoted by the writers of *The New Testament*. But as so often happens, this most ancient of all stories, and a knowledge of the prophecy it contained, eventually fell out of favor in the wake of certain political movements and was swept away, not to be seen again in the West for over a thousand years.

One man, set apart from all others, who was said to have talked with God, face to face, having a conversation that took place not in any earthly realm but at the very pinnacle of Heaven itself—a conversation written in a book for all humanity to read. Yet because of its startling and enigmatic message, it was deemed unsuitable for viewing by the common people, so sometime in the latter half of the fourth century of the Christian Era, it was banned and afterward thought lost by most of the world for more than a millennium.

And an array of sacred artifacts, each one a talisman said to emanate an uncanny power to affect the hearts and minds of those who encountered them. Although every one of these objects appear insignificant at first glance, according to legend, they are all more potent than any man-made weapon— The Ark of the Covenant, The Spear of Destiny, and The Shroud of Turin. The other object amongst this array, however, is not so much an artifact as it is a colossus of a structure—The Great Pyramid of Giza.

All these elements, then—a man and his heavenly conversation, a promise of "days," an ark, a spear, a shroud, a pyramid, and a book, that is to say, everything needed to demonstrate a startling proof of God's faithfulness— have for the first time been forged into a single storyline, to tell the story of *The Book of Days: In Search of the 5,500-year Prophecy Given to Adam About the Coming of Christ*.

From Out of Nowhere

BUT BEFORE I begin, one would do well to keep several important points in mind. Rest assured, although readers of this work will find themselves on a firm foundation of biblical truth, the process of investigating these origins will undoubtedly challenge their traditional view of *The Bible* as it is known today in the West. This is because a fundamental requirement in penetrating the veil that hides the truth concerning such matters is that one must first be willing to venture into territory familiar only to those who have encountered such works as *The Septuagint Bible,* one of the earliest known vernacular translations of *The Old Testament*—one of several books that, as we will soon discover, have all, at various times throughout their history, fallen in and out of favor.

This leads us, then, to important point number one: Throughout the entire course of history, the process of choosing which books were to be considered "acceptable" has been a veritable roller coaster of political correctness. As much as we would like to believe otherwise, the harsh reality is that the primary factor in deeming certain books as either inspired or heretical has been based not so much on matters of personal conscience as it has been on which political system was in power at a particular time and place. Still, this does not mean that these decision makers have always been able to enforce their political will in all places and at all times. More importantly, when it comes to the history of the formation of the Biblical Canon, what we are dealing with is, and always will be, an international struggle of global proportions. Ever since the Great Schism of the eleventh century, the Orthodox Church has occupied the East, while the Catholic and Protestant branches of Christianity have occupied the West. And because of this, the fact that some books are said to have been rejected and excised actually means that they were—contrary to popular opinion—not so much lost as they were marginalized and forgotten by a specific geographical segment of Christendom.[7] This fact, in turn, has several consequences that are critical to this present-day study, both of which have occurred as a result of the point of view of this work, which happens to be a Western Protestant one.

Important point number two that emerges from this admittedly Western view is that when we speak—as we often will in this work—about lost books, lost chronologies, and lost truths of *The Bible,* keep in mind that we are not implying that these things have ever been lost in the strictest sense of that word. What we are really saying is that they simply lost their foothold in the West, while remaining part of the orthodoxy in the East; or in some cases, what fell out of favor in the Protestant West held fast in the Catholic

---

7 *The Many Faces of Christ: The Thousand-Year Story of the Survival and Influence of the Lost Gospels,* Philip Jenkins, pp. 6-7

West. This more than anything else accounts for the apparently sensational aspect of the so-called "discovery" of manuscripts, all which had generally been thought to be lost forever.

It is also critical to realize—important point number three—that this sort of thing is not at all unusual in terms of the overall landscape of biblical history. The same idea undergirds our understanding of the so-called Lost Tribes of Israel. Although the northern kingdom of ancient Israel was punished and scattered throughout the nations, they were never truly lost in the sense of their having been totally annihilated; rather, they were driven "underground," so to speak. In fact, the prophet Hosea clearly spoke about this very thing, in that the ten tribes to the north were to be punished for their idolatrous ways but only for a divinely appointed period of time, after which they were to reappear upon the stage of world history, as if from out of nowhere.

This brings us to important point number four. I am one who firmly believes that this same phenomenon is at work when we as a Western people, dominated by a Protestant view of the Biblical Canon, are now the recipients of lost books that have all been—according to God's set time—rediscovered and restored to the West after centuries of having been deprived of their contents. And rather than scoff at such a possibility, one might humbly reconsider it in light of the facts that come forth from an in-depth look at these various manuscripts, many of which will prove to be more than capable of standing side by side with the traditional books of Scripture, as we will shortly demonstrate.

And finally, for important point number five. Unlike those who profess to believe in God's ability to protect His written revelation but reject the great antiquity alleged by the authors of that record, this writer believes that when *The Bible* declares that men like Enoch, the scribe—that is, *the writer*—received a message from God, which Enoch conveyed in books, that declaration should be accepted. Furthermore, if the biblical record states that these books were written prior to the Great Flood, then I, for one, have no problem believing that other books were also written many centuries before typical scholarship has been willing to admit. After all, is it not written: In the beginning was the Word, and through the same Word, the entire Universe was created?[8] How absurd, then, to relinquish the inevitable conclusion that if the Word of God communicated His truth to not only Enoch but also Adam before him that the end result of those communications would not have produced some form of written record.

---

8 *John* 1:1-3

The Unfolding Drama

IN 1650, ARCHBISHOP James Ussher published one of the most influential biblical chronologies ever set forth as the unassailable word of God. By using texts in *The Book of Genesis*, together with other passages from Scripture, Ussher calculated that the world was created on the 23rd day of October, in the year 4,004 B.C. To this day, most Christians would never think to dispute such a finding, and if ever challenged would defend this "fact" to the death, not knowing why, other than that it had been included in so many copies of their *Bible*. But sadly, as well-intentioned as these defenders of the faith are, they may, upon further review of all things scriptural, actually be defending a proverbial Trojan horse.

Nearly lost to history is the knowledge that long before Ussher offered his chronology as the "gospel truth," there was already another chronological system that had been universally accepted for the first fifteen centuries of Christendom. This chronology, derived from *The Septuagint Bible*, adhered to a 5,500-year period from the Fall of Adam to the Advent of Christ. And though it had withstood the test of time for so many centuries, it fell victim to one of the most ironic twists in history and was replaced by a more politically correct translation, which influenced all subsequent versions of *The English Bible* as we know it today. So, with *The Septuagint* having been officially relegated to the dustbin of apocryphal literature, the way was unwittingly paved for Ussher's "new and improved" chronology—one that most biblical scholars will admit is at odds with every known historical account, both Jewish and Christian.

Of course *The Septuagint* was not the first book to have suffered the wrath of ecclesiastical scorn. Included in the halls of the excised were such legendary texts as those ascribed to Enoch, the man who famously walked and talked with God. And though one can assume the truths conveyed in that conversation might be of great interest, this natural human curiosity was summarily short-circuited when religious authorities, declaring these books unsuitable for common folk, banned them. Such are the perpetual tug of wars—theologically-speaking—that have plagued the entire history of *The Bible* so that what was once perfectly acceptable is almost overnight deemed an object of holy revulsion. As a result, many of the world's most revered manuscripts, rejected and suppressed, have sadly been lost to history forever ... or so it would seem.

It is to the tumultuous story of these lost books, lost chronologies, and lost truths, then, that this work will turn in an effort to shed new light on what I believe to be the ultimate tale of God's intention toward humanity. To do so, this book—unlike any other that deals with such subjects as scriptural interpretation, biblical chronology, and religious artifacts—will not only offer evidence from history but also from the very books that have, down through the ages, generated so much derision and controversy. In the process, even the layperson will be able to judge for themselves what has, for so very long, been the exclusive domain of the elite and the scholar, the esoteric and the clandestine.

Consequently, readers will find themselves on an unprecedented journey in which the traditional notions concerning the so-called *Lost Books of The Bible* are turned upside down. What appears to be one of the great failures of history will, within the pages of this book, be portrayed not as having occurred in spite of God's best efforts to reveal His truth but as a direct result of His desire to hide it. No doubt Solomon had this in mind when he uttered his proverb: "God in His greatness has concealed many things, while kings have the honor of discovering them."[9] Simply put, in order to fully apprehend the manifold truths of Scripture — particularly as they pertain to the prophecy of the Great Five and a Half Days — one must come to grips with a peculiar paradox: In the course of the unfolding drama of history, God is far less concerned with how obvious He has made the truth than with how artfully He has hidden it in plain sight.

The Disclaimer

I WOULD NOW like to insert a disclaimer before I begin, which I feel is necessary because of the sensitive areas of knowledge into which a work like this delves. In order to present the material in its proper light, one must go into detail concerning the history of such controversial subjects as scriptural interpretation, biblical chronology, and religious artifacts, subjects that are still fraught by impassioned debates to this very day. As a result of this historical presentation, one inevitably runs the risk of stepping on numerous theological "toes," as it were.

Without a doubt, the following story involves just as many villains as it does heroes, and consequently, like all great stories, its villainous elements are often more intriguing — and therefore more interesting — than its heroic ones. Due to this ironic nature of storytelling, it is all too tempting to swing the sword of blame and accusation, especially when it comes to a story like this one that involves so many negative forces and characters. In order to tell the whole truth about the age-old controversy of why certain biblical books, chronologies, or truths were either sanctioned or banned, the story could never be written without having to insist that someone was "at fault" for having made a decision that was deemed unwarranted by some political or religious entity. As contemplative, questioning creatures, we simply cannot avoid this very real dilemma. For every controversial issue in life, one can

---

9 *Proverbs* 25:2

only confront the pros and cons of a given subject, and therefore, it is only natural to land on one side of the fence or the other.

My real concern, however, with this completely normal response, is the lengths to which some people will go to prove their point. By that I mean, if history teaches us anything about the debates that mankind is inevitably drawn into—especially when it comes to theological issues encountered in books like this—the quest for truth sometimes becomes so important that the participants lose sight of their original goals. In such a case, truth is no longer important, and the humble realization that we are all mere humans, reaching to know the unknowable, is swept aside. What began as a holy cause soon escalates into a holy war. Winning the argument, then, becomes the only goal, because it is often easier to appear the winner of the debate, while at the same time never coming one iota closer to the truth, which was the actual purpose for engaging in the quest in the first place.

As a matter of fact, this seems to me to be at the heart of every war that is waged in the name of "religion," or "truth," or "God," or whatever one chooses to call it, and it is this kind of thing that, above all else, I am committed to renouncing with every ounce of my being. Therefore, the contents of this work should never be construed as an effort on my part to deride any particular doctrine of faith, which I believe—as I am sure every true American believes—is a matter of strictest conscience, and as such is off-limits to criticism by anyone.

This, then, is the essence of my disclaimer. To anyone who reads the present volume, please keep in mind that I bear no ill will toward any person or group of persons, even while trying my best to present what I believe to be the unbiased facts that are central to this story. Just because certain individuals made decisions—as a result of their heartfelt convictions—that certain books should be excised from the Canon of Scripture and therefore suppressed from public circulation, does not mean that I hold those people to be evil or deluded. No one but God, I believe, is qualified to make such a judgment. Similarly, I feel no animosity or hatred toward any religion or denomination just because I point out from history that those who excised certain books belonged to a specific religious group.

And the reason I feel this is never an option is because of my own view on the nature of truth as I perceive it to be revealed in *The Bible* and by the One Who is the final arbitrator of the truth contained in it. To the best of my knowledge, I have never known the Jesus that I see in Scripture to have ever condemned an individual *per se*. What I do see Him condemning are the attitudes and beliefs of certain ones that have their origin in what can best be described as institutionally-oriented, or, to put it another way, system-oriented mindsets. In other words, Jesus seems less concerned with condemning individual sinners and more interested in attacking the root source of

what keeps those people spiritually, emotionally, and intellectually imprisoned by the state of sin into which all humans are naturally born. Simply
put, Jesus does not condemn people; He condemns institutions, or systems.

Now, before you insist that what I have just proposed is too absurd
to believe, and you do so based on the idea that only people and not institutions or systems can go to Heaven or Hell, please keep the following in
mind. There is an old adage, attributed to one Lord Acton, which states:
Power corrupts, and absolute power corrupts absolutely. Of this very thing
Abraham Lincoln spoke when he wisely observed: "Nearly all men can
stand adversity, but if you want to test a man's character give him power."
If there is any truth to such statements, then what follows is also likely to
be true: No individual in the history of mankind, that I know of, has ever
been corrupted by power while living alone on a desert island. It is therefore
axiomatic that the power that both Acton and Lincoln were referring to is
power that can only be exerted by an individual who exists within the matrix of an institution or system, whether it is political, economic, or religious
in nature.

Now, mind you, I am not trying to say that individual humans are sinless just because they withdraw from the world and live on a desert island;
that, sadly, is the fallacy of living the life of a hermit. What I am saying,
though, is what any social psychologist will tell you. The typical individual
left to his or her own devices is benign, but when you thrust that same individual into a decidedly hostile group, even if the sentiments and proclivities of that group are very different from that of the individual, a person
will eventually succumb to the herd mentality and align themselves with
the attitudes and beliefs of that group. Therein lies the logic of Jesus not
condemning people so much as the system or institution that indoctrinates
people with the attitudes or beliefs that He does condemn.

To see how all of this applies to the teachings of Scripture one need only
turn to the words and actions of Jesus Himself. When the Pharisees came
to Him demanding a sign to prove that He was the Messiah, Jesus flatly
informed them: "An evil and adulterous generation insists on seeking signs,
but none will be given to it except the sign of Jonah."[10] First, notice how
Jesus did not point an accusing finger at any of those individuals who were
standing right in front of Him. Was it because He was too timid to accuse
any single individual from within the group? Was He unsure of exactly who
were the guilty ones among the demanding crowd? I hardly think so. What
we have is simply a clear-cut example of what I am trying to point out. Jesus was less concerned about condemning individuals and more concerned
with warning them about the kinds of attitudes and beliefs that they should
avoid — attitudes and beliefs that only come as a result of associating with

---

10 *Matthew* 12:38-39

the institutions and systems that are united by like-minded individuals.

This becomes all the more evident when one takes the time to notice that Jesus did not say that a sign would be withheld from "them," that is, those "individuals" who made up the group that was addressing Him. What He did say was that a sign would be withheld from "it," that is, the "generation" that was demanding a sign from Him, which constitutes the world system, or present order. The same idea is expressed when Jesus spoke concerning those who believed in Him. "If you were of the world, the world would love you, but because you're not, the world hates you."[11] The Greek word being used here for "world" is *kosmos*, the word we transliterate directly into English as *cosmos*, a word that literally means "something ordered," as in an "ordered system." So what we see here is Jesus choosing to condemn a world system that is alien to His way of thinking, as opposed to targeting the individuals who had fallen victim to that system by virtue of their simply being born into it.

Next, we see that when Jesus came to the Temple at Jerusalem, He famously drove out those who were buying and selling there, even going so far as to overturn the tables of the moneychangers. "It is written," He bellowed, "My house will be called a house of prayer, but you've turned it into a den of thieves!"[12] What does this mean in the context of what I am trying to articulate by way of this disclaimer? Was Jesus condemning the people for the way they were presenting their offerings to God? Was He angry at the act of their buying and selling, as if one could actually buy or sell the favor of God with mere money? If so, then who did Jesus hold to be of greater guilt? Those who bought? Or those who sold? But, as usual, such a surface-oriented interpretation would miss the point entirely. Certainly, it was no more in the nature of Jesus to be angry with those buying or selling, any more than a doctor is angry with a patient for being sick. Undoubtedly, what disgusted Him was the fact that what had begun as a God-given impulse, that is, the desire to offer sacrifice to the Lord, had over time succumbed to the humanly-inspired forces that had crept in and undermined the original divinely-instituted purpose of giving the burnt offering. In other words, He was angry because what had begun as a sublime expression of a single heart offered to God had devolved as a result of the machinations of an institutionally-inspired system.

This same process can be seen repeatedly down through the corridors of history, like "*déjà vu* all over again," as it were. The Lord of the Harvest calls individual men and women of faith, who, in turn, teach their children the ways of God. In time, however, and always over the span of several genera-

---

11 *John* 15:19
12 *Matthew* 21:12-13

tions, the ways of God are slowly but surely subverted, and in their place a mere shell of their original intention is all that remains. In the end, the faith of "the one" has become the dogma of "the institution," which then creates a situation where God, as He does in every age, seeks the next individual who will heed the call in order to initiate the process all over again.

Therefore, when I attempt to convey the history of who decided which books should be excised from the Canon of Scripture, and in doing so, I quote certain ones who claim that "this person" belonging to "that religious group" made those decisions, remember I prefer to take to higher ground. And remember I, too, am less concerned by the actions of individuals and more interested in the process of institutionalization, which is constantly at work to undermine the original greatness of said person or group. In this, everyone is equally guilty or innocent, however the case may be, whether they are called Sethites, Semites, Hebrews, Israelites, Jews, Pharisees, Christians, Catholics, Protestants, Lutherans, Episcopalians, Methodists, Baptists, Presbyterians, Fundamentalists, *et al.*

In short, all these designations, in my view, are just like everything else in this God-ordained Universe of ours, which is to say, they are merely representative of both sides of the same coin. They are good when they willingly cooperate with the good as proscribed by the dictates of the One Who inspired their creation, and they are bad when they willingly succumb to the forces that forever seek to subvert the dictates of that same One. And because of this ironic nature of the human dilemma, I, for one, choose not to assign guilt or condemnation in regard to any of their particular actions; I only seek to report, impartially and with malice toward none.

Roll Call of the Intrepid

THE LAST THING I have to do before beginning is to express my gratitude to the intrepid pioneers I cite in this work. Just in case anyone thinks that I have concocted the following storyline entirely on my own, I would like to offer this list of discoverers, translators, and scholars whose monumental contributions have provided the biblical texts that form its backbone. For a more in-depth look at their lives and accomplishments, please refer to the *Selected Biographies* section in *The Credits*.

Among the discoverers who have restored to the world such an unexpected array of lost manuscripts, there are: Johann Grynaeus (1540-1617), a Swiss Protestant divine, professor of *The New Testament*, and collector of biblical manuscripts; Giuseppe Assemani (1687-1768), a Lebanese Orientalist and Vatican librarian; James Bruce (1730-1794), a Scottish explorer and travel writer; and E.A. Wallis Budge (1857-1934), a British Egyptologist, Orientalist, philologist, and author.

Among the translators who have turned many of these manuscripts into works that could be understood by an English-speaking world, there are: William Wake (1657-1737), a British clergyman, dean at Exeter, bishop at Lincoln, and archbishop of Canterbury; Richard Laurence (1760-1838), a British Hebraist, Anglican churchman, and regius professor of Hebrew at Oxford; Moses Samuel (1795-1860), a British author and translator of Hebrew works; S.C. Malan (1812-1894), a British biblical scholar and linguist of Oriental languages; William Wright (1830-1889), a British Orientalist and professor of Arabic at Cambridge; B. Harris Cowper (1822-1904), a British archeologist, historian, and translator; W.R. Morfill (1834-1909), a British professor of Slavonic languages at Oxford; and R.H. Charles (1855-1931), an Irish biblical scholar and theologian.

Among the scholars who invested their considerable skill and effort into making the various manuscripts accessible to the general population, there are: Theophilus of Antioch (c. 120-181), a Syrian theologian, apologist, author, and chronologist; Julius Africanus (c. 160-240), a Libyan historian, traveler, and chronologist; Hippolytus of Rome (c. 170-235), a Greek theologian, apologist, and chronologist; Ephrem the Syrian (c. 306-373), a theologian, deacon, and hymn writer; Giambattista Vico (1668-1744), an Italian historian, political philosopher, and apologist of classical antiquity; George Smith (1800-1868), a British historian, theologian, and author; Joseph A. Seiss (1823-1904), an American theologian, Lutheran minister, and author; E.W. Bullinger (1837-1913), a British clergyman and theologian; Louis Ginzberg (1873-1953), a Lithuanian professor of Judaism and Talmudist; Edgar J. Goodspeed (1871-1962), an American theologian and scholar of Greek and *The New Testament*; and Cyrus H. Gordon (1908-2001), an American biblical scholar and professor of ancient Near East culture and languages.

Thanks to the visionary efforts of "so great a cloud of witnesses," then, I hereby present the following work; I now present *The Book of Days: In Search of the 5,500-year Prophecy Given to Adam About the Coming of Christ.*

The Hidden Books

This Journey of Discovery

IN A WORLD where evil so often triumphs over good, several burning questions linger in the face of such tragedy and despair. Is the God of *The Bible* really in control of human history as the Scriptures declare? And if He is, does He actually keep His promises to mankind? Fortunately for us, these two questions are inexorably bound together, and they are bound in the following manner. God's control over history is clearly confirmed in direct proportion to His faithfulness to the promises He has made to humanity. In other words, to verify that God is in control, all one need do is confirm that He is faithful to the promises He makes. This leads us, then, to the next question, which is: Where does one look to confirm God's faithfulness to His word of promise? Naturally, the obvious solution to a problem framed this way would be: I guess one finds the answer in *The Bible*, right? Needless to say, though, as both believers and skeptics have discovered, such a straightforward solution is much more elusive than that. To begin with, one must first ask: To which promise of God should we look to confirm this faithfulness? And having decided upon which promise, how do we go about establishing a clear-cut way to determine whether or not God has kept that promise?

To that end, it would be useful to focus our quest. By that I mean that, out of the countless promises that fill the pages of Holy Writ, it would help if we could narrow down our choice. Fortunately, we do have the Apostle Paul to assist us in this matter. Speaking of Jesus, in his letter to the Corinthians, Paul said, "For all the promises of God find their 'yes' in Him."[13] Or as Weymouth's *New Testament* puts it: "All the promises of God, whatever their number, have their confirmation in Him."[14] In other words, if one were to gather together every promise that God has ever made to His people, they could all be confirmed by the fact that His Son came into this world to live and die and resurrect just as had been predicted. Therefore, if this Advent of Christ can be adequately confirmed, then — based on this verse in *Corinthians* — every other promise in the book can be counted on as well.

That said, it should be the mission of every student of Scripture to determine the extent to which the promises of God have been fulfilled in the Incarnation of Christ. Admittedly, this is not the easiest thing to do, consid-

---

13 *Second Corinthians* 1:20
14 Ibid. 1:20

ering all the roadblocks that stand in the way of one's quest for historical certainty. However, just because it is a difficult task does not mean that it is an impossible one. After all, although there are many pitfalls along the way, the God of *The Bible* does not hesitate to beckon us onward in this journey of discovery. Therefore, if one can appreciate that it is God Himself Who is guiding our quest, then it should come as no surprise that He is also the One Who has provided sufficient signposts to help us along the way.

With this in mind, one simply turns to the various ways in which *The Bible* portrays the manifestation of Christ in history, right? To which I must confess that — for me, at least — this is where things get a little tricky. Let me take a moment to explain what I mean by that.

Naturally, speaking as I am from an admittedly Christian frame of reference, I do look to *The Bible* as one of several sources for such evidence — that is, the traditional *Bible*. But notice how I said the traditional *Bible*. The reason I say this is because after more than forty years of research, I have become convinced that there is another source of God-inspired wisdom that is just as capable of confirming the truth of the divine promise concerning the Advent of Christ. Make no mistake, though, I am not referring to any literary source that has not, at one point or another, been considered part of Holy Scripture. On the contrary, what I am referring to are books that were once considered inspired by God but which have, over the course of time, been excised from the canon of so-called "accepted texts," generally for reasons that seem more motivated by the whims of politics than by the dictates of conscience.

I am referring to a body of ancient wisdom literature that has come to be known in modern parlance as the *pseudepigraphal* books of *The Bible*. *Pseudepigrapha* — chances are if you are neither a biblical scholar nor an archeology professor you may not even know what this word means or what it implies. According to the dictionary, the word is derived from two Greek words, *pseudo*, which means "false," and *epigraphein*, which means to "inscribe," thus, "to write falsely." By that definition, any book considered *pseudepigraphal* is one that is believed to be a "falsely attributed work," that is to say, a work that erroneously purports to be written by some noteworthy biblical personage. As such, any book labeled as *pseudepigrapha* is to be discounted as being outside of the canon of books that have been deemed truly inspired by God. In addition to labeling these books as *pseudepigrapha*, they are often designated as "apocryphal" literature because a number of these titles remain in a separate section of *The Catholic Bible* and *The Greek Orthodox Bible* called *The Apocrypha*. Among these books are *The Wisdom of Solomon*, *The Epistle of Jeremiah*, *The Prayer of Manasseh*, *The Book of Judith*, and *The Second Book of Esdras*.

One of the great tragedies, in fact, in the history of *The Bible* is that there is so much ignorance in regard to the peculiar assumption that we as a Western Protestant people received our Canon of Scripture like some hermetically-sealed document handed down from On-High. Fortunately, though, for the sake of those with the courage to examine this critical aspect of history, the work of intrepid scholars has greatly aided in dispelling such myopic thinking. Among them are Cyrus H. Gordon, professor of ancient Near East studies at Brandeis University, whose work shed much-needed new light on this age-old controversy. Said Gordon:

> *The Bible* is of a complex composition, varying in scope according to the different ecclesiastical bodies. The Samaritans include only the Five Books of Moses in their *Bible*, and it is evident from *The Dead Sea Scrolls* that before the start of the Christian Era *The Pentateuch* was the most stabilized part of the Hebrew Scripture. Normative Judaism embraces the conventional *Pentateuch, Prophets*, and *Hagiographa* of the familiar *Old Testament. The Septuagint*, however, is far more inclusive, containing as it does, *Apocrypha* and *Pseudepigrapha*. Qumranite and other sectarian Jews possessed still other sacred writings. *Protestant Bibles* usually contain the normative *Jewish Old Testament* plus *The New Testament; Catholic Bibles* have, in addition, *The Apocryphal Books*. Various Eastern Orthodox Churches include different *Pseudepigrapha*. Accordingly, there is no one biblical corpus; and the component books of either *Testament* are in many cases extremely heterogeneous individually.[15]

Concerning the variegated process of the formation of our *Protestant Bible*, Edgar J. Goodspeed, described as "America's greatest *New Testament* scholar,"[16] pointed out:

> *The Apocrypha* formed an integral part of the *King James* Version of 1611, as had all the preceding English versions from their beginning in 1382. But they are seldom printed as part of it any longer, still more seldom as part of the *English Revised* Version, and were not included in the American revision.
>
> This is partly because the Puritans disapproved of them; they had already begun to drop them from printings of their *Geneva Bible* by 1600, and began to demand copies of the *King James* Version omitting them as early as 1629... We moderns discredit them because they were not part of *The Hebrew Bible*, and most of them have never been found in any Hebrew forms at all.
>
> But they were part of *The Bible* of the early Church, for it used

---

15 *The Common Background of Greek and Hebrew Civilizations*, Cyrus H. Gordon, p. 278

16 *Edgar Johnson Goodspeed: Articulate Scholar*, James I. Cook, p. X

the *Greek* Version of *The Jewish Bible*, which we call *The Septuagint*, and these books were all in that version. They passed from it into Latin and the great Latin *Bible* edited by St. Jerome about 400 A.D., *The Vulgate*, which became the authorized *Bible* of Western Europe and England, and remained so for a thousand years. But Jerome found that they were not in *The Hebrew Bible*, and so he called them *Apocrypha*, the hidden, or secret, books.[17]

The Apocrypha, however, does not contain all of the books included in the pantheon of apocryphal literature. Most notable among the other titles are *The First Book of Adam and Eve*, *The First Book of Enoch*, *The Secrets of Enoch*, *The Book of Jasher*, *The Book of Jubilees*, *The Testaments of the Twelve Patriarchs*, *The Letters of Herod and Pilate*, and *The Gospel of Nicodemus*.

Grounds for Exclusion

OVER THE YEARS many reasons have been offered to justify the rejection of any book that is no longer found in many of our modern versions of *The Bible*. Chief among them are: One, they were written under assumed names; two, they contain historical errors; three, they were not quoted by Jesus; and four, they contain no prophetic elements. Yet ironically, these same objections, which seem to confirm the correctness of rejecting the apocryphal books, have also been leveled against books in the accepted Canon of Scripture.

For example, regarding *The Pentateuch*, or the first five books of *The Old Testament*, critics have often doubted the Mosaic authorship of *The Book of Genesis*. As their argument goes: While the last four books could have been written by Moses by virtue of the fact that he lived during the years described by the text, he certainly could not have been around to witness the events depicted in the first book. Yet according to most biblical scholars: "Long before the first century A.D., Moses was declared the author of *Genesis*, and Josephus, the first-century Jewish historian, in keeping with this tradition, accepted Mosaic authorship."[18]

Still other books in *The Old Testament* have had their authorship called into question, such as *Isaiah*, *Ezekiel*, and *Daniel*. Because they so precisely predict future events, these books, critics insist, must have been published after the fact and therefore must have been written under assumed names. Similarly, certain books in *The New Testament* have in recent times come under fire concerning their genuine authorship. Most notably are those attributed to the Apostles Peter and Paul. According to much modern-day scholarship, both epistles of Peter and several letters of Paul were allegedly

---

17 *The Apocrypha: An American Translation*, Edgar J. Goodspeed, p. v
18 *The Criswell Study Bible*, W.A. Criswell (Editor), p. 1

written as amalgamations by authors other than the ones to which Scripture has subscribed. Yet the simple fact is, though the identities of many of the best-known biblical authors remain subject to such doubt and speculation, the books that bear their names are still regarded as integral to *The Holy Bible*.

As far as rejecting certain books because they contain historical errors, again I should point out that this same argument applies to texts well within the accepted limits of scriptural sanctity. And again one need only turn to the first book in Scripture to prove my point, because as many biblical scholars are well aware it has been a longstanding bone of contention that the account of Noah's gathering of the animals into the Ark contains two contradictory versions. In one rendition, the animals enter in pairs,[19] while in another, they enter in groups of seven.[20]

The same thing occurs in *The New Testament* regarding Judas Iscariot, whose infamous demise is reported in two separate yet contradictory accounts. In *Matthew*, it is said that a grief-stricken Judas hung himself after betraying Jesus,[21] while Acts has him falling headlong into a field and being disemboweled in the process.[22] Naturally, scholars are quick to point out the various ways in which such contradictions can be logically reconciled, and justifiably so. Yet this still does not change the fact that there are obvious contradictions to be found in the received texts, which if they were found in books that critics were seeking to excise would be considered clear grounds for exclusion.

As for the claim that Jesus never quoted from any of the apocryphal books, one need only consider *The Testaments of the Twelve Patriarchs* to undermine such an objection. R.H. Charles, in his scholarly work on pseudepigraphal literature, said this about *The Testaments*:

> Its ethical teaching has achieved a real immortality by influencing the thought and diction of the writers of *The New Testament*, and even those of our Lord. This ethical teaching, which is very much higher and purer than that of *The Old Testament*, is yet its true spiritual child, and helps to bridge the chasm that divides *The Old Testament* and *The New Testament*.
>
> The instances of the influence of these writings on *The New Testament* are notable in the Sermon on the Mount, which reflects the spirit and even uses phrases from these *Testaments*. Saint Paul appears to have borrowed so freely that it seems as though he must have carried a copy of *The Testaments* with him on his travels. Thus,

---

19 *Genesis* 6:19-20
20 Ibid. 7:2-3
21 *Matthew* 27:5
22 *Acts* 1:18

the reader has before him in these pages what is at once striking for its blunt primitive style and valuable as some of the actual source books of *The Bible*.[23]

A perfect example of the way in which the apocryphal literature has made its indelible mark on the world of *The New Testament* can be seen in relation to *The First Book of Enoch*. Consider for a moment, if you will, the evidence of all four Gospels, in which Jesus refers to Himself as the Son of Man some eighty-one times. This is certainly a peculiar title when one considers the fact that most people assume Jesus was condemned for calling Himself the Son of God, not the Son of Man. The Jewish leaders repeatedly demanded to know if He claimed the title of the Son of God for Himself, but never once did any of the gospel writers record that Jesus did so. To a man, what they did reveal was, in response to this question, His reply was purely rhetorical. Said Jesus:

"From now on, the Son of Man will be seated at the right hand of the power of God."
And they all said, "Are you the Son of God, then?"
And He replied, "You say that I am."
Then they said, "What further need do we have of testimony? We heard it ourselves from his own mouth."[24]

But notice that Jesus never claimed here to be the Son of God; yet His enemies insisted He did. Was this simply a case of their having heard what they expected to hear, even though He never said what they claimed? Unfortunately, such an oversimplification is itself a product of wishful thinking by anyone who insists that Jesus never quoted from the apocryphal books, because all one must consider is that even though He never verbalized that He was the Son of God, His critics acted as if He did. But how?

In fact, they "heard" Jesus "say" so by way of His more than eighty references to Himself as the Son of Man. To the average listener, the title Son of Man carries no divine significance whatsoever, but to the Jewish religious community of that day, the Son of Man was an even more potent title than that of the Son of God. And much to the chagrin of the apocryphal naysayers, this disjointed string of logic in the minds of Jesus' enemies proves it, because the title Son of Man finds its origins in none other than *First Enoch*, as is demonstrated by the following excerpt:

There I saw the Ancient of Days, Whose head was like wool, and with Him stood another, Whose countenance resembled that of a

---

23 *The Apocrypha and Pseudepigrapha of the Old Testament, Volume 2*, R.H. Charles, p. 282
24 *Luke* 22:69-71

Man. His face was full of grace, like that of the holy angels. Then I asked one of the angels who had been showing me all of these secret things...

And he answered me, saying, "This is the Son of Man to Whom righteousness belongs ... and Who will reveal all the treasures that are concealed, because the Lord of Spirits has chosen Him, and His portion surpasses everyone else in everlasting uprightness. This Son of Man Whom you see ... will break the teeth of sinners. He'll hurl kings from their thrones and their dominions because they won't exalt or praise Him, nor humble themselves before Him, by Whom their kingdoms were granted to them."[25]

Hopefully, excerpts like this will put to rest any question as to whether or not Jesus quoted from the apocryphal literature. It should also help to explain the level of implacable hatred that the Jewish religious leaders displayed toward Jesus when this apparently ordinary man insisted on equating Himself with the loftiest and mightiest figure in their Hebrew pantheon.

A Thread of Prophecy

FINALLY, WE TURN TO the insistence that the apocryphal literature must be rejected because, unlike its legitimate counterpart of canonical Scripture, it contains no prophetic elements. This is perhaps the most spurious claim of all, because even a cursory examination of the many texts in this group will yield, on this point alone, a bounty far beyond the scope of this book.

In *The First Book of Enoch*, one finds innumerable descriptions of the future events concerning the long-awaited coming of the Son of Man and His subsequent judgment of mankind. Certainly, the most famous example of this is the quote by Jude in his *New Testament* letter: "Enoch, the seventh from Adam, prophesied, 'See, the Lord is coming with ten thousand of His saints to judge everyone, and to convict them for their ungodliness and all the defiant words they've spoken against Him.'"[26]

Again, there is *The Testaments of the Twelve Patriarchs*, which, while ostensibly a series of exhortations to Jacob's grandchildren, also provides a prophetic window into the future of Israel, one which speaks not only of the resurrection of Christ but also of the saints who were to rise in His wake. As Benjamin, the youngest son of Jacob, lay on his deathbed, he admonished his children with these words—both chilling and hopeful in their implications:

The Lord will send His salvation in the form of an Only-Begotten Prophet. He'll enter into the Temple and there be treated with out-

---

25 *First Enoch* 46:1-4
26 *Jude* 1:9

rage. He'll be lifted up on a tree, the veil of the Temple will be torn, and the Spirit of God will pass on to the Gentiles as a flame pours forth, and He'll ascend from Hades and pass from Earth to Heaven...

And then you'll see Noah, Shem, Abraham, Isaac, and Jacob, rising on the right hand in gladness. Then we'll rise, too, each of us at the head of our tribe, worshipping the King of Heaven, Who appeared on the Earth in the form of a Man with all humility.[27]

In *The Second Book of Esdras*, the visions of Ezra reveal the signs of the approaching messianic kingdom, the general resurrection of the dead, the final judgment, the New Jerusalem, and the coming of Messiah. In it, one finds the following prediction, written more than four centuries before the Advent of Christ:

> The time will come when the signs I've told you about will take place... Whoever is delivered from the evils I've predicted will see My wonders. For My Son, the Christ, will be revealed to those who are with Him, and those who are left will rejoice in Him, that is, in four hundred years, and it will be after those years that My Son Christ will die.[28]

Clearly, anyone who insists that the apocryphal books lack the prophetic elements that are in the canonical texts is blind by choice or by nature, but either way, they are blind to what even a rank amateur can detect, if only they are willing to honestly examine the evidence for themselves.

In our particular case, however, the extent to which we will be investigating this literature will be limited to a lone prophetic thread, though it is one that has everything to do with the all-important issue of the Advent of Christ. Unlike anything else in these ancient texts, this thread of prophecy is of paramount significance due to the fact that it weaves its way through no less than three of these books. Known as the prophecy of The Great Five and a Half Days, this messianic promise originates in *The First Book of Adam and Eve*, is then alluded to in *The Secrets of Enoch*, and finally culminates in *The Gospel of Nicodemus*. It is this prophecy, then, of The Great Five and a Half Days—which, as we will see, refers to a 5,500-year period from Adam to Christ—that will provide the framework we require to unravel the two mysteries this book has set out to solve. By verifying the historical reality of this *five and a half* "day" timeline, it is our intention to establish the criterion we are seeking to, one, demonstrate the Lord's control by way of His faithfulness to His promises, which is to say, "all the promises of God" that are

---

27 *The Testament of Benjamin* 2:6-9, 17-18
28 *Second Esdras* 7:26-29

"confirmed" in the Incarnation of Christ, and, two, demonstrate how this prophecy provides the key to revealing a hidden connection between the dimensions of the various sacred artifacts described throughout this work.

Meanwhile, at this moment, I can imagine the reaction of everyone who has ever studied biblical chronology and who are all asking the same question: "But what about Archbishop James Ussher's seventeenth-century timeline of 4,000 years from Adam to Christ? I thought it was the accepted version derived from *The Bible*." And to such a question, my response is: For many years I thought the same thing, too. I did, that is, until I encountered an alternate timeline—and, mind you, a timeline that offers a vastly superior method for verifying God's faithfulness to His promises. As it turns out, my original view changed in light of the evidence found not only in the apocryphal record but in the historical record as well—evidence that is still, to this day, being overlooked by the general public.

Just consider this potent statement offered by Nathan Rouse, who wrote in his 1856 book entitled *A Dissertation on Sacred Chronology*: "The important fact is … that for 700 years after the commencement of the Christian Era … the average estimation of the period from Adam to Christ was some 5,500 years."[29] Imagine that: For the first seven hundred years of Christianity, no one ever once considered the possibility of a 4,000-year period from Adam to Christ. Why? The reason for this was because, as historians like Rouse were right to point out, all the Church Fathers subscribed to a biblical chronology that was found in the earlier Greek Version of *The Old Testament* called *The Septuagint*—one that differed drastically from the later *Hebrew* Version, or *Masoretic* Text. Concerning this ecclesiastical controversy between the *Septuagint* and *Masoretic* Versions of *The Old Testament*, Rouse went on to say:

> Bishop Michael Russell in his observation on this subject, states that, "The *Septuagint* chronology was used before the Advent of Christ, was followed by the Church Fathers, and appears not to have been called into question until, in the eighth century, a disposition to exchange it for the rabbinical method of reckoning was first manifested by the Venerable Bede.
>
> "But his innovations were ill-received by his contemporaries. He was denounced as a heretic for taking it upon himself to assert … that the Redeemer of our race was not born in the sixth millennium of the world. Notwithstanding this attempt, however, and the high reputation which Bede possessed, his system was generally rejected and the *Septuagint* chronology prevailed. This will be evident from the following facts, for which we are chiefly indebted to Dr. William Hales.

---

29 *A Dissertation on Sacred Chronology*, Nathan Rouse, p. 20

"In the year 691 A.D., a general council was held at Constanti-
nople, and in its recorded acts it is stated that the members of this
council assembled in the Imperial City in the year of the world 6,199,
which places the Creation 5,508 years before Christ. This council,
it is true, was held in the nineteenth year of the life of Bede, and
therefore prior to his attempt to introduce the Hebrew numbers.
However, the date here assigned to the Creation was the act of a
general council, and as such it furnishes the most decisive evidence
that down to the close of the seventh century, the Christian Church
continued to use the *Septuagint* chronology."[30]

Not only was this particular chronology in place until then, but if one
takes the time to review the historical evidence, it will reveal that the lengthier time frame of 5,500 years from Adam to Christ was maintained by Orthodox Christianity for another eight centuries after that. It was actually not
until the Reformation—and then only as an unforeseen consequence of one
of the more ironic twists in history, to be discussed later in this work—that
the *Septuagint* numbers were finally replaced by those in the *Masoretic* Text.[31]
Concerning this fateful switch, Rouse wrote some three hundred years after
the fact:

A sufficiency of evidence shows that, notwithstanding the attempt
of Venerable Bede, the *Septuagint* chronology prevailed down to the
time of the Reformation… In this grand chronological blunder, however, the reformers stood alone and have continued to stand alone
to this day. It does not appear that any other church has followed
them in this path. They have the merit and glory of it entirely to
themselves. The Greek Church, as is well known, still adopts, as she
has always done, the *Septuagint* chronology. The Roman Church,
too, and … the Egyptian Copts, the Abyssinians, the Armenians,
the Ethiopians and the Georgians. So that, although the followers
of Luther … adopted the Hebrew numbers, all other churches have
continued to reject them to this day.[32]

It is to such evidence that the present work will turn in an effort to shed
new light on this critical lost chapter of biblical history. What is more, this
book will present, as far as I know, the first attempt to connect the 5,500-year
timeline of *The Septuagint Bible* with The Great Five and a Half Day prophecy so prevalent in parabiblical literature. And if this can be adequately accomplished, then it is my hope that they will never again stand apart; but
in their being brought together in a sublime continuum, they will finally be

---

30 *A Dissertation on Sacred Chronology*, Nathan Rouse, pp. 20-21
31 See *A Capstone to Time: The Five and a Half Days*
32 *A Dissertation on Sacred Chronology*, Nathan Rouse, p. 22

seen in the context that the God of *The Bible* originally intended for them.

Rest assured, however, this effort will not constitute some new revelation of my own conjuring. On the contrary, the storyline contained in
this work will stand as the inevitable ancestor of previous generations who
have paved the way with their courage and tenacity. Moreover, in turning
to these gems of forgotten wisdom—like *The First Book of Adam and Eve, The
Secrets of Enoch,* and *The Gospel of Nicodemus,* which provide us with the most
comprehensive scriptural view of this prophecy of The Great Five and a
Half Days—it will be just as it was intended by those intrepid scholars who
gave mankind the first modern translations of these books. According to
their mission statement:

> All of these apocryphal volumes are presented without argument
> or comment. The reader's own judgment and common sense are
> appealed to. It makes no difference whether he is Catholic or Protes-
> tant or Hebrew. The facts are plainly laid before him. These facts, for
> a long time, have been the peculiar esoteric property of the learned.
> They were available only in the original Greek and Latin and so
> forth. Now, they have been translated into plain English before the
> eye of every reader.
>
> The ordinary man has, therefore, the privilege of seeing upon
> what grounds the commonly accepted Scriptures rest. He can exam-
> ine the pile of evidence, and do his own sifting…
>
> In other words, the ordinary man is invited to take his place in
> that council chamber which accepts or rejects the various writings
> of Scripture. It is safe to say the conclusions desired can be left to his
> common sense.[33]

An Improbable Connectivity

WHAT MAKES *The Bible* such an amazing document actually arises from
the fact that even though it is a book written across the entire span of human history it still bears the unmistakable stamp of a singular point of view.
In other words, although so many hands have stirred the pot, although so
many perspectives have added to its mix, the integrity of the scriptural record still bears a remarkable similarity through in and throughout. From
age to age, what begins as a germ of thought in *The Old Testament* unfolds
with astonishing continuity in *The New Testament.* From author to author,
every book contained in *The Bible* echoes from cover to cover, clearly testifying that this cannot be the product of mere coincidence; it is undoubtedly
the greatest proof as to its divine authorship.

---

33 *The Lost Books of the Bible and The Forgotten Books of Eden,* Frank Crane (Contributor), pp. 1-2

Taking this into consideration, let us examine the internal logic of the apocryphal literature, that is to say, the way scattered references throughout these documents reveal a high degree of confluence, or textual continuity, from book to book. The greatest example of this internal logic can be seen in what has come to be known as the prophecy of The Great Five and a Half Days—a prophecy introduced in *The First Book of Adam and Eve*, then alluded to in *The Secrets of Enoch* and finally brought full circle in *The Gospel of Nicodemus*.

Part one of three: When Adam and Eve were expelled from the Garden of Eden, God promised them that they would someday be allowed to return to the place they had forfeited through their disobedience. This return, however, would not take place, explained God—though in typically veiled terms—for another *five and a half* "days." Confused, Adam and Eve thought that God was telling them they would only have to wait *five and a half* days in human terms.[34] But much to their chagrin, they discovered that God was really saying they would have to wait *5,500 years* before they could expect to return to the garden, at which time: "One would come to save them and their descendants."[35] Now anyone familiar with *The Bible* is already well aware that, from God's perspective, time is very different from our own. Typically, it is accepted, as per our understanding of Scripture, that one of God's "days" is equal to a thousand years from our human frame of reference.[36] In this way, the apocryphal and canonical records are in agreement. Okay, so far, so good.

On to part two of three: With the death and resurrection of Jesus of Nazareth, events came to a head in the confrontation between Pontius Pilate and the Jewish religious authorities who instigated the crucifixion of Christ. In a final showdown, as depicted in the pages of *The Gospel of Nicodemus*, Pilate demanded that Annas and Caiaphas come clean concerning their crime against Jesus. Then it happened. Smitten by guilt, compounded by the astonishment over numerous reports of the resurrected Christ, Annas, the chief priest at Jerusalem, made a startling confession. In checking the record of their own Scripture—described by Annas as *The Seventy Books*—they encountered a prophecy of the coming of the Messiah, a prophecy stating that, counting from the time of Adam, "After *5,500 years*, Christ, the most beloved Son of God, was to come to Earth."[37] What is more, Annas even went so far as to make a fascinating connection between this prophecy and the dimensions of The Ark of the Covenant. As he described it:

---

34 *First Adam and Eve* 3:2-4
35 Ibid. 3:6
36 *Second Peter* 3:8; *Psalm* 90:4; *Jubilees* 4:30
37 *Nicodemus* 22:11

We further considered that perhaps He (speaking of this Messiah) was the very God of Israel Who spoke to Moses instructing him to build The Ark of the Covenant with dimensions of *five and a half* cubits. From this we surmised that the Christ would likewise come in an ark, or tabernacle, of a body after *5,500 years*.[38]

In this correspondence of the dimensions of The Ark of the Covenant, it appears that there is again an uncanny agreement between the apocryphal and canonical records.

Now for part three of three: Before Adam and Eve were told about the promise of "days" and before Annas and Caiaphas learned about it, an event seems to have triggered God's choice for this numerical figure of *five and a half* in connection with the coming of the Messiah, an event recorded by none other than Enoch. Ironically, it exists as a mere sidebar — a "footnote," if you will — in *The Secrets of Enoch*. In it, Enoch describes Adam's creation on the sixth day, his subsequent fall, and the Lord's response to that first act of disobedience. "Finally, the seventh day arrived and God said, 'Because of what they'd done, I only allowed Adam and Eve to remain in Paradise for *five and a half* hours before I forced them to leave.'"[39]

The significance of this numerical value will no doubt escape those who are unfamiliar with what *The Bible* has to say about divine judgment but will not go unnoticed by those who are. The reason is this: Already firmly established in Scripture is that when it comes to God's decrees involving His chosen ones there is always a direct correlation between the nature of their crime and the severity of their punishment. In other words, when the people willingly rebel against God's commands, the Lord makes an extremely conscious decision to punish them in direct proportion — no more and no less — to the exact extent of their disobedience. So, according to this divine law of crime and punishment, *The Book of Jubilees* states that when Cain died it was as a result of his house collapsing on top of him.

And he was killed by its stones because he had killed his brother Abel with a stone, so in this way his death by stone was considered an act of righteous judgment. This is why it was ordained on the tablets of Heaven: With whatever instrument a man kills his neighbor, he will be killed with a similar object, and in whatever manner he wounds another, his punishment will be meted out in the same way.[40]

Louis Ginzberg, a Lithuanian professor of Judaism, provides us with some useful scenarios to illustrate this point in his book *The Legends of the*

38 *Nicodemus* 22:12-13
39 *Secrets of Enoch* 32:1-3
40 *Jubilees* 4:31-32

Jews. Of particular interest are the trials and tribulations of Joseph, the be-loved son of Jacob. When his jealous brothers sold Joseph to Ishmaelites on their way to Egypt, they received twenty shekels of silver in exchange for him; therefore, according to this law of crime and punishment, God commanded that every firstborn son of Israel be redeemed with the same amount. Also, every Israelite must annually pay the sanctuary this amount that each of Joseph's brothers received as their share for his sale.[41] According to Zebulun, the sixth son of Jacob and Leah:

> When the brothers sold Joseph as a slave, eight of them, including Simeon and Gad, bought sandals with the money. Having acknowl-edged that it was blood money, they refused to buy food with it. But because Joseph had prophesied that he'd eventually be their king, they wanted to see what would become of his dreams. Therefore, it is written in the Law of Moses that whoever refuses to raise up a descendant on behalf of his brother, his sandals will be removed and they should spit upon him.
>
> So because the brothers of Joseph wanted him dead, the Lord made sure that they'd have to remove the sandals they wore in their conflict with Joseph. That's why, when they went to Egypt, the ser-vants of Joseph forced them to remove their shoes and bow down to Joseph as the viceroy of Egypt. Not only that, but all the brothers were also spit upon, having been put to shame before the Egyptians, just as the Lord had decreed.[42]

Taking this into account, let us look at the most eloquent example of God's chastening of His people to be found in Scripture. I am referring to what is known as the Seventy Weeks of Daniel. Almost everyone who is familiar with biblical prophecy has heard of it. In this case, though, I want to focus on an aspect of the story that is often overlooked when discussing the implications of Daniel's prophecy, but first, let us set up our scene.

The prophet Daniel discovered while reading *The Book of Jeremiah* that God intended to extricate His people who had been in Babylonian captivity for seventy years.[43] He went on to say this seventy year bondage had been a microcosm of a greatly extended period of punishment — that is, seventy "weeks" of years — that the people of God were to endure, which would ul-timately conclude with the advent of a glorious millennial age ushered in by none other than the Messiah Himself.[44] Until that day, however, God would

---

41 *The Legends of the Jews, Volume 2: From Joseph to the Exodus*, Louis Ginzberg, p. 18

42 *The Testament of Zebulun*, 1:18-23

43 *Daniel* 9:2

44 Ibid. 9:24

be teaching His people to trust Him via incremental stages, which would gradually lead them from one phase of salvation history to the next.

Now, to the significance of all this for the purpose of our present study. Long before God decreed seventy years of Babylonian captivity, which prefigured the extended period of punishment, was the fact that when the people of Israel dwelled securely in Palestine there was an unusual law they were told to keep. Unfortunately, though, it was a law that was regularly neglected.

> For six years, you are to sow your fields, and harvest the crops, but during the seventh year let the land lie dormant, unplowed and unused. This way the poor and the stranger among your people may get food from it, and the wild animals may eat what they leave behind. Do the same with your vineyards and your olive groves.[45]

The reason for this prohibition was that, as every seventh day was a Sabbath day, every seventh year was likewise a Sabbath year. In doing this, God intended to not only nurture the Israelites' attitude toward the poor, the stranger, and the animals but also to nurture their trust in His divine provision during every seventh year of their existence in that land. But sadly, history records that they did not abide by this prohibition, and because they continued to farm their fields during those Sabbath years, God punished them with the Babylonian captivity, thereby ensuring that the land would remain untouched.

> So the Israelites were carried into captivity and became servants to the king of Babylon, and during the entire time of its desolation, the land finally enjoyed its Sabbath rests, until the seventy years were completed in fulfillment of the word of the Lord as it was spoken by Jeremiah.[46]

So, returning to our story of the first couple's exile from Paradise: Just as the Israelites were expelled from Palestine in direct proportion to the amount of time that they were in it, Adam and Eve were exiled from the garden according to a similar scale of divine judgment. But could these parallels of time-specific lengths of judgment really be a simple case of coincidence? Or is it possible that the God of Set Times actually built into the scriptural record these kinds of clues to His control over human history? And if so, what can one surmise from it? If Enoch wrote his texts long before such patterns of God's judgment were established, then it was certainly no mere whim that compelled him to mention seemingly trivial information like Adam and Eve living in Eden for *five and a half* hours prior to their God-ordained exile

---

45 *Exodus* 23:10
46 *Second Chronicles* 36:20-21

of *five and a half* "days." Naturally, from a strictly humanistic point of view, it might seem like an impossible leap of logic to assume such a thing, but, if one possesses a biblical view, it is not absurd at all.

One thing, however, is certain. We do have in our possession three separate manuscripts — *The First Book of Adam and Eve*, *The Secrets of Enoch*, and *The Gospel of Nicodemus* — all which were written long ago when the preservation of such ancient works demanded an improbable mixture of luck and determination. Yet they have somehow managed to survive to the present day. Even more astonishing to the modern mind, these manuscripts, which have all been scattered throughout time and geography, bear a similarly improbable connectivity, revealing a pattern that was generally believed to be confined to the Biblical Canon. Therefore, far from giving us the impression that they are the by-product of primitive human thought, they instead present a finely wrought synergy that no mere mortal, or group of mortals, could have ever conceived, separated by so many centuries, so many miles, so many improbabilities.

Shadow and Substance

Things to Come

ACCEPTS WE HAVE just seen, one of the greatest proofs of the authenticity of the apocryphal literature is its ability to reveal a coherence within the very fabric of its textual presentation. In short, there is an internal logic in the information found throughout the corpus of books deemed non-canonical. This internal harmony is revealed in the case of the prophecy of the Great Five and a Half Days, begun in *The First Book of Adam and Eve*, alluded to in *The Secrets of Enoch*, and fulfilled in *The Gospel of Nicodemus*. As detached prophetic wisps, they float about as disjointed blips on the divine radar screen, but stitched together they coalesce into a genuine pattern, obvious to even the most obtuse observer of biblical timelines.

Having established this kind of logical structure, which binds the apocryphal and canonical record into a cohesive whole, I would now like to proceed further in light of this newfound awareness. Next, we will examine the extent to which the apocryphal record lends itself to deepening our understanding of the biblical doctrine known as typology. In theological terms, typology is the doctrine that expounds the idea that certain events, persons, or statements in *The Old Testament* are "types" that represent "shadows" that prefigure specific attributes relating to the Advent of Christ, which, as you will recall, constitutes our primary focus in demonstrating God's control and faithfulness. Paul articulated this idea best when he said, "Don't let anyone judge you about food, or drink, or festivals, or new moons, or Sabbaths, which are all but *shadows of things to come*, but the substance is Christ."[47] This very thing, as we have already seen in the last chapter, is what happened when Annas confessed to Pilate that because they had discovered that Moses had been instructed to build The Ark of the Covenant with the dimensions of *five and a half* cubits, they deduced from this seemingly random bit of information that the Messiah was to arrive on the stage of world history 5,500 years after Adam. In this, both Paul and Annas were doing exactly what Jesus had done when He compared the experience of Jonah in the belly of the whale with the death and resurrection of the Son of Man.[48]

That said, my purpose in analyzing the role of typology in apocryphal literature is to provide answers to questions that have, down through the ages, plagued anyone attempting to either believe or dismiss the truths

---

47 *Colossians* 2:16-17
48 *Matthew* 12:40; *Luke* 11:30

found in *The Bible*. For those who wish to believe them, I would like to offer fresh hope in their quest to ground their faith in the promises of God; and for those who wish to dismiss them, I would like to offer an alternative to their outmoded conclusions based on short-sighted interpretations.

These questions pertain to so-called "truths" offered up by various preachers that, on the surface, may sound correct, but due to stale repetitions of shallow traditional views, they instead constitute so much useless pabulum. According to Paul, God has given "gifts" to His Church in the form of apostles, prophets, evangelists, pastors, and teachers, whose job it is to administer His word, which when done faithfully accomplishes God's stated purpose.

> His people are to be equipped to do His work in order to build up the Church, the body of Christ. That way we'll all come to such unity in our faith and knowledge of God's Son that we become mature in the Lord, measuring up to the full stature of Christ. Then we'll no longer act like children, forever changing our minds just because someone's told us something different or because they deceived us by making a lie sound like the truth.[49]

All too often, however, humans want the purpose of God's Church to revolve around them and their needs, that is, to heal them, bless them, prosper them. But Paul insisted that the true purpose of these gift ministers is to bring the scattered individuals who comprise the Church into a "unity of faith," which can only come from a "knowledge of God's Son." Therefore, it behooves those who are attempting to become part of this body of Christ to find someone who can adequately inform them about what the Scriptures say about faith in Jesus Christ. Sadly, though, much of today's *Bible* teaching focuses on catering to the human needs of its parishioners as opposed to God's specified desire to build a body of believers who truly understand Who Jesus is.

Part of the problem, as I see it, rests squarely on the shoulders of those individuals who—while claiming to be gift ministers of God's word— willfully insist on feeding their unsuspecting congregations the same old stories, regurgitated from their pet *Bible* commentaries. Never mind that intelligent people with the courage to ask difficult questions prefer meaningful answers rather than trite homilies. Never mind that these so-called "gift ministers" seem to be so oblivious to the inconsistencies in their own teaching of God's word, in spite of the glaring contradictions that their worn out clichés attempt to gloss over. We are simply expected to marvel at their well-intentioned genius while we politely resist the urge to ask any question that might make our fellow saints think we have lost faith in the traditional

---

49 *Ephesians* 4:11-14

interpretation of the brethren.

For example, as long as I can remember, I have been taught that when God asked Abraham to offer his son Isaac as a burnt offering on Mount Moriah, it was supposedly a "type" of God offering up His Son Jesus as a sin offering on Calvary. In this comparison between Abraham and God, and between Isaac and Jesus, I could clearly see a direct correlation in theological terms. What is more, because I already had an appreciation for such cinematic concepts as "foreshadow" and "payoff," this interpretation of biblical history seemed quite plausible, as though God, the Cosmic Director of the Universe, had planned it so that we could not fail to recognize a connection between the two events. In fact, never once in all my years have I ever felt that such "parallels in time," so to speak, were not consistent with God's attempts to convey the truth of His plan of redemption throughout the ages.

To this very point, Cyrus H. Gordon spoke most eloquently:

> Scripture makes it quite clear that … Isaac was conceived through divine agency. Like the Mycenaean Greek heroes, Isaac could claim paternity at two levels; the human and the divine. His human father, through whom he obtained his specific position in his people's history, was Abraham; but his superhuman quality was derived from the deity that visited Sarah. This is of a piece with the dual paternity of Homeric heroes, who hold the office of their human fathers, but are supernatural because of their divine fathers… It is in every way conceivable that some of the original Isaac Cycle survived to re-echo in Christianity. Jesus derives His human office of Messianic King from Joseph, but His divine quality from His Divine Father. Moreover, the Church tradition that connects the sacrifice of Isaac with the sacrifice of Christ apparently rests on sound exegesis, for the sacrifice of Isaac would have meant not only the sacrifice of Abraham's son but of God's.[50]

Understood in this context, then, it has always made perfect sense to me that if Abraham were the father of faith, one could easily accept the view that Isaac was the son of faith. What I did find confusing, though, was the seemingly incomplete picture that the canonical record seemed to offer in the actions of Isaac in relation to those of Jesus. Let me explain what I mean.

To begin with, if Isaac is supposed to be a "type" of Christ in this scenario, then why does *The Book of Genesis* depict him as an ignorant, little boy who has no idea what his father is planning for him? In my view, this could never adequately fulfill the typology of Christ, Whom the Scriptures tell us, repeatedly, was a willing participant in drinking from the cup of suffering

---

50 *The Common Background of Greek and Hebrew Civilizations,* Cyrus H. Gordon, pp. 290-91

prepared by God. "I'm the Good Shepherd," Jesus said. "The Good Shepherd lays down His life for the sheep. The reason My Father loves Me is because I lay down My life — only to take it up again. No one takes My life, but I willingly offer it on My own."[51] So if I am to believe in the unerring word of God, how can the traditional picture of an ignorant son of Abraham qualify as the devoted Son of God? To me, this has always presented a lingering contradiction, even as I have tried to reconcile this blatant gap in terms of what *The Bible* is supposedly offering as God's control over every stream of history. No wonder intelligent people continue to question the teaching of preachers who sanctimoniously offer up the Lord as the Omnipotent Master of the Universe, yet He Himself, it seems, is just as determined as they are to sidestep such nagging inconsistencies in His word.

So imagine my reaction when I came upon the story of Abraham and Isaac in the apocryphal literature. In *The Book of Jasher*, I had finally come upon a rendering that satisfied my desire to prove that God actually knew what He was doing with Isaac when He set out to prepare humanity to recognize what He would someday accomplish with Jesus at Calvary. In *Jasher*, we are presented with a picture that adequately fleshes out the idea that not only did Jesus fulfill His destiny as the obedient Son of God, but Isaac also fulfilled his role as a genuine type of Christ when he made that fateful journey to Mount Moriah with his father.

But before we look at the scenario presented in *Jasher*, let us take a moment to examine what would be required of Isaac to ensure that he might truly be called a type of Christ. First of all, unlike the canonical record implies, Isaac could not have been a mere child who was not yet old enough to act on his own accord. If Isaac had been a child, then he still would have been under the jurisdiction of Abraham, and any action performed by Isaac, the boy, could not rightly be compared to those being performed by Jesus, the adult. Furthermore, Isaac would have to know why he was going to Mount Moriah with his father. He would have to fully appreciate the fact that he was going to be killed and presented as a burnt offering to the Lord. And above all, he would have to willingly consent to the wishes of Abraham in what was being done to him. Without any one of these necessary components, the idea that Isaac represents a type of Christ is simply not consistent with any form of logic that I am aware of; and anyone who says otherwise is either stubbornly ignorant, or worse still, downright hypocritical. But fear not, God is quite capable of making sure that all the streams of history conform to His will, because as the story is revealed in *Jasher*, all these criteria have been adequately met. Let us see for ourselves, then, how all these elements come together in *Jasher*'s depiction of the drama of Isaac as it pertains to Abraham's most important mission to Moriah.

---

51 *John* 10:11, 17-18

When Isaac was thirty-seven years old, Ishmael was visiting him in his tent.

"I was thirteen," said Ishmael to Isaac, "when the Lord told Father to circumcise us. I gave my life to Him, and since then I've never disobeyed."

"Why brag to me about something like that?" asked Isaac. "You cut off a piece of your skin because the Lord told you to. As the God of Abraham lives, if He told Father to cut me into pieces and burn me as an offering, I wouldn't hesitate. I'd gladly consent."

And when the Lord heard what Isaac said to Ishmael, He decided that it would be exactly how He would test Abraham.[52]

The first thing that one cannot help but notice in this account is that according to *Jasher*, Isaac was not a mere child as the canonical record implies. He was actually thirty-seven years old. So why would *Genesis* describe Isaac as a lad? The word *lad* denotes a child, not a thirty-seven year old man. Why the discrepancy, then? Did Moses make a mental error when he penned *Genesis*? The discrepancy lies, I believe, in the simple fact that when Moses wrote his version of the story, he knew full well that human beings lived much longer in those days. Based on the apocryphal record, when Abraham was eighty-seven years old, his great-great-grandfather Reu, the son of Peleg, died at the age of two hundred and thirty-nine.[53] And when Isaac was one hundred and ten years old, Shem, the son of Noah, died at the ripe old age of six hundred.[54] These numbers are also borne out by the canonical record, so by no means was Moses making a mental error when he described Isaac as a mere lad; he was simply describing the situation based on his understanding of the life spans of that era.

In retrospect, the discrepancy lies not in the numbers given to us by Moses but in the fact that we all judge things in relation to our own particular frame of reference. And when this reality, which was simply taken for granted by the biblical authors, is accounted for, it seems quite natural that Moses would call Isaac a lad, even though we moderns would never describe a thirty-seven-year-old man in that way. With this in mind, then, one can easily see that Isaac was, in reality, an adult, and as such can now be considered responsible for any of his own decisions, just as any normal adult might be.

The next thing one will notice is that, far from being ignorant of his father's intention in offering him up as a sacrifice to God, Isaac was actually the one who first thought of the idea. Of course, at the time, he could have never anticipated the possibility that God might actually take him up on his

---

52 *Jasher* 22:41-45
53 Ibid. 16:22
54 Ibid. 28:24

brash offer. Meanwhile, I can almost hear some people ask the inevitable question: Why would God make Isaac go through such a harrowing ordeal simply because he was the one who suggested it first? Is He some kind of cosmic sadist? If by that do you mean to ask: Is God in the habit of helping people perform any and all foolish acts because He enjoys watching people suffer? Then, no, He most assuredly is not a sadist.

Instead, what we have here, when one cares to examine *The Bible* as a whole, is simply another situation where God finds someone who has chosen to do something that He can use to communicate His purpose to an onlooking world. The same could be said when Enoch agreed to go along with the angels in his ascension to Heaven. Before God found that He could use Isaac to communicate what it means to be a type of Christ, He found Enoch. Though fearful of losing his life in the process, Enoch willingly accepted the inherent risk in ascending into the very presence of Almighty God. Thus, he became a heavenly mediator of His word, just as Jesus ascended to His Father where He continues to act as the eternal mediator between God and humanity.[55]

Subsequent to Enoch and Isaac, there was Moses, who also functioned as a type of Christ. In turning his back on the riches of Egypt in order to fulfill his calling as the deliverer of the Hebrews, Moses foreshadowed what one day Jesus would do, in emptying Himself of His divine power in the Incarnation and dying a cruel death on a Roman cross in order to provide a ransom for the people of God.[56]

In the case of Abraham and Isaac, then, God saw the same potential to lay down a shadow of things to come concerning the death and resurrection of His own Son, Jesus, when Isaac volunteered himself as a sacrificial offering. And though Isaac's desire to demonstrate his love and devotion to his father was a noble one, he certainly must have regretted it while having to follow through with his pledge by actually going to Mount Moriah with Abraham. Naturally, from a strictly humanistic point of view, Isaac could never have imagined that God would eventually provide a substitute in the form of a ram, who having appeared out of nowhere was sacrificed by his father instead of him. In this, the canonical record is again misleading. According to *Genesis*, Isaac, in being led up the mountain, appeared completely ignorant as to his father's intention.

> As the two of them went on together, Isaac spoke up and said to Abraham, "Father?"
> "Yes, my son?"
> "The fire and wood are here," said Isaac, "but where is the lamb

---

55 *Secrets of Enoch* 1-68
56 *Hebrews* 11:24-27

for the burnt offering?"

And Abraham answered, "God Himself will provide the lamb for the burnt offering, my son."

And the two of them continued on together.[57]

In *Jasher*, however, Isaac is portrayed in a much different way. To be sure, he is afraid of the situation into which he has gotten himself. He does undeniably waver, quite naturally. Who among us would not have done so if we were thrust into that same situation? He was, after all, only human, and in this it was to be the same with the human side of Jesus. Though the Son of God, the Incarnate One in human flesh, yet He likewise prayed in His darkest hour that the cup of God's wrath might pass from before Him. Still, as the obedient Son that He was, He willingly accepted the role that had been foreordained for Him before the foundations of the world had been laid. And as Jesus revealed His own humanity in a moment of overwhelming dread, so, too, did Isaac momentarily buckle under the pressure. Says *Jasher*:

And Isaac carried the wood for the burnt offering while Abraham held the torch and the knife. After walking along in silence for quite a while, Isaac stopped and turned to Abraham. "Father, I see the fire, and I see the wood, but where's the lamb to burn on the altar?"

"Oh, Isaac, you already know that the Lord has chosen you to be the burnt offering, not a lamb."

Isaac tried his best to smile. "Yes, Father, I know. Then, I'll happily do everything the Lord told you."

"You don't think what we're doing is wrong, do you?" asked Abraham. "Tell me now, son. Please, don't try to hide anything from me."

"As the Lord lives, Father, nothing is going to keep us from doing what God wants. I'm completely resolved. In fact, I thank the Lord for choosing me to be a burnt offering for Him."

Relieved, Abraham hugged his son, and they resumed their journey.

Soon, they arrived at the place that the Lord had described, and Abraham began to build an altar on that mountain. He cried as Isaac went around gathering stones and mortar to help him complete it. Then, placing the wood on the altar, he began tying up Isaac.

"Make sure the rope is good and tight, Father. That way I can't roll around. I don't want to ruin the offering by breaking loose when your knife cuts me."

So Abraham tied him securely with cords and carefully placed

---

57 *Genesis* 22:6-8

him atop the pile of wood.

"And Father, please, promise me you'll take some of my ashes to Mother. Tell her: This is the sweet-smelling savor of Isaac. But make sure you don't tell her if she's sitting near a well or anywhere high up. I don't want her throwing herself off trying to come after me."

Abraham cried even more. His tears spilled onto Isaac, who started crying, too. "Hurry, Father, do with me as God has instructed."

Strangely enough, though, their hearts rejoiced in what the Lord had told them to do. Outwardly they wept, while inwardly they celebrated. Then, Isaac stretched his neck out for his father, and Abraham raised the knife, preparing to cut his son's throat.[58]

From all this added detail, found only in the apocryphal record, one can clearly see that Isaac was not at all ignorant of what his father had in store for him. Though Abraham's son was human and Jesus was both human and divine, the two were yet one in spirit. Both were adults of sound mind and body, both willingly offered themselves to their father's will as supreme proof of their love and devotion, and both completed their journeys to the bitter end. Away forever, then, with the idea that just because the canonical version unnecessarily waters down a genuine parallel between these two heroes of *The Bible*, never let it be said that Isaac, the faithful son of Abraham, was not in every respect a worthy type of Christ, the obedient Son of God, after all.

Patterns of History

IN EXAMINING THESE historical patterns found in Scripture, we are driven to the inevitable question: What, exactly, is the point of all this so-called "typological" evidence? Simply put, because God understands how stubborn and skeptical we humans are as a species, He has deigned to communicate the vastness of His truth by way of the patterns of history, which, by their very nature, are hidden in plain sight. As such, these patterns through time are uniquely designed to be recognized by some but not by others. In this way, the truth of God conveyed by these patterns exists like so much gold lying about in a treasure chest, but which is only open to the virtuous who will use this wisdom to find their way home, while remaining inaccessible to the unscrupulous who would squander such riches on their own selfish purposes.

Therefore, in terms of our present study on shadow and substance, we are hopefully better able to appreciate the "predicament of God," if you will,

---

58 *Jasher* 23:49-65

so that in the case of Adam and Eve, we can see their exile from Eden was not an unfortunate aberration in the plan of God, as it has so often been portrayed. It was, in fact, a necessary cog in the wheel of the ultimate—dare I say—evolution of the redemption of mankind.

Notice, though, I did *not* say the evolution of *mankind*. In using the word *evolution*, I am not referring to a biological process but to a historical one, which we—limited as we are by our human perspective—have only come to grips with as the centuries roll on and our understanding of the divine roadmap matures. What I am speaking of here is the evolution of the *redemption* of mankind, in that the salvation of the world was never something that was going to take place overnight, would never happen without the sacrifices that such a miraculous redemption demanded. By necessity, it has been nothing short of an agonizingly slow procedure, much akin to that of the alleged process of biological evolution.

Mind you, however, I am not talking about the godless sort of evolution that seeks to eliminate the role of divine intervention from human history. What I am talking about is a God-ordained process of historical evolution— one that requires numerous messianic figures who lead each generation of the faithful to the next level of awareness of God's plan for humanity, which ticks away like some great celestial clock, with its persistent, methodical unfolding of time.

To reiterate: When God revealed to Adam that He would rescue him and his righteous descendants, He said it would take place in *five and a half* "days." Naturally, Adam did not understand until it was explained to him that it would not occur after just five and a half days as they were perceived in human terms. These *five and a half* "days" represented days from God's perspective, in which a day for Him constituted a thousand years from humanity's view. That is to say, the redemption that God spoke of would occur upon the completion of a period that encompassed 5,500 years. And not only did Adam misunderstand the actual time frame that was involved in this salvation, but he was also just as ignorant about its progressive nature. From God's point of view, this process of rescuing us from the clutches of death, Hell, and the grave has taken just a few days to fulfill, but from our perspective, it has required many long and excruciating centuries for this rescue effort to unfold.

So for us, this protracted process—where we are literally spoon-fed a gradual knowledge of God's redemptive plan—requires our understanding of the types of Christ in each succeeding generation. Moreover, because of the incremental nature of this awareness, it is entirely incumbent upon us to have a new revelation for each wave of mankind, much in the same way a traveler requires a series of milestones along the roadside so they may complete their journey without getting lost. In other words, without a clear understanding of who — and what — God is calling us to pay attention to in our journey of discovery, which is leading us back to Paradise, we are like sheep without a shepherd, in need of the sort of guidance that only the Lord of the Sheep can provide.

This is why, when Jesus asked His disciples Who they thought He was, they were actually expressing an awareness — however limited — of this age-old dilemma concerning the gradual dispensation of God's revelation. In the disciples' responses were telling clues to anyone who has taken the time to understand that their various answers were not merely random guesses along the way to solving some sort of cosmic whodunit. So Jesus asked His disciples: "Who do people say the Son of Man is?" And they replied: "Some say John the Baptist. Others say Elijah. And still others, Jeremiah or one of the prophets."[59]

In light of our present study, which demonstrates the extent to which both the apocryphal and canonical records converge in this exegetical tool of shadow and substance, one can better understand the disciples' view of this guiding principle. To a man, the disciples had all been born and bred into Hebraic messianic theology, and as such, they were trained to expect not just anyone who came along talking about God. They were seeking Someone Who conformed to a timeless tradition of prophetic utterances — a specific Man Whose birth and appearance among men had been precisely predicted.

Above all, they were seeking a Man Who fit a particular mold in terms of the heroes of faith who had all foreshadowed the coming of this Promised One, that is, the Son of Man spoken of so prominently in the books penned by Enoch. So when Jesus continually referred to Himself as the Son of Man, He was unreservedly confirming this tradition of messianic figures who in succeeding generations had prefigured one another until His very day, and this was the hidden meaning behind the disciples' apparently random answers, which to the untrained reader might seem like so many guesses. But to those in the know, their answers actually revealed the extent to which this messianic view of world history had been digested by the people of Israel in that day and age. And when the disciples replied that the people thought Jesus was John the Baptist risen from the dead, or instead a reincarnation of Elijah, Jeremiah, or some other messianic figure in their pantheon of heroes, they were actually testifying to something that only makes sense in light of our study of typology.

This is especially evident when Jesus Himself attested to this phenomenon to which His disciples obviously subscribed. Matthew described the scene where Jesus was speaking about John the Baptist. He asked the crowd what they had expected to see and hear when they came out to the desert to find John. "A prophet?" asked the Lord. "Yes, of course, and more than

59 *Matthew* 16:13-14

a prophet, I tell you. In fact, this is the one of whom it was written: I'll send My messenger ahead of You, who will prepare the way before You. And if you're willing to accept it, he is Elijah who was to come."[60]

Once again, Jesus in His own unique way was demonstrating the validity of typology as it is portrayed throughout *The Bible*. According to Him, God has always been in the business of foreshadowing the events of His salvation throughout the ages. So when Jesus spoke of John the Baptist as being the one of whom it was written, He was actually quoting from *The Book of Malachi*, the last book of *The Old Testament*. In it, Malachi was expressing the lament of God at the perpetual infidelity of His chosen people. Eventually growing weary of their unjustified complaints, the Lord had no choice except to turn away from them; but, in a moment of divine inspiration, Malachi prophesied a different fate for God's people:

> "See, I'll send My messenger who will prepare the way before Me. Then suddenly the Lord you're seeking will come to His Temple; the Messenger of the Covenant, Whom you desire, will come," says the Lord Almighty.
>
> But who can endure the day of His coming? Who can stand when He appears? For He'll be like a refiner's fire or a launderer's soap. He'll sit as a refiner of silver. He'll purify the Levites like gold and silver. Then the Lord will have men who will bring righteous offerings to Him, and the offerings of Judah and Jerusalem will be acceptable to the Lord, as in days gone by, as in former years.[61]

So what can one make of all this in light of our new understanding of typology? The first thing to notice is how Jesus locks into the portion of Scripture that pertains to His coming to the Temple as the Messiah Who has the way prepared for him by Elijah, whom He clearly saw as typifying John the Baptist. The next thing one cannot help but notice is that Jesus did not continue beyond the point that represented His First Coming. "Then suddenly the Lord you're seeking will come to His Temple; the Messenger of the Covenant, Whom you desire, will come," says the Lord Almighty.[62] Beyond that point of the mission of Messiah, He did not relate, because hidden in the plan of God—the mystery so difficult for the disciples to grasp—was that there were two distinct phases that comprised the coming of the Deliverer and not just one, as had always been believed by the people of Israel.

The same thing happened when Jesus read aloud from *The Book of Isaiah* in the Temple concerning the acceptable year of the Lord—a time that involved the healing, deliverance, and liberty of God's people. Closing the

---

60 *Matthew* 11:7-14
61 *Malachi* 3:1-4
62 Ibid. 3:1

book, He stopped midsentence at the very point that segued to the day of God's vengeance.[63] Similarly, Jesus at that moment in history spoke only of "the Messenger of the Covenant, the One Whom you desire, Who will come." But He did not continue with the next part of the text in *Malachi* that spoke of the future phase of His coming in which His life would no longer function as a ransom for sin but as the refiner's fire.

Therefore, in both the quoting of the portion of Scripture that pertained to His present situation and the omitting of the part He chose to avoid, there was a clear and telling message, which in the context of shadow and substance reveals a great deal about the mind of Jesus. The most obvious thing is that, in light of the challenges facing Him in communicating God's unfolding plan, Jesus focused on the portions of Scripture that illuminated the most misunderstood aspect of salvation, that is, the nature of His First Coming as the Kinsman Redeemer Who would give His life as a ransom. In order to do this, Jesus made it a point to echo what He found in *The Old Testament* that spoke of this phase of His work, while avoiding what did not.

This is why Jesus sought to highlight the fact that in the person of John the Baptist, they were witnessing the very messenger of God who had been prophesied to prepare the way for the Christ Who was to come. By referring to *Malachi*, Jesus was impressing upon them the lengths to which God had undergone to first raise up Elijah so that they could more readily accept the genuineness of John's role in the redemptive scheme of things. In doing this, God was revealing an enduring truth not only to them but also to an onlooking world. The Lord of the Harvest has forever been in the business of confirming His word by means of this process of shadow and substance—a fact which, as we have seen thus far, is clearly borne out in both the canonical and apocryphal records.

In light of this truth, an understanding of the history of mankind can ultimately be divided into two camps. One view states that history is a series of random actions that results in an endless array of open-ended and meaningless outcomes. The other view states that, however random the actions of humanity appear, there is an underlying principle that is unifying the events of historical time, particularly as they pertain to the so-called "people of God." According to this latter view, specific events in the past foreshadow future events in such a way that the past, the present, and the future are all intertwined so that one day they will ultimately confirm the controlling influence of the God of the Universe.

All this leads one, then, to ask the next question: Is there no easier way for God to get His message across? The answer, I am convinced, is quite an obvious one. But before one can entertain a possible answer to such a ques-

---

63 *Luke* 4:16-22

tion, one must first understand the underlying problem that the answer is intended to address.

The initial hurdle one is confronted with has everything to do with the nature of communication. By that I mean that it is a problem that rests squarely on the shoulders of the fact that we are neither God-like, nor are we capable of communicating in a God-like manner. As a result, we, as a species, are devoid of the necessary tools to communicate with a God-like being. To which one might reasonably respond: Of course, that is a given; so what is your point? My point is this. If we lack the ability to communicate with God, as we normally communicate with one another, then how might God choose to communicate with us? He is, after all, the One Who first conceived of this thing we understand as language, is He not? Certainly He does not lack the ability to communicate. Therefore, if anyone has a problem with this process of communication between God and humanity, I would have to assume that the problem lies with us.

From an awareness of this ironic nature of communication, which affects not only mankind's relationship with God but also with itself, one is confronted with the oldest complaint ever introduced into a conversation that ponders whether or not *The Bible* can be trusted as a valid source of truth. Naturally, this complaint is argued all the more passionately by those who proudly embrace their skepticism in the face of anything that even remotely postulates the communicative power of a higher being such as God. Their arguments generally run as follows: How can anyone believe in the divine origin of a book that was written by so many different people, living in different times and places, and speaking different languages? Everyone is familiar with the infamous parlor game where a line of people attempt to convey a message introduced at one end of the line and then passed on from person to person until eventually it comes out completely different on the other end. Is not this exactly what has happened with the countless regurgitations of *The Bible*?

To which I would respond: Yes, madam, or, yes, sir. I completely understand your dilemma. I would never think to argue with you on such a point. On this one thing we can all agree. This is certainly the true nature of the problem we are facing when it comes to depending on a compendium of books that have clearly been translated via a plenitude of language frames. Only a fool would try to dismiss such a valid criticism; a fool, or worse still, a simpleton—neither of which I am sure God needs to affirm His ability to communicate with His own creation. Therefore, any attempt to unravel such a mystery without addressing such an obvious objection would constitute a complete failure on the part of anyone who was endeavoring to validate the truth of *The Bible*.

Admittedly, when one addresses the dilemma in these terms, our problem certainly does appear hopeless, does it not? Yet this is exactly the series of obstacles that the biblical record as a whole is claiming to surmount. But how? Could it be that there is actually a key to unlocking the mysteries of *The Bible* as so many throughout the ages have suggested? And if there really is a key of interpretation, then why has mankind been unable so far to establish some kind of consensus with this process?

A Universal Language

STRANGELY ENOUGH, I believe, the answer to such a conundrum is really quite simple, if by the word simple one inserts the word *non-mystical*, because, contrary to popular opinion, finding the answer does not involve delving into the murky realm of *Bible* codes but rather into the all-too-human domain of the cinema. For in the cinema, one is presented with a very specific language—a language not comprised of words but a dialectic of visual imagery, that is to say, a series of images made more meaningful via their sequential arrangement. In the more than one hundred years of its existence, this international art form has managed to accomplish what was best described by American film director D.W. Griffith. "We've gone beyond Babel, beyond words. We've found a universal language."[64] As a result, this language of the cinema—composed entirely of images, of symbols, of meanings—is uniquely capable of imparting a message that transcends any known language barrier. Moreover, it is this simple usage of symbolism to convey meaning—as opposed to a more arcane approach—that most closely resembles the way in which *The Bible* manages to articulate its deepest truths.

Consider this: Prior to the industrial revolution of the late eighteenth century, the world remained compartmentalized—geographically, culturally, ideologically. As a result of industrialization, there came an explosion in mass transportation technology in the form of steam locomotion, which within a few short decades laid the foundation for everything that followed. With electrification came the telegraph, the telephone, the phonograph, the automobile, the cinema, the radio, and the airplane, which physically connected the world in a manner previously unimaginable. But, while all these inventions abolished the barriers between physical spaces, none of them could provide the much-needed means to eliminate the psychological barriers that remained. Consequently, a world without geographic barriers has only managed to create an environment where previously disparate regions of the globe began to commingle in unanticipated ways. Rather than unite the world, the abolition of borders has done far more harm than good, as ev-

---

64 *Screening Out the Past: The Birth of Mass Culture and the Motion Picture Industry*, Lary May, p. 60

idenced by two world wars, followed by decades of regional war ever after.

Amidst all this technologically-induced strife, only one invention has succeeded in rising above the mayhem of clashing titans, of south rising against north, of east rising against west. Only the cinema has provided humanity with the potential to bridge the psychological gap that was laid bare in the wake of the tearing asunder of physical barriers, and only masters of the cinema have learned over the course of time to perfect an art form that has managed to transcend all cultural and ideological boundaries, proving that the peoples of the world are not so different after all. North, south, east, west: When seen through the eyes of the universal language of the cinema, these so-called "pockets of ideology" bear a striking, if not haunting, similarity to one another.

It is this unique language of imagery, symbolism, and meaning, then, that, I am convinced, is the key to understanding God's message in *The Bible*; not the vague, surreptitious sort that only a computer genius can hope to decipher, but one that is laid bare for all to see on pages of black and white. This is why, when pioneers of the cinema sought to distance their product from their childish reputation as mere nickelodeons, they did so by cleverly embedding the universal message inspired by Holy Writ. By virtue of this infusion, the world's first patently modern art form soon took on an unprecedented maturity. Inspired by the timeless tapestry of biblical history, prescient producers breathed new life into their creations: Heroes and heroines alike strove against overwhelming odds, brother pitted jealous will against brother, merciless overlords sought to enslave the free, and amidst it all, the Divine One dipped His benevolent hand into the well of human misery. In theaters around the globe, themes of tragedy and hope, of crime and punishment, of ruin and rebirth, resonated deeply, from city to city, state to state, and country to country.

Furthermore, in a truly ironic fashion that I am sure no one has yet to fully appreciate in terms of its prophetic significance, for its first thirty years of existence the cinema was forged into being without uttering a single, spoken word. The silver screen was above all a silent one. To be sure, the written word was periodically inserted, but primarily it was an art form that conveyed its story entirely by way of a series of visual images. Concluded British film critic David Robinson: "This was the most truly international era in which was created a new art of great subtlety and sophistication."[65] Through all manner of metaphor, allegory, and simile, the cinema perfectly conveyed its poetic vision in a way that could be understood in every corner of the globe without an ounce of its intended message ever being lost to mistranslation.

---

65 *Seventy Years at the Movies: From Silent Films to Today's Screen Hits*, David Robinson (Consulting Editor), p. 7

This to me is what God—in His preponderance for using types and shadows—had in mind when He set out to communicate His truth to mankind. He speaks through dramas that transcend interpretation, that is to say, through universally recognizable symbols of dramatic significance that supersede the brute limitations of the intellect and speak directly to the heart and soul of humanity. This is why *The Bible* repeatedly focuses on the enduring elements that constitute the human condition in all its ignominious glory—of courage and cowardice, of sacrifice and greed, of faith and doubt, of honesty and deceit, of revenge and mercy, of loyalty and betrayal, of love and hate. This is why the truths of Scripture are so often couched in double and triple parallels of events that span many generations, as when the likes of Isaac, Joseph, Moses,and Jonah all foreshadow the life of Jesus.

In this way, the Lord demonstrates His acute awareness that we, as members of a fallen race, require this process of foreshadow and payoff to apprehend the true nature of the Divine, much like an audience sitting in a darkened theater requires the necessary clues to penetrate the mystery that is being played out on the screen before it. And though we can only gaze in rapt anticipation upon these iconic dramas, as those who "look through a glass, darkly," we are still able to grasp the truth conveyed in these scattered moments through time, and perceive in them a remarkable synergy that no mere mortal could have ever contrived.

The Author of the Universe

IN REVIEW, WHAT can one surmise from all of this? If it can be summed up concisely, I guess our storyline would run as follows. If God has apparently gone to such great lengths to speak to mankind by way of types and shadows, then He must have done so because He understands that, more than anything else, we are creatures with brains that are uniquely tuned to these tried-and-true storytelling elements. In an attempt to prove such a point, we not only have the biblical texts to offer up as evidence, but we also have a continuing record of many millennia in which humans, as a species, have spent endless amounts of energy in the business of telling stories.

As for the precise origin of storytelling, there is much debate as to how far back one must look to discover history's first example, particularly in respect to its conveyance in written form. This is due primarily to the fact that the modern view simply cannot accept the idea that the ancients were—as *The Bible* clearly implies—recipients of a "written tradition" prior to the so-called "oral tradition." In this way, a strictly humanistic interpretation of world history has won the day in its ability to rewrite an unabashedly biblical one. According to this humanistic view, primitive mankind simply lacked the necessary cognitive skills which were required for such things as writing—a skill that would only later supersede the more "primitive" phase of human development indicated by a "simpler" oral transmission of cultural wisdom.

Unfortunately, because this present analysis on the function of story-telling is a limited one, we have neither the time nor space to delve into the arguments for or against such a view. Suffice it to say, this work em-braces a biblical frame of reference in opposition to a humanistic one that assumes that storytelling began with caveman drawings. As such, we view its true origins as having occurred with the production of written works like those attributed to Enoch, the first narrator of *The Bible*. And should any-one ask why there is no evidence for this written tradition prior to the oral tradition—apart from the straightforward testimony of Enoch's texts them-selves—one may simply point out that this "missing chapter" of history was entirely in accordance with the plan of God, in that these earliest examples of storytelling were meant to be lost for a time. Only later, following a peri-od similar to that of the Dark Ages of medieval Europe, would writing give birth to the more traditionally accepted version of storytelling as it has come to be known today.

Needless to say, however, the importance of telling stories as a cultural phenomenon, both past and present, can hardly be overstated. In fact, many historians and anthropologists believe storytelling to be one of the most widely influential factors in the development of civilization, the common denominator that binds our collective humanity. Since time immemorial, stories that define the human race have been handed down from generation to generation. Many are viewed as merely myths, legends, fables, or fairy tales; others are deemed epics, adventures, or morality plays. But in every case, at the heart of the tale that stands the test of time, is a story of what it means to be human—or more specifically—what it means to become "more" human. In other words, at the center of all the stories that have carved out this universal tradition of storytelling is an element of *transformation*.

As the old adage goes: The only constant in the Universe is change; and just as it is with the Universe, so it is with every great story. Transforma-tion, metamorphosis, transcendence, call it what you will. Whether literally or figuratively, characters that speak to the human heart are ones who are striving to become something more than what they started out to be. And in this process of "becoming"—as when a caterpillar morphs into a butterfly, thereby becoming something altogether different—mankind is face to face with God's age-old work of recession and renewal, of extinction and rebirth, of death and resurrection. Old things are passed away; behold, all things have become new.[66] Death is swallowed up in victory,[67] and resurrection—whether literally or figuratively—has provided a brand-new start.

---

66 *Second Corinthians* 5:17
67 *First Corinthians* 15:54

This, then, is the essence of drama and the reason, I believe, that God Himself is to be considered the Author of the Universe. After all, did not John, in the opening chapter of his Gospel, state that the Word of God created all things?[68] According to this view, the Godhead spoke the Universe into existence by way of the articulated word. "And God 'said' let there be light."[69] From this, one might gain some insight into the biblical passages that refer to Jesus as the Author of the Universe. The Apostle Peter called Jesus the "Author of Life."[70] Additionally, Paul referred to Jesus in much the same vein, twice calling Him the "Author of Salvation," and once, the "Author of Faith."[71]

No wonder that all the processes in the known Universe, both natural and supernatural, are undergirded by this same articulated word, which speaks of the irresistible cycle of life and death. According to both biological and spiritual precepts—each according to its own frame of reference—the death of an organism is but a gateway to another form of life, however mystifying that new life form appears from our limited view. In scientific terms, matter is never lost; it is regenerated into a different form. Similarly, in theological terms, spirit is never lost; it, too, is retranslated into a new dimension.

The Wondrous Circle

SO WHAT IS the point of all the foregoing analytics? The point is: If God is the Author of the Universe, then it should no longer come as a surprise that He determined every aspect of creation would embrace the message of redemption that He uttered to Adam and Eve. In fact, given this understanding of God as Author, it makes perfect sense that He would choose a messianic figure like Enoch to proclaim the first prophecies of the Son of Man Who would one day carry out this mission of saving Adam and his descendants. It would similarly follow that—as critical as the articulation of such a message was—this message of Enoch, and others like him, would have been rejected and subsequently lost for many long ages. And finally, when the time had finally come to initiate a new era of spiritual awakening, it seems only natural that this Author God would do so via this same articulated word, specifically uttered for the sake of the chosen people of His calling.

More to the point, this is why I am convinced that God has chosen to convey His message not in terms that stifle the faith of His people, that is to say, in the trivial details of laws, regulations, and restrictions, which invoke

---

68 *John* 1:3
69 *Genesis* 1:1
70 *Acts* 3:15
71 *Hebrews* 2:10; 5:9; 12:2

such a burden of guilt and shame that it does nothing but quench the Spirit of Truth. Instead, God, as the Author of the Universe, has chosen to manifest His redemption via the power of the dramas of life and death, of war and peace, of doom and deliverance, as they are portrayed throughout the history of His chosen ones. As it was written by the hand of the Apostle Paul: "Faith comes through the hearing of God's word."[72] And again he wrote: "So I ask you, does God give you His Spirit and work miracles among you by the works of the Law or by your believing what you have heard?"[73]

In other words, God's plan has always been to rescue mankind by way of its response to the message He has entrusted to His light-bearers who have woven their artful tales, of the rising and falling of the human spirit, of the rebellion and rebirth of the human heart, of the death and resurrection of the human body. In this way, these inspired tales of wonder and awe have fulfilled their divine purpose in being spread abroad and received by those individuals who simply have eyes to see and ears to hear.

Such are the enduring tales like those penned by Enoch, which were handed down to inspire subsequent generations of prophetic genius, producing such works as *Jasher, Genesis, Isaiah,* and *Daniel.* All this until finally the One Who had set His redemptive plan of *five and a half* "days" into motion strode upon the stage of world history to give His life as a ransom to fulfill that promise made to Adam and Eve.

In turn, we would one day partake of the drama of their lives in such a way that—though dead and buried long ago—they would impart meaning to us, not in a didactic way that leads to disenfranchisement and despair but one that conveys truth that resonates from age to age, from life to life. In examining the meaning of these lives, we would in some special way detect in them a way of interpreting the meaning of our own lives, and as a result of this peculiar connection, which stretched to us in our own time, we, too, though destined to die like Adam, would be able to reach for the impossible and thus be imbued with the same force that transformed Jesus' mortal coil from death to life.

In this way, the wondrous circle of life as God has intended it is made complete. In the beginning was the Word; from age to age, it is the Word that sustains the Universe; and through to the very end, it will be the power of this Word that communicates His eternal purpose to all the world. And one day a generation will arise—perhaps this generation—that Enoch spoke of so long ago when he recorded his conversation with the Lord, Who said:

> I'll describe two mysteries for you, Enoch. First, many rebels will violate the word of truth. They'll speak incredible things and pro-

---

72 *Romans* 10:17
73 *Galatians* 3:5

nounce many lies. Tremendous civilizations will be created, and many books will be composed in their own words.

But My people will begin to write all My words properly in their own languages without altering or diminishing their meaning. They'll perform the task correctly, and then they'll possess everything I've said about them from the beginning.

The other mystery to tell you about concerns the faithful and wise, who will be given books of joy, integrity, and remarkable wisdom. And having received the gift of those books, they'll believe in what they have to say. They'll rejoice in them, and all the faithful ones will acquire the knowledge of every righteous path through them and be rewarded.

And someday, they'll call out to the people of Earth and make them listen to their wisdom.[74]

---

74 *First Enoch* 104:7-11

BOOK TWO

Why should I speak of ... the Phoenicians or ... the Chaldeans? For the Jews, deriving their origin from the descendants of Abraham ... have handed down to us ... the number of 5,500 years as being the period up to the advent of the Word of Salvation.

Julius Africanus, *On the Mythical Chronology of the Egyptians and Chaldeans*

Enoch as: The Go~Between

A Bridge Between Worlds

FOUND WITHIN the pages of the biblical record is the strange story of a man by the name of Enoch. Anyone familiar with *The Bible* is familiar with him. In both *The Old Testament* and *The New Testament*, it is related, in no uncertain terms, that "Enoch walked with God, and he was not, because God took him."[75] According to biblical scholars, Enoch is a man who holds the peculiar distinction of being the only patriarch whose life story does not end with the words: "And he died." What is more, Paul elaborated on his story when he said, "By faith, Enoch was taken from this life so that he did not experience death. He could not be found because God had taken him away. But before he was taken, he was commended as one who pleased God."[76]

So in the mouth of multiple witnesses, we have one of the most remarkable biographies—however brief—in all of Scripture, not to mention, this is the same man who supposedly penned numerous books as a result of his encounter with God. Yet flying in the face of such testimony, many of these same scholars—who all presumably believe in God's ability to communicate—have chosen to repudiate the idea that Enoch actually wrote the books that bear his name. Attributing them instead to later writers, who allegedly borrowed Enoch's name to lend authenticity to their own works, these so-called "experts" have categorized these texts as *pseudepigrapha*. In doing so, these remarkable books were stigmatized, and have ever since been tainted by equal parts of skepticism and doubt.

Even after the pioneering work of men like James Bruce and Richard Laurence, most biblical scholars insisted that *The First Book of Enoch* could not have existed during the time of *The New Testament* world, having placed its origins some three centuries *after* the birth of Christianity. That is, they did until 1947, when the unprecedented discovery of *The Dead Sea Scrolls*, in the Judean Desert, sparked a fervent, new wave of inquiry. Amongst the more than seven hundred fragmented documents discovered at Qumran, believers and skeptics alike were amazed to find remains of ten manuscripts of *First Enoch*, as well as several other works in the Enochic tradition, such as *The Book of Jubilees* and *The Testament of the Twelve Patriarchs*. Using carbon-14 dating, these ancient manuscripts were estimated to have been writ-

---

75 *Genesis* 5:24
76 *Hebrews* 11:5

ten at least as early as 200 B.C. No longer could anyone argue that these documents had not been produced *before* the birth of Christianity, or that these works were not in a position to influence those who walked and talked with Jesus of Nazareth.

More importantly, since those heady days of discovery, books like those ascribed to Enoch are no longer the sole property of cloistered scholars who discuss such arcane matters amongst themselves in darkened rooms, walled away from the rest of humanity, which is, according to them, bereft of their learned perspective. Now, thanks to today's open-ended world of mass communication technology, those of us who choose to read these texts for ourselves are now in a position to come to our own conclusions, based on a comparison of them with their more familiar canonical counterparts. The fruits of such a labor are positively astounding. Far from lending credence to the *pseudepigraphal* theory of Enochic authorship, the resulting examination—free from the bias that often accompanies institutionally-sponsored reviews—demonstrates that these texts reveal an array of striking parallels between the teachings of Enoch and Jesus. In fact, it has been estimated there are at least one hundred known references in *The New Testament* that can be traced directly to the books ascribed to Enoch. In light of such a connection it appears that, more than any other figure in biblical history, Enoch stands as a veritable bridge between worlds, between that of *The Old Testament* and *The New Testament*.

Parallels of Thought

IN THE GOSPELS OF both Matthew and Luke, for example—when Jesus spoke of the resurrection of the dead, where people will refrain from marriage because they will be like the angels of Heaven—it turns out that He was actually quoting Enoch.[77] "But from the beginning you (speaking of the angels) were made spiritual, living a life that is eternal; therefore, I (God) have not made wives for you because your dwelling place is in Heaven."[78]

Elsewhere, John has Jesus speaking of "rooms" in Heaven.[79] But what most people never realize is that before Jesus mentioned them Enoch spoke of the "habitations of the elect."[80] Speaking to his children, Enoch said, "In the great time to come, there are innumerable mansions prepared for men— good ones for the good, and bad ones for the bad."[81] Later, Paul would echo this same idea when he wrote: "If the earthly tent we live in is destroyed, we

---

77 *Matthew* 22:30; *Luke* 20:35-36
78 *First Enoch* 15:6-7
79 *John* 14:1
80 *First Enoch* 41:1
81 *Secrets of Enoch* 61:1

have a building from God, an eternal house in Heaven, not built by human hands."[82]

Furthermore, one of the titles Jesus gave Himself to convey His unique role in history, that of the Son of Man—repeated eighty-one times in *The Gospels*—finds its source in none other than Enoch. Mark has Jesus saying, "At that time, mankind will see the Son of Man coming in clouds with great power and glory, and He will send His angels to gather his elect from the four winds, from the ends of the Earth to the ends of the Heavens."[83] In this passage, one can see that Jesus was referring to *First Enoch*, when the patriarch prophesied that:

> The kings, princes, and all who possess the Earth will glorify the Son of Man, Who was concealed from the beginning, in complete secrecy, by the power of the Most High and revealed only to the elect. He will sow the congregation of the saints and the elect, and they will stand before Him on that day.[84]

Another remarkable evidence for the authenticity of *First Enoch* is revealed when one considers the disciple's description of the transfiguration of Christ: "And a voice came out of the cloud, saying, 'This is My Beloved Son: Hear Him.'"[85] Matthew, Mark, and Luke all record this same event, each describing the scene in similar terms—with one exception, however. Luke, in his description, provides a unique distinction that was sadly omitted by the *King James Bible* translators, an omission that obscures the true meaning of Luke's rendition, which was clearly spelled out in the original Greek. Fortunately for us, later generations of translators who had access to the Greek manuscripts were not so worried with the Elizabethan concern for textual uniformity, and have admirably noted Luke's subtle but all-important distinction. According to *The Expanded Bible*, in Luke's recounting, we discover what the voice out of the cloud really said. "This is My Son, My Chosen One: Listen to Him."[86]

In this version, the translators compare this exalted title to one that is found in the forty-second chapter of *The Book of Isaiah*. Most render Isaiah's description as: "Behold, My Servant Whom I uphold, My Chosen, in Whom My soul delights."[87]

Clearly, one can see the parallels in the language of Isaiah with that of Luke's, when he records the circumstances of the transfiguration event. Of

---

82 *Second Corinthians* 5:1
83 *Mark* 13:26-27
84 *First Enoch* 61:10-11
85 *Matthew* 17:5; *Mark* 9:7; *Luke* 9:35
86 *Luke* 9:35
87 *Isaiah* 42:1

greater importance still is that Isaiah's title of "My Chosen " is often rendered as "My Elect." Sources for this variation include the esteemed *Geneva
Bible*, a translation that predated the *King James* Version by more than half a
century, and one that accompanied the Pilgrims on the *Mayflower*. The reason that this distinction is so important is because the title of the "Elect One"
is found *fifteen* times in *First Enoch*.

> In that day, the Elect One will sit upon a throne of glory, and their
> spirits within them shall be strengthened when they look upon My
> Elect One, because they've fled for protection to My holy and glo-
> rious name. In that day, I'll cause my Elect One to dwell in their
> midst.[88]

Assuming, then, that this book was known to the disciples of Christ, one
can only imagine their considerable astonishment when the "voice out of
the cloud" told them concerning Jesus that "This is My Son, My Elect One,"
the very One Who was promised in *The First Book of Enoch*.

Could it actually be possible that such precise parallels of thought are
the result of books that were not divinely inspired? Furthermore, who in
their right mind would even concern themselves with the hackneyed controversy of who did or did not write these books when they have been
linked with the teachings of none other than Jesus, Isaiah, Matthew, Mark,
Luke, John, and Paul? Clearly, this book—and others just like it—have been
treated as genuine sources of truth by some of the greatest seers in the history of the world, and just because a bunch of well-intentioned "experts"
have cast these books into the realm of doubt and suspicion does not mean
that free-thinking, rational minds should henceforth be kept from coming to
their own conclusions.

So away with the outmoded verdict of self-appointed geniuses, who,
in their timid ignorance, refuse to sanction the books of such luminaries as
Enoch, who, as the canonical record clearly states, walked and talked with
God. Let the light of truth shine forth as it has always been meant to do,
and let no one presume to hold back what God has intended by way of the
revelation of Jesus Christ, the Elect One Who "dwelled in their midst,"[89] the
Son of Man Who, though once "concealed by the power of the Most High,"[90]
has now "chosen to reveal the secret of God's kingdom to His saints and His
elect."[91]

---

88 *First Enoch* 45:3-4
89 Ibid. 45:4
90 Ibid. 61:10
91 *Matthew* 13:11; *Mark* 4:11; *Luke* 8:10

The Man From Forever

THE STORY of Enoch, the seventh from Adam, is an incredible tale of a man who walked and talked with God, a man who was said to have soared through a hole in space and time, where space was without limit, and time stood still. There was only the man and his journey, and this journey took him to a land where all legends and lore collide, where the man found himself standing before the Face of God, the Lord of Eternity Who holds space and time in the palm of His hand.[92]

When Enoch asked the Face why he was there, he was told simply that he should tell the tales of forever. Then he was given a pen of quick-writing and told to write them down as fast as he could.[93] So for what seemed like but a moment, the man beyond time wrote down everything he heard. He wrote stories of everyone's lives, of those who *have* lived, of those who *were* living, and of those who *were yet to* live.[94]

And after he was done writing, he awoke on his couch, wondering what he should do next.[95] Until finally, he realized that he had no choice in the matter, because unless he did what he was supposed to do, no one else would ever know the tales of forever, because no one but him had witnessed the things that he had. So he looked in the mirror and understood what he alone had to do, because he recognized the face staring back at him, and it was the face of the man from forever.

---

92 *Secrets of Enoch* 22:1-7; 39:3
93 Ibid. 22:11
94 Ibid. 23:2; 39:2; 40:1-2
95 Ibid. 38:2

A Prophecy of Days

A Time for Everything

TIME IS A FUNNY thing, it is said. Time is fleeting, we are told. Time—"ticking away the moments that make up a dull day," sings Pink Floyd, the seventies British progressive rock band. "And then one day you find ten years have got behind you. No one told you when to run; you missed the starting gun."[96] Everywhere one turns, there is an obsession with time—time is up, time to go, time is money. Clocks chime, watches beep, phones chirp. Everywhere some kind of device is reminding us of what time it is. Even so, long before the modern world became obsessed with the concept of time, *The Bible* declared its importance in the plan of God. "There is a time for everything, and a season for every activity under Heaven—a time to be born and a time to die, a time for war and a time for peace."[97] The prophet Isaiah referred to the "time" of God's favor.[98] Daniel spoke of the "set times" of the Lord,[99] and twice he spoke of the "appointed time."[100] Jesus spoke to His disciples about the importance of His doing things at the "right time."[101] Paul, too, spoke to the Corinthians about an "appointed time,"[102] and to the Romans, he described how at just the "right time" Christ died for us.[103]

No wonder that when God spoke to Adam and Eve about restoring them to their original state in Paradise, He designed His rescue effort in accordance to a timeline of His own choosing. The first thing God did, as depicted in *The First Book of Adam and Eve*, was to explain: "I have ordained days and years for you and your descendants, Adam, until those days and years are fulfilled; and when those *five and a half* days are fulfilled, I will send the Word to save you."[104] Of course, when Adam heard about this prophecy of The Great Five and a Half Days, he had no idea what God meant. At first, he thought the Lord was saying that the end of the world would be taking place in just *five and a half* days, so he begged God to explain this to him.[105]

---

96 *Time*, David Gilmour, Nick Mason, Roger Waters, Richard Wright
97 *Ecclesiastes* 3:1-2, 8
98 *Isaiah* 49:8
99 *Daniel* 7:25
100 Ibid. 8:19; 11:29, 33
101 *John* 7:6
102 *First Corinthians* 4:5
103 *Romans* 5:6
104 *First Adam and Eve* 3:1-2
105 Ibid. 3:3-5

That is when the Lord informed Adam that the *five and a half* "days" He was referring to actually represented 5,500 years, after which, "One would come and rescue him and his descendants."[106]

Now, at this point, I imagine that certain ones reading this still might insist on objecting to such a prophecy on the grounds that no comparable prophetic timelines can be found in the canonical record. There are, you may point out, prophecies regarding future events, say, ones predicted by Jeremiah, which involve a *year*-oriented prophecy, as in *seven times seventy* "years." But nowhere have biblical scholars ever mentioned anything similar to this one regarding The Great Five and a Half Days. At which point I would have to strongly object; because there is, in fact, a clear precedence in the realm of biblical scholarship with regard to such a *day*-oriented prophecy. Let me explain what I mean.

A Sliver of Hope

CONTAINED IN *The Old Testament* is a story that has, for centuries, perplexed biblical scholars who have sought to understand its meaning. It is the story of the prophet Hosea. Although classified as one of the Minor Prophets, due to its subordinate relationship to others like *The Book of Isaiah* and *The Book of Daniel*, the book bearing his name is actually one that plays a major role in terms of its prophetic significance. The most intriguing thing about Hosea, though, is that his prophecies have clearly been overshadowed by the peculiar life that he led as a result of God not merely giving him a series of prophetic utterances to deliver but instructing him to live out the very message he was inspired to preach. To drive home the full impact of how God felt about His people's penchant for idol worship, Hosea was instructed to marry a prostitute. Then, via the choice of names for their children, God dramatically revealed His attitude toward the people of Israel. The first child, a son, was called Jezreel, because God was going to scatter the inhabitants of the land and thereby put an end to the northern kingdom of Israel. The second child, a daughter, was called Loruhamah, because God was going to withdraw His love from the House of Israel to the north and only care for the House of Judah to the south. And finally, the third child, another son, was called Loammi, because the northern kingdom would no longer be treated as God's people, and He would no longer be considered their God.[107]

To a lesser degree, the same thing happened when God inspired Isaiah to walk around Jerusalem — naked and barefoot — as a "sign of things to come." In this case, the "thing" that would be happening to the inhabitants

---

106 *First Adam and Eve* 3:6
107 *Hosea* 1:4-8

of the land was that they, too, would walk naked and barefoot as they were being led into captivity because of their trusting the Egyptians rather than the Lord.[108] Similarly, to foretell the imminent destruction of Jerusalem, God instructed Ezekiel to shave his head and beard, and to divide the hairs into three piles. One pile was to be burned, one was to be struck by a sword, and one was to be scattered to the wind. Yet from each pile, a few strands of hair were to be tucked away in the folds of Ezekiel's garment—all this to typify the coming destruction of the majority of the population, while but a remnant was to be spared by God.[109]

Just like Isaiah and Ezekiel, then, Hosea was forced to dramatize the message he was entrusted with so that the recipients of his message would not only have to hear it but would be forced to live it, too. Fortunately, though, for the northern kingdom of Israel, Hosea did foresee a sliver of hope in the catastrophic events that lay ahead, because no sooner did he proclaim the abandonment and scattering of the kingdom to the north than Hosea prophesied a much different outcome in their distant future. Notwithstanding the period of desolation and humiliation that the Israelites were to endure, Hosea foresaw the day when "the Israelites would be as the sand of the sea on the seashore, which cannot be measured or counted, and in the very place where it was said of them, 'You are not My people,' they will be called the 'children of God.'"[110]

In many ways, this period of alienation and restoration of the House of Israel constitutes a unique parallel in biblical history with that of the House of Judah. Just as Jeremiah prophesied seventy years of desolation upon the Judahites to the south, followed by their eventual return to Jerusalem, Hosea pronounced a similar sequence of events as they pertained to the Israelites to the north. And so it is with this unique relationship of events that connect the prophetic timelines of both the northern and southern kingdoms—which comprise the totality of the nation of Israel—that we are now able to bring all these apparent loose ends of our discussion to a point of convergence. Let us review to this point.

More than Poetry

WE BEGAN BY EMPHASIZING the importance of timing in the plan of God. In this, the Scriptures are abundantly clear. If nothing else, the God of *The Bible* is a God of Set Times Who fulfills His word of promise at "just the right time." We then considered the possibility that God might have revealed this notion of His "appointed times" from the beginning when Adam

---

108 *Isaiah* 20:1-6
109 *Ezekiel* 5:1-17
110 *Hosea* 1:10

and Eve were originally expelled from Paradise. In the apocryphal record, we discover the very moment when God explained that even though He had banished them because of their disobedience He would not abandon them forever. Someday, according to God's first prophetic timeline for humanity, He would allow them back into their garden home upon the completion of The Great Five and a Half Days, or rather — from Adam and Eve's point of view — after 5,500 years.[111]

Next, we brought up the issue of whether or not this same principle of a *day*-oriented prophecy could be found in the Biblical Canon. Or, to put it in the form of a question: Are there any rescue efforts in the traditional texts depicting a prophecy of "days" like the one in *First Adam and Eve*, as opposed to those utilizing the more familiar timeline of "years" like the one in *Daniel*? In order to answer this question, I then led us to the prophecies of Hosea, Isaiah, and Ezekiel. There we discovered a consistent pattern of God lifting His provision and protection of His people in times of punishment, and in this pattern, I believe, we have the evidence that we are seeking. In all of this, the reoccurring pattern that emerges is: Again and again, whether it is Adam and Eve, or Israel and Judah, the chosen ones begin in a state of blissful ignorance, believing themselves to be the perpetual darlings of God. Then, complacency and pride creep in, slowly but surely eroding the established order, followed by willful disobedience and outright rebellion. Finally, after all the stern warnings of the Lord are ignored comes His reluctant, though necessary, punishment as depicted in the first couple's fall from grace and both the kingdoms of Israel and Judah's deportation into slavery. Yet according to a similarly persistent pattern, God places a time limit on this period of judgment. Instead of destroying the people of His calling, His chastisement ultimately leads to repentance and renewal, thereby bringing them to a higher level of responsibility and awareness.

In the case of Hosea, one comes face to face with this principle when he reassured the Israelites that although they would be abandoned and characterized as "not God's people" they would yet, in the very place of desolation and retribution, someday be called "the children of God."[112] But when was this future restoration and exaltation supposed to take place? Fortunately for us, not only can we find the answer to that question, but in doing so, we will also finally be able to answer our question as to whether or not there is any evidence for the kind of prophecy of "days" in the canonical record like those in the apocryphal record. However, to find that out, one must delve even further into *The Book of Hosea*. First, we read that Hosea ended the fifth chapter with a severe word of warning:

111 *First Adam and Eve* 3:1-6, 16
112 *Hosea* 1:10

For I will be like a lion to Ephraim, like a great lion to Judah. I will tear them to pieces and go away. I will carry them off with no one to rescue them. Then, I will go back to My place until they admit their guilt and seek My face. In their misery, they will earnestly seek Me.[113]

Then, Hosea began the sixth chapter with a hauntingly familiar message of hope:

Come, let us return to the Lord. He has torn us to pieces, but He will heal us. He has injured us, but He will bind up our wounds. After two days, He will revive us. On the third day, He will restore us so that we may live in His presence. Let us acknowledge the Lord. As surely as the Sun rises, He will appear. He will come to us like rain in winter, like the spring rain that waters the Earth.[114]

So there it is. A prophecy of "days" is in the canonical record after all. "After two days, God will revive us. On the third day, He will restore us." And just like God's timeline for Adam and Eve, this exiling of the nation of Israel was destined to involve a prophetic period that would be comprised of a similarly constituted set of preordained "days."

And just in case anyone is liable to think that this prophecy of "days," located in the Canon, is some kind of fluke or aberration, let us take a moment to examine the precision of the scriptural record as it pertains to this particular chapter of prophetic history. To Ephraim, synonymous with the northern kingdom, Hosea proclaimed that God would attack like a lion, and to Judah, the southern kingdom, He would attack like a great lion. In this declaration, Hosea was not merely uttering a poetic turn of the phrase. He was precisely predicting the way in which God was planning to vanquish the two kingdoms.

The northern kingdom of Israel was to be conquered by Sargon the Second, whose power was depicted, throughout that country's architecture and sculpture, by none other than the lion. In 722 B.C., the Assyrians, led by Sargon, vanquished the capital of Samaria, located in the territory of Ephraim, and carried away captive the majority of the population. Then, in 586 B.C., the southern kingdom of Judah came to an ignominious end; this time at the hands of the Babylonian Empire. And what was their national symbol of power? Naturally, just as Hosea had warned them so many years earlier, it was the lion of Babylon, Nebuchadnezzar, who performed God's will in humbling the kingdom to the south.

My purpose in mentioning all of this is two-fold: First, I hope to con-

---

113 *Hosea* 5:14-15
114 Ibid. 6:1-3

vey the precision with which Hosea presented his message. In other words, for Hosea, the words that God entrusted him with were more than poetry. When he proclaimed to a rebellious nation that unless they changed their idol-worshiping ways the Lord would attack them as a lion, he was accurately predicting the way in which God eventually raised up both Assyria and Babylon to perform the work of His hands. In this, it was exactly as Moses warned the nation in *The Book of Deuteronomy*:

> If you do not obey the Lord your God, and do not carefully follow all His commands, all these curses will overtake you: The Lord will cause you to be defeated by your enemies. You will come at them from one direction but will flee from them in seven, and you will become a thing of horror to all the kingdoms of the Earth — an object of scorn and ridicule to all the nations where the Lord will drive you.[115]

Second, just as his predictions of doom were more than merely poetic in nature, so also were his predictions of salvation. Therefore, when Hosea reassured the people that God would "revive them after two days; and restore them on the third day," he was being just as precise in his meaning. In this case, of course, we are much more sophisticated in our understanding of the ways of God when He stated that His intention was to restore the nation in three "days" time. Certainly no one in the present age would ever be so naïve as Adam when he thought that God was going to rescue him after just *five and a half* days as they are reckoned from our earthbound perspective. Naturally, when God speaks of doing things according to His days, He is always referring to a period that is, according to our human perspective, equal to a thousand years.[116]

On the Third Day

STILL YOU MIGHT BE asking: Why, then, are there no biblical scholars who have ever published anything about this *day*-oriented prophecy of Hosea? Oh, but there are. The most eloquent of these is Adam Rutherford, the British biblical chronologist, who, in his book *Israel-Britain*, wrote:

> Israel was finally smitten and carried captive into Assyria at the close of Hoshea's reign, their chief city, Samaria, having fallen after a three year siege.[117] But God promised that after Two Days — which, according to His days of a thousand years each, are equal to two thousand years — He will revive them. All are agreed that the captivity of Israel occurred in the eighth century before Christ,

---

115 *Deuteronomy* 28: 15, 25, 37
116 *Second Peter* 3:8; *Psalm* 90:4; *Jubilees* 4:30
117 *Second Kings* 17:5-6

therefore, two thousand years later is the thirteenth century of the Christian Era. We are now more than halfway through that Third Day, and just look at the raising up of Israel under the modern name of the Anglo-Saxon race as it takes place before our very eyes.[118]

Rutherford then goes on to compare Hosea's prophecy of the Three Days with Ezekiel's more familiar vision of the Valley of Dry Bones.[119] He continued:

The restoration of the whole House of Israel, so often spoken of in the Scriptures, is beautifully pictured in Ezekiel's vision of the Valley of the Dry Bones. In this famous vision, the prophet saw an open valley full of dry bones. On Ezekiel's being commanded by God to prophesy that these bones come to life, "there was a noise and a shaking, and the bones came together, bone to his bone." And then, "the sinews and the flesh came upon them, and the skin covered them, but there was no breath in them." The prophet was then asked to prophesy that God would cause these slain ones to live. Then, "breath came into them, and they lived and stood upon their feet—a vast army." God then said to Ezekiel, "These bones are the whole House of Israel."

Notice the close correspondence between Ezekiel's vision of the Valley of Dry Bones and Hosea's Three Days. Each deals with the House of Israel, and each are in three stages. Hosea's First Day corresponds exactly with the first stage of Ezekiel's vision. The valley of dry bones spoke eloquently of the sad picture of the scattered, hopeless, and lifeless condition of Israel during the First Day. It depicted dispersion, disorder, and death.

Hosea's Second Day saw the luring and the gathering of the tribes into the "appointed place." This resembled the second stage of Ezekiel's vision, where there was a shaking, and bones were sorted and gathered "bone to his bone." Order was evolved out of chaos, but it was not yet orderly life. "There was no life in them yet."

Hosea's Third Day was one of resurrection to national life. "On the third day, He will raise us up, and we will live in His sight." So it was in Ezekiel's vision. The Spirit of God breathed upon "these slain ones," and "breath came into them, and they lived and stood upon their feet—a vast army." It was a vision of life, order, power, and invincible might.[120]

---

118 *Israel-Britain*, Adam Rutherford, 1934, p. 161
119 *Ezekiel* 37:1-14
120 *Israel-Britain*, Adam Rutherford, 1934, pp. 181-82

A Capstone to Time

One Final Twist

*T*HE BOOK OF DAYS chronicles a two-fold drama of paramount importance, to hardcore biblical scholars and casual readers of Scripture alike. The first of these pertains to the little-known prophecy of The Great Five and a Half Days — introduced in *The First Book of Adam and Eve*, alluded to in *The Secrets of Enoch*, and finally culminating in *The Gospel of Nicodemus*. Prior to this work, the scattered bits of this prophetic tapestry lay strewn about like so many disassembled pieces of a puzzle abandoned long ago, but herein they have all been reconnected, and a continuous dramatic narrative has been constructed.

As the story goes: Soon after their tragic expulsion, Adam and Eve were told by God that He intended to allow them back into the garden home they had forfeited; but not until the completion of *five and a half* "days" from His perspective. Why *five and a half* days? They were to be banished for that length of time because, as Enoch stated in his record of events, Adam and Eve had resided in Eden for *five and a half* hours. So, just as the Israelites neglected to keep God's command to let the land lie fallow during His Jubilee years and were consequently exiled, the Lord of Time deigned to establish the prototypical pattern of His judgments in the lives of our first parents and were thereby exiled for *five and a half* "days."

Thus, having established the prophetic timeline of The Great Five and a Half Days, the drama came full circle when Pontius Pilate confronted Annas, the chief priest at Jerusalem, who confessed that he had also become aware of this promise of "days." Quite unexpectedly, Annas had discovered a passage in their most sacred text, in the first of *The Seventy Books*, as he described it himself, in which the archangel Michael was said to have told Seth, the third son of Adam, that the Christ was to appear on Earth after 5,500 years. Furthermore, he deduced that because Moses had constructed The Ark of the Covenant with dimensions of *five and a half* cubits, this doubly confirmed that Christ would come in an ark, or tabernacle, of a body, according to this same time frame.[121]

All this leads us, then, to one last bit of information — "one final twist," as it were — regarding the prophecy of The Great Five and a Half Days, which concerns the second drama depicted in this work, that of Enoch, the scribe, who was entrusted with a knowledge of the entire span of human

---

121 *Nicodemus* 22:10-13

history. Still you may be asking: How can anyone believe that a mere mortal could possibly perceive the history of all mankind—of those who *had* lived, who *were* living, and who *were yet to* live?[122] Certainly, it is impossible for anyone to know something so far beyond the pale of human cognition, is it not? Admittedly, such questions are perfectly valid ones, and in our attempt to address such impossibilities, we will offer the following possibilities.

Detectives of History

WHEN GRAPPLING WITH mysteries like this, we have focused on certain key strategies. Primarily, we have centered our investigation upon what I have called the dramas that transcend interpretation. In other words, when faced with the dilemma of what can and cannot be trusted in our search for scriptural truth we—as veritable detectives of history—have focused on events that have been repeated over and over again. In the case of Enoch, history's most articulate type of Christ, this means we should collect clues that correlate his life and teachings with Jesus, the articulated Word of God, that is to say, the substance of Enoch. In this way, the greater the extent to which we find parallels between Enoch and Christ, the greater the probability that the improbabilities in question might not seem so improbable after all.

So, what are some of the ways that Enoch, "as shadow," and Christ, "as substance," are displayed throughout biblical history? Like Jesus of Nazareth after him, Enoch was anointed with a very special connection with God that provided an acute awareness of the divine presence that no one else possessed. This eventually led Enoch into a one-on-one encounter with God Himself, where the patriarch was given a prophetic message for the sake of the chosen—an event that in many ways foreshadowed the transfiguration of Christ. Upon returning to his family that was convinced he had been killed, Enoch was received by them as one who had been figuratively brought back from the dead. And finally, having gifted his family with the books he had written, Enoch ascended to Heaven in the sight of everyone, just as Jesus would likewise do after His death and resurrection.

Naturally, because of these striking parallels, skeptics have argued that later authors must have edited the events of Enoch's life in order to create these connections after the fact, much in the same way they have maligned the prophecies of Daniel because of their unprecedented level of historical accuracy. Of course, much of this criticism falls by the wayside in light of the findings at Qumran, where the contribution of *The Dead Sea Scrolls* has demonstrated that the books attributed to Enoch preceded the Christian Era by at least two centuries. In this way, one might better appreciate the role

---

122 *Secrets of Enoch* 23:2; 39:2; 40:1-2

that the life of Enoch plays in foreshadowing that of Jesus', and, considering the relationship between these two miraculous figures, Enoch's insight into the fate of all mankind.

That said, I would like to return to the point I made earlier in this chapter when I mentioned that you may not be aware of one final bit of information regarding the prophecy of The Great Five and a Half Days. Thus far, in our mystery grappling, we have employed the use of dramas that transcend interpretation. Next, we will turn to another form of examining biblical history, one that is also used because of its ability to nullify the inherent problems that occur with the numerous translations of *The Bible*. In this case, we will be interpreting the biblical record in terms of another tool, which, like that of the drama, is universal in nature, regardless of culture and/or language, that is to say, mathematics.

But where some would seek to find mathematical messages in Scripture in the form of obscure codes, which may or may not exist, the ones I will be discussing are the kind that are clearly visible, though hidden in plain sight. Moreover, while some would try to expound complicated mathematics that only a genius might hope to appreciate, I will be discussing the kind that even a child can understand. In this case, the mathematics we will be dealing with pertain to one of the most ancient monuments ever dedicated to the knowledge of God — The Great Pyramid of Giza, renowned throughout history as The Pillar of Enoch, due to his reputed role as its architect.

Fear not, however, those of you who have already encountered the stupefying mysteries surrounding this enigmatic structure. We will not be delving too deeply into the multitude of cryptic meanings encased in its marvelous design. No, that, I can assure you, is quite beyond the scope of this particular essay. What we will be looking for, though, is the possible link between Enoch, as architect, and The Great Pyramid, as The Pillar of Enoch. Hopefully, we will establish this link by way of investigating the following questions. Do the allegedly prophetic implications built into the design of The Great Pyramid of Giza reveal a connection to the hidden hand of its supposed architect, Enoch? How might this help to explain the way that this mere mortal could have perceived something as unknowable as the fate of all mankind? And in what ways might the testimony of the alleged "word of God in stone" corroborate the validity of the alleged "word of God by the hand of Enoch"?

The Pillar of Enoch

LET US TAKE A MOMENT, then, to examine some of the things that might offer the necessary links we are seeking. First, how does *The Bible* even begin to consider mere stone as a form of witness to the word of God? In fact, a passage in *The Book of Isaiah* has something very interesting to say about it.

As in the construction of any grand edifice, which requires a precise plan of measurement, the following verses provide a unique benchmark into the meaning of the divine metaphor of the *stone*. Said Isaiah:

> Listen to what the Lord says to all you skeptics who rule the people in Jerusalem, because you've said, "We've made a covenant with death and Hell. The overwhelming scourge will not reach us when it passes by, because we've made falsehood our refuge, so as to conceal ourselves with lies."
>
> Therefore, the Lord God says, "Look and see how I've placed a stone in Zion—a tested stone, a precious cornerstone as a firm foundation. Whoever believes in it will not be shaken. I'll make justice the measuring line, and righteousness the level. Then, hail will sweep away the refuge of lies, and the waters will overflow the secret place."[123]

What can one deduce about the meaning of the "stone" in the context of the preceding statement? Apparently, Isaiah is revealing that God and His creation are at odds. On one hand, there is the deceitfulness and myopia of the human race, while on the other hand, there is the perfection of God's justice and righteousness—a perfection conveyed by what Isaiah described as a tested stone that functions as a cornerstone. Furthermore, he continues his metaphor by saying that God's justice is like a measuring line and His righteousness is as a level, all of which—a cornerstone, a measuring line, and a level—are devices used in the construction of a building. Is this building merely a metaphorical building? Or, instead, is Isaiah thinking of an actual structure? The answer, I believe, is one that any beginner student in the study of The Great Pyramid is already well aware of. Immediately, one thinks of an earlier chapter in *Isaiah*, which has the prophet saying:

> In that day, there will be an altar to the Lord in the midst of Egypt, and a pillar of God at its border. It will become a sign and a witness to the Lord of Hosts in the land of Egypt, for they'll cry to God because of the oppressors, and He'll send them a Savior and a Champion to deliver them.[124]

One of the foundational passages in the canonical record, this verse is cited by all advocates of Pyramidology in an attempt to verify the scriptural integrity of their subject matter. Because Egypt just happens to be divided into upper and lower sections, this description, they say, is perfectly fulfilled by the fact that The Great Pyramid sits on the very spot that constitutes both its center *and* its border.

---

123 *Isaiah* 28:15-17
124 Ibid. 19:19-20

The next clue to this verse, say the experts, pertains to the Hebrew meaning of the words for "sign" and "witness." In order to dismiss the possibility that The Great Pyramid is nothing more than a by-gone funerary heap built for some heathen Pharaoh, pyramidologists quickly point out that the words used by Isaiah leave no margin for error in this regard. According to *Strong's Exhaustive Concordance of The Bible*, the word translated as "sign" conveys the meaning of a signal, a beacon, a monument, and/or evidence.[125] The word translated as "witness" is derived from a word that means to testify, to admonish, to charge, and/or give warning.[126] Together, these words uniquely express the idea that in the land of Egypt, God will provide a monument that will stand as evidence, as a beacon, as a testimonial, bearing witness in a form that encompasses both an admonition and a warning.

To that end, advocates of Pyramidology will proceed with endless explanations as to the latent meaning revealed in the dimensions of the many passageways and chambers in this ancient megalith, each intended to mathematically predict nearly every important event in world history, both sacred and secular. Building off the work of such nineteenth-century pioneers as John Taylor, C. Piazzi Smyth, Robert Menzies, and Joseph A. Seiss, modern scholars like John Garnier, David Davidson, and Adam Rutherford have inspired the next wave of researchers, all with a single conviction held in common across the generations. That is to say, every one of them is convinced that this remarkable structure was divinely inspired to convey a message of God's control over human history. But this message, they insist, is not one that is expressed in the form of words, which can become misconstrued over time or through mistranslation. In fact, it is conveyed via the incontrovertible science of mathematics. According to this way of thinking, because the God of *The Bible* is a God of Set Times, the mathematics of The Great Pyramid are expressed by way of the specific measurements of the passageways and chambers within it. These measurements, in turn, create a time-oriented chronology of the pivotal points in the biblical timeline, such as the Exodus of Israel out of Egypt, the birth, death, and resurrection of Christ, and the Reformation. Similarly, conveyed by the internal dimensions of The Pyramid, there are turning points in world history to be found, such as the invention of the printing press, the year of global revolution, and the beginning and end of World War I.

Having pointed that out, however, I did already explain this would not constitute the primary focus of this chapter, because attempting to confirm or deny the truth of all the intricate mathematics involved in the dimensions

---

125 *Strong's Exhaustive Concordance of The Bible: Dictionary of Hebrew Words*, James Strong, p. 10

126 Ibid. pp. 85-86

of this remarkable edifice would lead us down a far different path than I hope to take. Rather, what I am attempting here is to focus on any links that might connect Enoch's role — as the first prophet of history — with whatever prophetic message is encrypted into The Great Pyramid of Giza. I merely mention the prior evidence provided by pyramidologists to demonstrate that just as Enoch has been connected with the gift of prophecy, so also has this most famous of all megaliths been connected with the notion of prophetic wisdom.

So much for this introduction to the way in which The Great Pyramid relates to the history of mankind. How, then, does its architecture reveal the hidden hand of Enoch as its original designer? Granted, one is facing numerous disadvantages in seeking the answer to such a question. If Enoch had drawn the schematics of this Pyramid, he might have signed his name at the bottom; but without such obvious evidence, one is left with only the structure itself as a clue to provide a potential answer. Moreover, as most researchers will confess, a megalithic work of this nature does not easily lend itself to the process of authentication. Except for the counterfeit hieroglyphs placed there by an overzealous explorer — erroneously identifying the pharaoh Khufu, a.k.a. Cheops, as the architect — The Great Pyramid, alone among all others, has never been found to contain a single stroke of writing. As a result, the only way to determine who might have designed it comes in the form of detective work. That is to say, one must look for other clues to reveal their true identity. In this case, because we are dealing with a stone edifice with passageways and chambers, we have a unique opportunity at our disposal in that a specific pattern emerges when one takes the time to examine its structural design. As such, a building's construction can actually convey a recognizable signature, much in the same way that certain architectural features reveal whether a Michelangelo or a Christopher Wren might have designed a particular building.

More about this approach in determining Enoch's role as The Pyramid's architect will follow a little later. First, though, let us continue to build up a picture of the structural design that The Great Pyramid presents to us.

By all accounts, the primary feature built into The Pyramid has to do with revealing a timeline of historical events of biblical proportion, but is this the only architectural feature that might provide us with the truth of who designed it? As a matter of fact, no, it is not.

In addition to revealing biblical chronology in stone, the dimensions of The Great Pyramid also display a unique insight into the nature of the physical construct of our Earth, which, according to the experts, includes, among other things, its weight, its mean density, and its distance from the Sun. So while researchers might disagree as to the "where and when" of historical events alluded to via The Pyramid's dimensions, there is one thing that they have a much harder time disagreeing about — the verifiable dimensions of our solar system. This is not to say that science does not have different ways of measuring such things as the distance from the Earth to the Sun, the weight of the Earth, or its mean density. Nevertheless, while so much of biblical prophecy resides within the realm of personal opinion, the discrepancies encountered within the realm of physical matter are infinitely more reconcilable. In fact, these dimensional clues as to the physical nature of the Earth and Sun seem to stand out as a clear punctuation mark in the overall investigation of the more metaphysical aspects of Pyramidology. In other words, it seems as if whoever designed The Great Pyramid fully anticipated the skepticism of humanity that would one day ponder the mystery of its construction, and in order to substantiate its prophetic possibilities, they included these more tangible clues concerning the physical nature of the solar system.

With this in mind, we will examine the way in which the number three hundred and sixty-five is commemorated within the architectural design of The Great Pyramid. This number, more than any other, constitutes a unique signature, which — in conjunction with the ubiquitous legends that call it The Pillar of Enoch — goes a long way toward indicating Enoch as its architect. Again, as any student of Pyramidology will tell you: The reason this number is so thoroughly associated with Enoch is that this was his age when *The Bible* records a peculiar event: "So all the days of Enoch were three hundred and sixty-five years. And Enoch walked with God and was not because God took him."[127]

But what, you may ask, is so unusual about this event? Is it because of the ambiguous nature of this "taking"? Certainly, this has always been a bone of contention with students of *The Bible*. However, in the context of our discussion, it is not, I am afraid, even pertinent to the topic. What is pertinent is the patriarch's *age* when he was "taken," because in an antediluvian age, when men were reported to have lived an average of nine hundred years, this man was said to have lived a measly three hundred and sixty-five years. Why?

As usual, the answer resides in "the eye of the beholder." In other words, if you are the kind of person that dismisses Scripture as being purely imaginative, with no basis in fact, then you probably see this as a random lifespan. If, however, you are a believer in God's control over history, then you probably see this as no accidental occurrence. Add to this the apocryphal record that has Enoch being given a guided tour of the cosmos, and one might very likely accept that God purposefully removed him from the Earth so his very lifespan would convey a truth that would resound for generations to come.

---

127 *Genesis* 5:23-24

Either way, the fact is, long before modern man ever determined the actual length of the solar year, the lifespan of Enoch perfectly portrayed it in terms that even a child in Sunday school can appreciate.

The first occurrence of this numerical value of three hundred and sixty-five becomes evident when one considers the exterior of The Great Pyramid, which nineteenth-century British archeologist Flinders Petrie discovered in his pioneering work of measuring the structure's base perimeter. Having measured the four sides of the megalith's foundation, Petrie found that they were slightly indented at the middle. In time, subsequent researchers became intrigued that three distinct measurements of its base, indicated by this apparently random indentation, bore a striking resemblance with the three known variations of the solar year—the tropical, at 365.242 days, the sidereal, at 365.256 days, and the anomalistic, at 365.259 days. (For further details on this phenomenon, please refer to page 65 of E. Raymond Capt's introductory study to Pyramidology entitled *The Great Pyramid Decoded*.)

Furthermore, inside The Great Pyramid is another example of this numerical value of three hundred and sixty-five, or—more specifically, in terms of the precise length of the solar year—365.242. Lying at the nucleus of The Pyramid's interior is what scholars have christened the King's Chamber, where there is an empty granite Coffer, or open strongbox. In order to enter the King's Chamber, one must first pass through another smaller chamber, dubbed the Ante-Chamber. Upon measuring this room, explorers found that within its dimensions a circle drawn inside yielded a circumference of 365.242 pyramid inches—a unit of measurement which, by the way, differs from the British and American inch by just 1/1000th of an inch. As a result of this discovery, this circle is referred to as The Enoch Circle. In addition to this, the distance from the midpoint of the Ante-Chamber to the south wall of the King's Chamber again measures 365.242 pyramid inches. (For a more in-depth explanation on the origins of the so-called "pyramid inch," please refer to pages 290-304 of C. Piazzi Smyth's book entitled *The Great Pyramid: Its Secrets and Mysteries Revealed*.)

And just in case you think that this is all by chance, let me offer the following quote from one of the leading pyramidologists of the last century, Adam Rutherford. More important still to our present investigation, this statement provides additional evidence in our attempt to connect this grand edifice with its true architect; and I quote:

> The entire geometric design of The Great Pyramid is built upon the Enoch Circle—its circumference, diameter, and radius, which are respectively 365.242, 116.26, and 58.13 geometric, or pyramid, inches. So, by geometric symbolism, the representation of Enoch is stamped on the entire Pyramid from top to bottom, inside and out.

No wonder that The Great Pyramid is traditionally associated with Enoch, and that Masonic tradition alludes to this Pyramid as The Pillar of Enoch.[128]

Not only is this numerical value of 365.242 built into the dimensions of The Great Pyramid, but also inexorably linked to it is a number that is revered by mathematicians and scientists alike — pi. Considered the Universe's one great constant, pi is defined as the ratio of a circle's circumference in relation to its diameter, and as such is approximately equal to 3.14159. Concerning the ubiquitous nature of this value within The Pyramid's construction, this is never more evident than at its very heart, that is, in both the Ante-Chamber and the King's Chamber. The length of the floor in the Ante-Chamber just happens to measure 116.260 pyramid inches, or 365.242 divided by pi. Inside the King's Chamber, we find that its length, east to west, is 412.131 inches, or 2 times 365.242 divided by the square root of pi. Its width, north to south, is 206.065, or 365.242 divided by the square root of pi. Its height is 230.388, or the square root of 5 times 365.242 divided by 2 times the square root of pi. The floor's diagonal length is 460.777, or the square root of 5 times 365.242 divided by the square root of pi. The east and west wall's diagonal length is 309.098, or 3 times 365.242 divided by 2 times the square root of pi. The diagonal length of the north and south walls is 472.156, or the square root of 21 times 365.242 divided by 2 times the square root of pi. And finally, the distance from either the north or south wall to the end of the Open Coffer is 58.13, or 365.242 divided by 2 times pi, while the combined distance to the north and south walls at either end of the Open Coffer is 116.26, or 365.242 divided by pi.[129]

In all, the preceding equations constitute no less than nine separate occurrences in which the dimensions of The Great Pyramid's architecture indicate a consistent relationship between the numbers that represent both our solar year and pi. Still, I can hear the skeptics out there who are insisting that this is all sheer coincidence. Besides, one must go to an awful lot of trouble in order to arrive at such equations. Not only that, but what could have possibly prompted someone to go to such lengths to hunt and peck for numerical relationships like that in the first place? In point of fact, equations like these did not materialize overnight. The discovery of such permutations, hidden deep within the dimensions of this astonishing stone structure, came as the result of generations of researchers who successfully built upon the work of their predecessors.

---

128 *Pyramidology: Book I*, Adam Rutherford, p. 83
129 *The Great Pyramid Decoded*, Peter Lemesurier, pp. 375-76

The Bible in Stone

THE FIRST MAN TO approach The Great Pyramid in a scientific manner was a British professor of astronomy at Oxford by the name of John Greaves, who, in 1646, produced a book on the subject entitled *Pyramidographia: A Description of the Pyramids in Egypt*. As a result of his publication many more intrepid explorers would be drawn into the never-ending labyrinth of trying to solve the enigma that is The Great Pyramid of Giza. Even one of the most influential scientific thinkers of all time, Isaac Newton, became intrigued by Greaves' work and wrote his own paper, entitled *A Dissertation upon the Sacred Cubit*, which was posthumously published in 1738, some ten years after his death.

It was not until 1859 that British mathematician John Taylor was credited with being the first to determine an actual link between the ancient megalith and modern science when he suggested that the numerical value of *pi* had been deliberately factored into its design. Next came C. Piazzi Smyth, astronomer royal of Scotland, who then elaborated on Taylor's theories in his 1864 book *Our Inheritance in the Great Pyramid*. Greatly influenced by his personal correspondence with Taylor, Smyth went to Egypt at his own expense, where he measured every conceivable dimension of The Pyramid, both inside and out, and was the first to photograph its interior passages. Subsequent to this hands-on investigation, Smyth postulated the idea of the "pyramid inch," which he claimed was the architect's intended unit of measurement with which to interpret the structural and chronological aspects of The Pyramid's design.

Then, in 1865, Robert Menzies inaugurated the next chapter in the story of The Great Pyramid when he began exploring the notion that its various passageways and chambers had been constructed to reveal — in accordance with the very dimensions that Smyth had been documenting — a divinely-inspired chronology of historical events, particularly those of a biblical nature. A decade later, an American theologian and Lutheran minister by the name of Joseph A. Seiss wrote what undoubtedly stands as the most eloquent book on the subject, which became quite popular among evangelical Christians. Entitled *The Great Pyramid of Egypt: Miracle in Stone*, Seiss' landmark publication was the first to refer to the marvelous megalith as "*The Bible* in Stone."

With the turn of the century came the work of John Garnier, who published his 1905 book *Great Pyramid: Its Builder and Its Prophecy*, which further elaborated on the idea that the chambers and passageways inside The Great Pyramid not only provided a chronology of fulfilled biblical events but also contained a prophetic timeline of future events. In the following decades, several more individuals would help popularize the study of Pyramidology, as it came to be known, most notably, a British structural engineer by the name of David Davidson, who published his findings in 1924 with *The Great Pyramid: Its Divine Message*. After him came Adam Rutherford, whose exhaustive work entitled *Pyramidology*, was published in four volumes between 1957 and 1971. More recently, books like the 1972 publication *Secrets of the Great Pyramid* by Peter Tompkins, and the 1977 international bestseller *The Great Pyramid Decoded* by Peter Lemesurier have fueled further interest in the study of Pyramidology. Admittedly, these two latter works contained a much greater emphasis on the esoteric aspects of their subject matter as opposed to earlier works that focused more on a scientific approach to their message.

In this way, each man's work was enriched by the direct influence of his predecessor, causing a chain reaction to occur. One discovery led to another; one realization became the impetus for the next, until finally every conceivable geometric and prophetic relationship had been considered and calculated. And whether all these dimensional relationships in The Pyramid are real or imagined one thing remains constant in unlocking the mysteries of this greatest wonder of the world: Its very existence defies any attempt to casually dismiss the possibility that it might actually contain the ultimate expression of truth. To this point, the words of Joseph A. Seiss speak most eloquently:

> This great monument itself gives palpable demonstration of what cannot be rationally explained... Materialistic and skeptical science has determined that mankind has had to educate himself upward to be what he is today, from a troglodyte, if not from something much lower... But no such philosophizing can hold up in light of the construction of The Great Pyramid.
>
> If primeval man (*of the type that supposedly built this ancient megalith*) was nothing but a gorilla or troglodyte, how, in those far prehistoric times, could the builders of this mighty structure have known what our profoundest *savants*, after scores of centuries of observation and experiment, have only been able to find out imperfectly? How could they know how to make and handle the tools, machines, and expedients indispensable to the construction of an edifice so enormous in its dimensions, so massive in its workmanship, that to this day it is without rival upon the Earth? How could they know the spherical nature, rotation, diameter, density, latitudes, poles, land distribution, and temperature of the Earth, or its astronomic relations? How could they solve the squaring of the circle, calculate the *pi* proportion, or determine the four cardinal points? How could they frame charts of world history and dispensations, true to fact in every particular for the space of 4,000 years after their time, and

down even to the final consummation?

And how could they know to put all these things on record in a single edifice of masonry without one verbal or pictorial inscription, yet proof against all the ravages and changes of time, and capable of being read and understood down to the very end of the world?[130]

How could they, really? That is the question. But in my mind, at least, the question as to *how* they could have known such things is thoroughly tied up in the question of *who* built The Great Pyramid, or, to be more specific, who *designed* it. If one is capable of ascertaining the mystery of *who* designed its impossibly complex construction, then the answer as to *how* they could have known such things seems a foregone conclusion. To reiterate Seiss' view, according to the edicts of science, the historical period for the building of The Great Pyramid simply does not sync with the traditionally accepted level of knowledge of the supposed builders. In other words, the prehistoric date for The Pyramid's construction presents one with an insurmountable gap between the actual level of technological skill required to construct it and the assumed level of mankind's skills at that point in world history. Clearly, then, as it pertains to our present inquiry, a merely scientific explanation will not provide the answer to our *"who-then-how"* mystery.

So, where can we look for the answer of who built The Great Pyramid? Can we look to those of a theological bent? Surely they are in a position to provide us with the sort of answer we are seeking, right? Ironically, even those who proclaim to believe in the divine origins of The Pyramid's construction seem far too timid in their attempts to answer such a question. Displaying no lack of courage in declaring their far-reaching prophetic calculations, they quite uncharacteristically fail, in my opinion, to grasp the true significance of the facts that they are professing to believe in. As a result, the theologians' choice of who designed and built The Pyramid of Giza falls as far short as that of their alleged opponents, the scientists. Whereas the humanist-inspired scientists insist it was built by Khufu, or Cheops, depending on your language frame, the divinely-inspired theologians insist that it was built by, among others, Job, Shem, Melchizedek, or Noah.

In their defense, scientists point to the cartouche bearing Khufu's name, which was "discovered" inside one of The Pyramid's chambers, all the while ignoring that modern inquiry has led researchers to conclude that an overzealous explorer, hoping to secure additional financial backing for his vaunted efforts, fraudulently placed it there. Likewise, in their defense, theologians point out that certain ones in the halls of God's great accomplishments — men like Noah — were clearly in a position to be uniquely instructed in building projects of world-changing importance. Or, if Noah was

---

130 *The Great Pyramid of Egypt: Miracle in Stone*, Joseph A. Seiss, pp. 115-16

not the one who built it, then certainly it might have been built by that ever mysterious personage known as Melchizedek, who was reputedly involved in the construction of that blessed city of God, Jerusalem. Another of those who professes to believe in the prophetic aspects of The Pyramid has even alleged a connection that equates Shem — the son of that colossal boat build-er, Noah — with Cheops, claiming that an etymological link reveals him as its architect. Still others, in an attempt to prove their theory, have pointed to a biblical book, which admittedly contains the most obvious allusion to The Pyramid in all of Scripture.

> Then, from out of the storm, the Lord spoke to Job: "Who is this that obscures My plans with words devoid of knowledge? Brace yourself like a man; I'll question you, and you'll answer Me. Where were you when I laid the Earth's foundation? Tell Me, if you un-derstand. Who marked off its dimensions? Surely you must know! Who stretched a measuring line across it? Upon what were its foot-ings set, or who laid its cornerstone while the morning stars sang together, and all the sons of God shouted for joy?"[131]

Concerning these verses, Seiss, again, has much to say:

> The speaker is God, and the subject is the creation of the Earth. The picture is the building of an edifice. Elsewhere in the same book, the Earth is said to be hung upon nothing; so we cannot pretend to be ignorant of the real facts when here the Earth is being compared to a building that rests on foundations... Behold the architecture of God! The terms are those of the Geometer, the Master Builder. Here is the base ... the measures ... the lines ... the cornerstone! The style of the building is unquestionably The Great Pyramid. That "cornerstone" is spoken of in the singular, which is clearly distinct in relation to the "foundations," while the singing and shouting of the heavenly host as a result of the mighty achievement at the laying of that par-ticular cornerstone requires the proper pyramidal edifice.
>
> This picture cannot be interpreted any other way. That corner-stone could not be at the base because others were there against which no such distinction was made, and its laying would then have been at the beginning, at which time this celestial celebration would be out of place... And as this celebration, according to God Himself, is at the laying of that cornerstone, it must, by necessity, be a top stone — a cornerstone at the summit — whose placement has completed the edifice and displayed the whole work in finished per-fection. But for such a cornerstone at the summit there is no place in

---

131 *Job* 38:1-7

any then known form of building, save only The Pyramid, of which it is characteristic. Nor is it only to the pyramidal form in general that the allusion is, but to a particular pyramid. By that strange reference to the sunken feet or planting of the foundations in "sockets," we are conducted directly to The Great Pyramid of Giza.

In 1799, two sunken "encasements" in the rock were found under two of its base corners by the French *savants*, which were, in 1837, again uncovered and described by Colonel Richard Howard-Vyse. And as God here speaks of such a fastening down of the foundations in general, Professor Smyth was persuaded that there were corresponding "sockets" at the other two base corners, and when search was made for them in 1865, they were found by William Aiton and Thomas Inglis, assisted by Professor Smyth. Here, then, are all four "sockets" or fastened foundations. Nothing of the sort exists in the construction of any other known pyramid. They are among the distinctive marks of The Great Pyramid of Giza. They are the enduring tracks of its feet cut into the living rock, by which Almighty God Himself identifies it for us as the original image from which His own description of the creation is drawn. Men may treat the matter as they will, but here are the facts showing a divine recognition of this particular edifice as the special symbol of the Earth's formation![132]

My purpose in presenting the preceding in such great length is twofold in nature. First, I consider it essential in my attempt to cement the idea that a study of The Great Pyramid constitutes more than the vain pursuit of wishful thinkers who are dissatisfied with the simple tenants of Scripture. In light of such eloquence, one can clearly see why some of the greatest theological minds have found a biblical connection with the most thought-provoking monument known to humanity. Second, I inject such worthy scholarship into the mix because I wish to demonstrate how someone as astute as Seiss is still capable of falling short in his honest attempt at solving the mystery of who designed The Great Pyramid. On the subject, he said, "The more I study *The Book of Job* ... the stronger and more satisfying to me becomes the likelihood that here is the mighty prince and preacher of Jehovah from whom we have that monument."[133] Moreover, his choice of Job as the designer of The Pyramid came with the following explanation:

He was a true man of God, a public instructor in sacred things with whom Jehovah communicated, and whom the Spirit of God inspired. The Almighty speaks to him in Chapter 38 as if he were the

---

132 *The Great Pyramid of Egypt: Miracle in Stone*, Joseph A. Seiss, pp. 61-62
133 Ibid. p. 110

identical person who had laid the measures of The Great Pyramid, stretched the lines upon it, set its foundations in their sockets, and laid its capstone amid songs of exalted triumph. Chapter 19:23-27 looks like a description of the high intent of The Great Pyramid, and a prayer that it might endure with its glorious freight, even to the end of the world.[134]

Unfortunately, however, I must wholeheartedly disagree with such a conclusion, and notwithstanding my admiration for such an eloquent spokesperson, I must do so for two reasons. In the first place, when I read the thirty-eighth chapter of *Job*, I do not get the feeling that God is speaking to, as Seiss put it, "the identical person who had laid the measures of The Great Pyramid." If anything, it reads to me as if God is chiding Job, if not downright mocking him: "Brace yourself like a man, Job; I'll question you, and you'll answer Me. Where were you when *I* (not *you*) laid the Earth's foundation? Tell Me, if you understand."[135] So, if God is mocking Job — quite unlike Seiss' view of this scene — then this could never, in my opinion, at least, constitute an affirmation of his alleged role in The Pyramid's creation.

The second reason I disagree with Seiss originates entirely from the biblical text itself, as opposed to God's tone of voice in speaking to Job. Let me explain what I mean by that. The last portion of the biblical passage in question states: "Upon what were its footings set, or who laid its cornerstone while the morning stars sang together, and all the sons of God shouted for joy?"[136] But who, exactly, is Job referring to when he mentions *morning stars* and *sons of God*? The answer, I believe, will shed a great deal of light in our quest to discover who both designed *and* built The Great Pyramid. And as strange as it may seem, I am fully convinced that this seemingly insignificant portion of canonical Scripture holds the key to solving this ancient mystery. In order to make this point clear, though, one must first analyze all of the details involved in our quest.

Geometer of Heaven and Earth

IN THE GREAT PYRAMID, one is faced with an innumerable list of perplexing anomalies. Not only does it confound us with the sheer impossibility that its dimensions might somehow reveal a prophetic timeline, but its very existence is also a blatant contradiction to modern-day assumptions, based as they are on a scientific worldview. In an age before pulleys, wheels, or iron tools, the builders of The Pyramid still managed to enlist the use of an estimated two and a half million stone blocks, each averaging two and a

---

134 *The Great Pyramid of Egypt: Miracle in Stone*, Joseph A. Seiss, pp. 109-10
135 *Job* 38:3-4
136 Ibid. 38:6-7

half tons. The result was a colossus that covers nearly sixty-four thousand square yards, weighing an estimated six million tons, and which, for more than four millennia, stood as the world's tallest structure. In today's terms that would mean that enough stones were employed in its construction to build thirty Empire State Buildings or sixty-five Washington Monuments. Yet for all its massiveness, scientists have determined that it is more closely oriented to true north than any other edifice known to mankind, only missing the mark by less than three minutes of one degree. Modern man's best efforts, on the other hand, as exhibited in the Paris Observatory — completed in 1671 — produced results that were six minutes off course.

Add to this the fact that the dimensions of this mammoth megalith incorporate the numerical values of both *pi* and the solar year throughout its construction, and one is faced with an insoluble conundrum. Even if one could explain how these pre-Iron Age builders erected such an edifice, this still cannot explain how they knew to incorporate knowledge that was not discovered until centuries after the assumed date of its construction — in the case of *pi*, around 1,650 B.C., and the solar year, around 150 B.C. Furthermore, when one considers the added occurrence of its numerous other astronomical design features — among them, the spherical nature, rotation, diameter, density, and temperature of the Earth — one is forced, by the sheer process of elimination, to reject every potential candidate that either the scientific or theological community has to offer. In the final analysis, then, neither Khufu, Noah, Shem, Melchizedek, nor Job possessed all of the requisite skills to complete a structure of such multitudinous splendor.

More importantly, none of the previously mentioned personages had any known connection with those mysterious entities that we recently encountered in the thirty-eighth chapter of *Job*, in that time when "the morning stars sang together, and all the sons of God shouted for joy." Fortunately, for the sake of our investigation, there is someone who does fit such a profile — a man who was knowledgeable in the realms of both celestial mechanics and structural engineering. That man was Enoch. Having walked and talked with God, he is alone among men in having possessed all the necessary ingredients to fit the bill of being the genuine architect of The Great Pyramid of Giza. In addition, he is the only man whom the biblical record portrays as having had an association with that peculiar race of angelic beings known as the Watchers, a.k.a. the "sons of God," the very ones that "went to the daughters of men and had children by them, which became *Nephilim*, or giants."[137]

As one can imagine, there has been no end to the intense theological debate regarding the true identity of these so-called "sons of God," but like most controversial issues of this nature, the debate always seems to hinge

---

137 *Genesis* 6:4

more upon the *a priori* position of the one who is making the argument as opposed to said facts of the argument itself. As such, most modern biblical scholars, who are offended by an apparently outmoded view of the Universe, favor a less spiritual interpretation of the meaning of the "sons of God." As a result, they tend to believe that this term simply refers to the righteous lineage of mankind through Seth, the third son of Adam. On the other hand, most of the earliest expositors of Scripture leaned toward the view that the Hebrew words used to translate "sons of God," that is, *bene ha Elohim*, clearly meant that these personages were of non-human origin, and so they had no difficulty at all in accepting them as angelic beings. Among those who held this view were Philo, Josephus, Justin Martyr, Irenaeus, Clement, Tertullian, Eusebius, Ambrose, Jerome, and Augustine.[138]

Naturally, critics who cling to the purely humanistic view — that the "sons of God" were mere children of Seth — do so because they believe that in *The Book of Genesis* there is simply no tenable support for their opponent's theory. Therefore, lacking any further scriptural evidence, they conclude that their interpretation offers the safest road to correct thinking. But alas, they do so by ignoring every other biblical source that is readily available to any modern-day truth seeker, because if they were to simply pull their proverbial heads from the sand, they would be truly amazed at the tenuousness of their allegedly *Bible*-inspired position. Let me take a moment to elaborate. More to the point, let me do so in such a way that our inquiry into the mystery of who designed and built The Great Pyramid does not steer too far off course.

To reiterate, we are seeking to gather together in a single architect all the necessary requirements for The Pyramid's construction, an architect so inspired by God, the Geometer of Heaven and Earth, that he was able to doubly convey his prophetic genius in both stone and book form. Not only that, but it should also be remembered that we are attempting to do this in order to connect said architect with the little-known prophecy of The Great Five and a Half Days. Are you still with me on all that? If so, then let us continue with all the preceding concepts in mind.

Sons of God

TO THE BEST OF our ability, we have narrowed down our choice for The Pyramid's architect to a single candidate: Enoch, who alone possessed an understanding of the divine mysteries associated with both the celestial mechanics of the Universe and the prophetic knowledge of the history of mankind. This, then, offers us a potential answer as to who could have known the things passed down to humanity in stone and Scripture alike. Yet this

---

138 *Complete Books of Enoch*, Ann Nyland, p. 20

still does not adequately answer the question as to how Enoch managed to turn this special knowledge into the enigmatic megalith that is The Great Pyramid. It is, after all, one thing for God to reveal such mysteries to Enoch, and have him, with the aid of angelic helpers, write the books that depict the future of mankind. It is, however, a different matter altogether to convey this knowledge in terms of everything involved in The Pyramid's actual construction, requiring as it does some two and a half million stone blocks, which together form an internal network of passageways and chambers that have all maintained their geometric relationships in spite of centuries of the crushing weight bearing down on them.

This is particularly pertinent when one considers the added presence of what is certainly the most perplexing feature of The Pyramid's interior, that is, the four so-called "air shafts" located within its interior. Two shafts lead from the King's Chamber diagonally up to its exterior, one connecting with the north face and the other with the south face; while two more similar shafts were discovered leading from the Queen's Chamber. Strangely enough, though, these particular shafts were not evident for quite some time because, as it turns out, both ends of this pair had been sealed by The Pyramid's builders. Ignoring, then, all the various interpretations of their true significance, these shafts present yet another glaring conundrum to anyone who considers the incredible lengths that such design features would impose upon their builders, causing many an investigator to scratch their head as they contemplate the staggering difficulty in engineering not just one but four such shafts that cut through more than two hundred feet of solid core masonry, and all in an age prior to pulleys, wheels, or iron tools. No wonder that such insoluble mysteries have caused some to speculate that because no earthly technology could have accomplished such an impossible feat, The Great Pyramid must have been built by some otherworldly race of beings.

Ironically, though, such apparently outrageous conclusions might, as so often happens, actually contain the germ of truth that we are pressing toward, because the final ingredient in the personality profile of the architect of The Great Pyramid does, in fact, involve an eerie offshoot of this very notion. Remember how we mentioned that, not only does Enoch fit the bill concerning his knowledge of celestial mechanics and prophetic wisdom, but he is also the only candidate associated with those strange characters known as the Watchers — angelic beings thought by many biblical scholars to be the same ones referred to in the sixth chapter of *Genesis*? And remember my statement that I believed a single, insignificant verse in *Job* might hold the key to the mystery of who designed and built The Great Pyramid? I certainly hope you have not forgotten about that. What was that verse again? It was: "Upon what were its footings set, or who laid its cornerstone while the morning stars sang together and all the sons of God shouted for joy?" Do I have you caught up so far? Good, then it is time to pick up that thread again and hopefully tie all of our loose ends together.

Even if Seiss is wrong in his view that Job was the architect of The Great Pyramid, he still deserves credit for having correctly surmised that these verses reveal a genuine insight into its construction as being symbolic, from God's perspective, of the Earth's creation. As a matter of fact, if anything at all has been ascertained about this Pyramid it is that in every possible way its dimensions represent the Earth in microcosm. And if the last verse of this passage is any indication of divinely-inspired truth, then the construction of this miniature version of Earth was completed in the presence of those entities that *The Bible* describes as the "sons of God," or *bene ha Elohim*. That said, it should not seem so far-fetched to imagine that these same angelic beings might have actually been the "construction crew," as it were, that saw to it that Enoch's heavenly blueprint was turned into a reality. After all, it is well known to any biblical scholar the extent to which angels have played a pivotal role in accomplishing God's purposes throughout human history, particularly in regard to their superhuman strength and abilities.

After King David presumptuously tallied the number of fighting men throughout his kingdom, God sent an angel to teach David an excruciating lesson. During this encounter, which a single angel executed, it was said, "from the morning until the end of the designated time, seventy thousand people from Dan to Beersheba died, and when the angel stretched out his hand to destroy Jerusalem, the Lord relented concerning the disaster and said to the angel who was afflicting the people, 'Enough! Withdraw your hand.'"[139]

Then there was the time when Sennacherib, king of Assyria, after marching his army to the very outskirts of Jerusalem, threatened Hezekiah, king of Judah, with swift annihilation, but because Hezekiah earnestly prayed to the God of Israel, he successfully invoked divine deliverance. So, "that night an angel of the Lord killed one hundred and eighty-five thousand men in the Assyrian camp, and when the people woke up the next morning, they saw dead bodies lying everywhere."[140]

Additionally, just in case anyone has forgotten, one of the most famous incidences involving angelic strength occurs in *The New Testament*. There it is said that on the day Jesus rose from the dead, a violent earthquake occurred as a result of an angel coming down from Heaven. Going to Christ's tomb, the angel rolled the massive stone away from the entrance and sat down on it, whereupon the Roman guards, terrified by what they had just seen, fell down like corpses.[141]

---

139 *Second Samuel* 24:15-16
140 *Second Kings* 18:13, 17, 25; 19:1, 15-20, 32-35
141 *Matthew* 28:2-3

Several things can be surmised from the preceding examples of angelic activity. First, notice how these supposedly incorporeal beings are quite capable of affecting the substantive realm of human beings. Contrary to popular opinion, the angels of *The Bible* do not simply float about like ephemeral nothings, incapable of exerting tangible results in the so-called "real world." Second, notice the immense impact that a single angel can have when they have been commissioned by God to intervene in human affairs. What would otherwise require a veritable army of men and machines, apparently just one angel can accomplish. And third, notice that angels are not only capable of dispensing a death blow to mere flesh and blood, but they are also more than capable of moving something as immensely solid as a stone. It is important to understand here the nature of the sort of stone doors implemented in sealing the entrance to a typical Jewish tomb. Weighing an average of one to two tons, they were enormous circular stones that were rolled down a slot into their final resting place, and considering that these stone doors were never intended to be removed once they had been secured, one can imagine how much easier they were to roll into position as opposed to rolling them away from the entrance.

Taking all this into consideration, then, one can see how a biblical perspective of angelic intervention sheds new light on how the construction of The Great Pyramid of Giza might have been achieved. Of course, all that is very nice, you may say, but how could anyone make such a speculative leap in proposing that angels could have been involved in building The Great Pyramid? To quote the more conservative theologians: "Besides the fact that there is no scriptural support that angels were involved in The Pyramid's construction, there is no evidence that *Genesis* 6 is even describing angels when it speaks of 'sons of God.' To the contrary, the prevailing theological position concludes that this passage is simply referring to the sons of the righteous lineage of Seth rather than those of the evil line of Cain." To which I would encourage such timid ones not to be so hasty. After all, whenever I read the sixth chapter of *Genesis*, I always find myself intrigued by the latent possibilities that I see there. What do I mean by latent possibilities? Well, when I read the text with unbiased eyes, I notice certain incongruities to which few, if any, seem to pay attention. Let me explain.

Monsters Crashing About

A FEW ENIGMATIC verses in the sixth chapter of *Genesis* paint what is undoubtedly the grimmest picture in the entire biblical record.

> When the sons of God came to the daughters of men, they bore them children, who became mighty men, which were heroes of old, men of renown. And God saw the wickedness of mankind had become

great in the Earth ... and He grieved that He had made mankind ...
so He said, "I'll destroy mankind whom I've created."[142]

So why do I call these verses enigmatic? I do so because — in my mind, at
least — they have always raised a red flag. As long as I can remember, I have
felt that there was something about these verses that was clearly not right
in terms of their logical continuity, either human or divine. In a nutshell:
Mighty men are born, the wickedness of mankind increases, and in response
God decides to destroy the Earth — just like that, no ifs, ands, or buts. Certainly, anyone who has ever contemplated this familiar sequence of events
has been similarly perplexed by their apparent abruptness. Certainly, I
could not be alone in wondering how a loving, merciful God could have decided to wipe out the whole world so quickly and casually simply because,
as the Scriptures state: "The Lord saw how great mankind's wickedness had
become."[143] I do not know about you, but this to me has never seemed like
an adequate reason for such an all-consuming punishment. If God is truly
a divine being of supreme justice, then how does the punishment fit the
crime? On that basis alone, judgment in the form of a worldwide deluge has
never seemed like a commensurate outcome. Yet since time immemorial we
have simply been told by those who are supposedly in the know that we
should never question such mysteries of the faith. Quite frankly, we have
had it so relentlessly drummed into our heads that "God's ways are not our
ways," we have had no choice but to turn off our brains while we are forever left to scratch our heads and wonder: "Who is the bigger jerk here? Me,
them, *or worse* ... God?"

So what is one to do in the face of this well-intentioned onslaught against
questioning such obvious biblical incongruities? Fortunately, as we have repeatedly seen, the solution is to allow the apocryphal record to provide the
necessary context for God's anger in His apparently incommensurate act of
destroying the world in the Deluge. *The First Book of Enoch* clarifies the mystery for us with this stark description:

> It so happened that after mankind began to multiply in those days
> daughters were born to them, elegant and beautiful, and when the
> angels, the sons of Heaven, saw them, they became enamored of
> them, saying to each other, "Come, let's select wives for ourselves
> from among these humans, and let's beget children."
>
> Then their leader Samyaza said to them, "I'm afraid you may
> not go along with me in carrying out our plan, and that I alone will
> suffer the consequences of such a terrible crime." And they said to
> him, "Then we'll swear together, and bind ourselves by a mutual

---

142 *Genesis* 6:4-7
143 Ibid. 6:5

oath, in order to confirm that we won't change our minds but execute our projected undertaking." Then they all swore together...

So they took wives, each choosing for himself whom they ap-
proached, and with whom they cohabitated, teaching them sorcery,
incantations, and the dividing of roots and trees, and the women
conceived and gave birth to giants, whose stature was each three
hundred cubits. These devoured all that the labor of men produced,
until it became impossible to feed them any longer.

Therefore, they began to turn against mankind in order to de-
vour them, and began to injure birds, beasts, reptiles, and fishes, to
eat their flesh one after another, and to drink their blood... Impiety
increased, fornication multiplied, and they transgressed and corrupted all their ways... And men, being destroyed, cried out, and
their voices reached to Heaven.[144]

Now in order to put such a horrific scenario into perspective, try to
imagine the size of these giants that are being described here. The text states
that they were three hundred cubits tall. Naturally, as members of a modern
society, which utilizes measurements quite foreign to that distant time, it
is very difficult for us to get a genuine sense of what it means to look upon
a human being—if it can still rightly be called that—who is three hundred
cubits tall. Nevertheless, we can get an idea of the immensity of such creatures if we compare these proportions with other things with which we are
familiar.

For example, *The Bible* speaks of two very large things of which we do
have a sense, that of Goliath and Noah's Ark. To get an idea of how impossibly huge these *Nephilim* were, consider this. Goliath is said to have stood
just over six cubits tall.[145] That would mean these giants were more than
fifty times the size of Goliath! Likewise, the immensity of the Ark, which
famously harbored not only Noah and his family but also all those animals,
was said to be three hundred cubits in length.[146] Imagine, then, standing
the Ark straight up, and one of these antediluvian giants would have stood
stem to stern with it! According to our best estimates, modern science has
determined that three hundred cubits is roughly equivalent to four hundred
and fifty feet.

Therefore, having achieved a sense of the enormity of these creatures,
imagine the horror of an entire race of these gigantic monsters crashing
about the countryside, snatching up both humans and beasts, tearing them
limb from limb, drinking their blood, and devouring their flesh. Certainly,

---

144 *First Enoch* 7:1-7, 10-15; 8:2, 9
145 *First Samuel* 17:4
146 *Genesis* 6:15

a revised scenario such as this might better explain why God decided to destroy the planet in the Great Flood; not simply because, as *Genesis* implies, mankind got a little racy.

At this point, I would next like to take some time to investigate the origin of these giants. Could the gigantism of these creatures simply have been a function of their being sired by angelic beings? Certainly, there is no scriptural foundation that post-Flood giants like Goliath received their enormous stature from this sort of intermarrying of species. In fact, history is replete with the existence of numerous gigantic human beings, but all born — and this is the important thing to note — *after* the Deluge, because, as one will recall, God specifically designed the Flood to remove the *Nephilim* from the planet, once and for all. So, if giants have existed both before *and* after the Flood — though not in such gigantic proportions afterwards — then there must be another explanation for the enormity of this peculiar race of *Nephilim*. But what? Again, the clues to solving this mystery are all around us, though, as usual, one must do a bit of detective work to apprehend the solution.

He Who Descends

OUR FIRST ORDER OF business is to search out what modern scientific thinking has to say about the human body and its potential for the kind of biological mutation displayed by these infamous offspring of the Watchers. Like all questions regarding the wonders of the human body, science has done a remarkable job in ascertaining the role of DNA, genes, and chromosomes in all of its processes. Accordingly, the unique combination of chromosomes that a human being inherits from their parents determines their physical traits. These chromosomes are themselves made up of hundreds to thousands of genes, which, in turn, contain their own unique sequence of DNA molecules. Based on this view, then, a person's height is biologically determined by their inherited genes, which combine to affect such human traits as growth, appetite, muscle mass, and activity level.[147]

Therefore, considering the importance of this biological component in determining the height of any given human being, who among the descendants of mankind could have supplied these *Nephilim* with the necessary genetic material? Is there any evidence in the biblical record, either canonical or apocryphal, which might point us in the right direction? I do believe there is, yes. In fact, I believe it can be found in the opening chapters of our canonical record of *Genesis*, just as one might expect when delving into the origin of the human species and all its peculiarities. Let me present a series of ideas, and hopefully this will provide us with an entirely new way of

---

147 *The Merck Manual: Home Edition, Genes and Chromosomes*, David N. Finegold

looking at the situation.

In this first book concerning the father of mankind, one finds the all-too-familiar story of Adam having just eaten the Forbidden Fruit that God had warned him about. Upon eating it, says *The Bible*, he realized that he was naked, and because of his subsequent shame he tried to hide among fig trees, where he found an abundance of leaves in his attempt to cover himself. Then, God arrived in the cool of the day and asked, "Where are you, Adam?"[148] Of course, the telling of this story is almost universal the world over. As such, most biblical scholars are unanimous in offering the same old appraisal of what God meant by asking such an obvious question: "Where are you, Adam?" Certainly God knew where he was, right? After all, He is God. Why, then, would He have to ask Adam where he was? To which these same scholars intone with utter self-assurance that what God was really doing was engaging Adam in a rhetorical argument in the hopes that he might confess to having eaten the Fruit. This way, say the scholars, Adam might somehow gain an insight into just how far he had fallen from grace. The problem with that logic is, assuming the foreknowledge of God and the nature of the Fall, the idea that Adam could have had a genuine self-awareness of his moral bankruptcy at that moment in time makes about as much sense as God holding out that Adam would have taken personal responsibility for his own actions. No, I am afraid that this stale, worn-out interpretation simply does not fit the facts of Scripture. So, what reaction might this question have been meant to illicit in Adam?

To answer that question, I would like to return to Louis Ginzberg, who paints a much more vivid picture in his book than the one found in *Genesis*. According to Ginzberg, prior to their fall from grace, Adam and Eve could never have hidden among the fig trees, because before he committed his trespass against God, Adam was a giant of a man, so much so that any attempt to describe his colossal size bordered on the utterly fantastic.[149] Citing a widespread tradition found in a variety of rabbinical sources, Ginzberg said:

> The dimensions of his body were gigantic, reaching from Heaven to Earth, or, what amounts to the same, from east to west. Among later generations of men, there were only a few who in small measure resembled Adam in his extraordinary size and physical perfection. Samson possessed his strength, Saul his neck, Absalom his hair, Asahel his fleetness of foot, Uzziah his forehead, Josiah his nostrils, Zedekiah his eyes, and Zerubbabel his voice.[150]

---

148 *Genesis* 3:6-8
149 *The Legends of the Jews, Volume 1: From the Creation to Jacob*, Louis Ginzberg, p. 76
150 Ibid. p. 59

It was only after Adam and Eve had eaten the Forbidden Fruit and were stripped of their former glory that they were reduced to their present size. Concerning this momentous turn of events, which occurred as a result of Adam's fall from grace, Ginzberg continued:

> It cannot be denied, the words, "Where are you?" were pregnant with meaning. They were intended to bring home to Adam the vast difference between his previous state and his present state—between his supernatural size then and his shrunken size now.[151]

Based on the foregoing information, then, we may have discovered the "missing link," as it were, between not only the reason for this outcropping of antediluvian giants but also for those individuals who exhibit similar traits of gigantism after the Flood, though not nearly so exaggerated as the *Nephilim*. Either way, what we seem to be dealing with, as far-fetched as it sounds, is actually a genetic throwback, which was undoubtedly triggered by the biologically-encoded DNA buried deep within the father of mankind. If this is true, then the real father of these monstrous *Nephilim* was not the Watchers but Adam.

Meanwhile, anyone reading this may already be wondering: What does any of this have to do with who built The Great Pyramid of Giza? And the reason I have taken this apparent detour is to drive home one very important point—a point that can actually best be summarized by asking a question that is directly linked to the history of the Watchers and their role in instigating God's judgment of the Great Flood. And that question is: If the Watchers, in conjunction with their offspring, the giants, were the ones who were responsible for humanity's downfall prior to the Flood, what in the world could God have been thinking in allowing such a disastrous intermingling of species in the first place? By any stretch of the imagination, it seems like a perfectly idiotic move by a God Who presumably should know better than to unleash events that He knew full well would lead to such a monstrous outcome. Not only that, but considering the complete absence of logical congruity as far as mankind's alleged guilt in eliciting the Flood, it also adds more fuel to the fire in the view of anyone who doubts God's claim to be a loving and merciful Creator.

Taking all this into consideration, then: What could possibly explain any of these apparent incongruities? Where does one even begin to look to shed light on such a multifaceted mystery? And the answer, as we have seen, time and time again, is the apocryphal record. In this case, we need only turn to *The Book of Jubilees* to find out what God's purpose was in allowing these Watchers to interact with humanity.

---

151 *The Legends of the Jews, Volume 1: From the Creation to Jacob*, Louis Ginzberg, p. 76

In the second week of the tenth Jubilee, Mahalaleel took a wife, Dinah, the daughter of Barakiel, his father's brother, and she bore him a son... And he called his name Jared because in his days the angels of the Lord descended to the Earth, those who are called the Watchers, in order that they should instruct mankind, and that they should execute judgment and uprightness.[152]

Several important points can be ascertained from the preceding passage that are critical to understanding the mystery of God's original purpose in allowing this angelic interaction. The first thing is how this verse reveals that these Watchers who descended to Earth did so prior to the birth of Enoch, because as we know from biblical history Jared is, in fact, Enoch's father, which would explain how Enoch could have been in a position to interact with these mysterious personages. Next, this verse in *Jubilees* explains why God would have allowed these Watchers to descend to Earth in the first place. They did not just wander onto the scene of their own accord, as it might appear at first glance. The Watchers were specifically commissioned by God Himself to perform a divinely-appointed task.

The next thing to take note of in this verse is the way that it helps to clarify the true nature of these Watchers. To anyone still clinging to the spurious notion that the "sons of God" of *Genesis* 6 were nothing more than the sons of the righteous lineage of Seth, *Jubilees* provides us with clear corroborating evidence that they were not mortal beings, as so many traditional expositors of Scripture have insisted. Notice the portion of the verse that states, "He called his name Jared because in his days the angels of the Lord descended to the Earth." I wonder what these expositors would have to say about this verse. Do they actually expect us to believe that this righteous son of Adam, Mahalaleel, was inspired to name his son Jared, which any scholar understands to mean "he who descends," because he wanted to convey the idea that the sons of Seth would one day be characterized as such?

Furthermore, this practice of naming the patriarchs because of their connection with some great milestone in biblical history was by no means an isolated incident. In fact, it is one of the bulwarks of scriptural exegesis, whereby God repeatedly deigned to communicate the marvelous nuances of His master plan. There is even an entire school of theological thought which has determined that the name of each and every patriarch in the genealogy from Adam to Joseph, the father of Jesus, typifies an aspect of the Christ Who was to Come. God's purpose in this was to lay down a clearly discernible pattern in order that fallen humanity might better understand the nature of this Coming One.

According to this view, the name of Adam and Eve's third son, Seth,

---

152 *Jubilees* 4:15

contained a double meaning when *The Bible* recorded: "Adam knew his wife again, and she bore him a son, and called his name Seth because, said Eve, 'God has appointed me another son to replace Abel, whom Cain has slain.'"[153] The underlying application of this name, however, had to do with the hidden, alternative meaning in which Seth represented one of the earliest known types of Christ Who, as the Second Adam, was "appointed" by God as a replacement son for the first Adam who had, in a spiritual sense, been slain by Satan in the Fall.

Similarly, when Noah was born, *Genesis* tells us: "This same one will comfort us concerning the toil of our hands, because the Lord has cursed the ground."[154] Again—to the discerning—the double meaning is obvious. Not only would Noah comfort mankind from God's cursing of the ground, but Christ—of which Noah is a type—would also provide eternal comfort from the curse that was pronounced upon Adam. And just in case you doubt the possibility of such an interpretation, it should be noted that the Hebrew word used here for "ground" is *adamah*, a word that is clearly linked etymologically to that of Adam.

To deny, then, the validity of this pivotal passage in *Jubilees*, regarding this added dimension in the naming of Jared—as so often happens within traditional circles—would sadly constitute a failure of nerve at the very moment when truth could shine its most illuminating beacon of light. Yet such is the habit of the pernicious heart, "always learning but never coming to an awareness of the truth."[155] As it stands, this single verse provides us with several important clues in our ongoing attempt to solve the mystery of who designed and built The Great Pyramid. Above all, it provides corroborating evidence to support the idea that these "sons of God," these *bene ha Elohim*, these Watchers, were never initially of this Earth, but they were of such a nature that they had to "descend to it." As far as the double meaning of the name of Jared, not only did it refer to these Watchers who descended from Heaven, but it also foreshadowed the coming of Christ, Who famously chided His critics with the words: "You are from below, but I am from above; you belong to the Earth, but I am not of this world."[156]

This, then, leads us to the next point that this verse provides us, which is that, contrary to the opinion of most people who have ever heard of these Watchers, they were not demonic in nature. If all that someone did was to take their cue from *First Enoch*, we would have no way of seeing these Watchers as anything more than a veritable fountain of evil, and therefore assume that these creatures were just another class of demons. But far from

---

153 *Genesis* 4:25
154 Ibid. 5:29
155 *Second Timothy* 3:7
156 *John* 8:22

reinforcing such an interpretation, *Jubilees* states, in no uncertain terms, these Watchers are not to be counted among Satan's original horde of demonic minions; on the contrary, these were angels of the Lord, angels who had to descend from Heaven above in order to initiate contact with mankind below. If the preceding statement is true, then we have our first real insight into the activity of these Watchers, who, though originally commissioned by God to perform a specific task among humanity, obviously took it upon themselves to instigate, of their own volition, a little "extra-curricular" activity upon completing their tour of duty. How familiar does that sound?

Naturally, all this leads one to ask the next series of questions: What was the nature of this God-ordained mission in which the Watchers were to, as *Jubilees* states, "instruct mankind, and execute judgment and uprightness"? What were they supposed to teach mankind, and how were they supposed to convey their message? How, exactly, would this teaching constitute a form of judgment and uprightness? Why assign the job to angelic beings whose offspring would create a monstrous race of giants? And what was so important about their mission that God would send them even though it would lead to the most devastating calamity the world has thus far experienced?

Could I really be the only one who is led to ask such questions? If I am not, then quite possibly I am not the only one who thinks that in the very asking of these questions lie the answers to this ongoing enigma of who, how, and why The Great Pyramid of Giza was built, and hopefully with these answers, we might come full circle in our discussion, and by way of this matriculating route proceed to a clear-cut, satisfying conclusion.

The Architecture of God

LET US BOIL DOWN the aforementioned questions into a single train of thought. Such a question might be framed in the following manner: What sort of mission could have been so important that, in order to achieve His goal, God would be willing to risk sending angelic beings who were not only characterized by their teaching ability and superhuman strength but their freedom to abuse that tremendous power? Would you agree that this is a question that sufficiently embraces all of the preceding facts in our mystery story? If so, then quite possibly the answer might be attained by way of the methodology known as *Ockham's Razor*, a problem-solving technique devised by William of Ockham around the turn of the fourteenth century. Simply put, it states, "All things being equal, the simplest explanation is generally the correct one."

In this case, we might frame our explanation in the following way — as easy as one, two, three: One, God said, "Where were you, Job, when I laid the Earth's foundation? Surely you must know! Who stretched a measuring line across it? Upon what were its footings set, or who laid its cornerstone while the morning stars sang together and all the sons of God shouted for joy?" Two, Seiss declared, "Behold the architecture of God! The terms are those of the Geometer, the Master Builder. Here is the base ... the measures ... the lines ... the cornerstone! The style of the building is unquestionably The Great Pyramid." And three: All this occurred at a moment in history when — having laid the foundation, footings, and cornerstone, or, in the case of The Pyramid, a chief cornerstone — this display of architectural splendor culminated in a choral celebration in which all the "sons of God" shouted for joy.

Or to state our conclusion more specifically, based on all the previous points: "Enoch, prophet-architect *extraordinaire*, joined forces with the Watchers, angelic ambassadors sent to Earth by God, and together they constructed a megalithic pillar of testimony, uniquely designed to communicate a divinely-inspired knowledge of the destiny of mankind via a language frame that is capable of transcending any and all linguistic barriers."

The Sands of Time

THIS BRINGS US to the next phase of our study. Thus far, we have retraced the two-fold path that is depicted in *The Book of Days*, that of the storyline concerning the prophecy of The Great Five and a Half Days, and of Enoch as the narrator of our story. In the process of this retracing, I then alluded to a hidden link between these parallel storylines that has until now gone unnoticed by the public. But before I would reveal this link, I chose to engage in a lengthy dissertation retracing the age-old debate over who designed and built The Great Pyramid of Giza. So as not to entirely lose our original thought process, I would like to explain why this was so important.

My purpose in the previous matriculating was to establish overwhelming evidence for a series of ideas prior to my revealing this hidden link. The first thing to understand addresses an obvious question asked by anyone who examines the mystery of The Great Pyramid, which is: Why would the person who designed such an important monument — built as a testimony to God's truth and justice — conceal his identity? As usual, before I simply blurt out the answer, I would first like to lay a foundation by highlighting the repeatable aspects inherent in all our points of discussion. Such a foundation might be formulated by asking this preliminary question: What, exactly, is the common denominator in the special wisdom embodied in the person of Enoch? There are the prophecies contained in the books that have been attributed to him; there are the numerous parallels between the lives of Enoch and Jesus; and there are aspects of the architecture of The Great Pyramid that clearly allude to Enoch as being its architect. Each is an example of divine manifestation in the world, which was first rejected by mankind, was then lost for long epochs of history, and eventually rediscovered at some future "set time," thereby restoring them to their rightful place in the hierarchy of God's creation. This sequence of events, then, constitutes a blueprint that undergirds every aspect of messianic history—rejection, disappearance, and rediscovery.

So to return to our previous question: Why would Enoch deliberately conceal the fact that he was the architect of The Great Pyramid? The answer is: He never did. Yet for two primary reasons this authorship would remain a mystery to all but the most discerning of truth seekers. The first reason that Enoch's architectural role has been so difficult to ascertain is because, to whatever extent his authorship exists, it was encrypted in the same "language" used in the rest of The Pyramid's message, which is to say, mathematically. And just like every other form of messianic truth, it was destined that this knowledge—designed as a numeric time capsule—would be set aside as being irrelevant, and then lost amidst the sands of time. Only later, with the arrival of a far distant future generation, would its encoded message be revealed, understood, and restored.

The second reason for the difficulty in recognizing Enoch's role as architect is that it was never his intention to reveal himself as such. What does that mean? It means that Enoch was more interested in conveying messianic truth than he was in revealing his own genius or personal contribution to The Pyramid's construction. As a result, he would never have intentionally "signed," as it were, his architectural masterpiece. Ironically, the ubiquitous nature of the numerical value of 365.242 has led researchers to correctly surmise a connection between this all-important number and its designer, but any attempts to make a case that it constitutes a personal signature on Enoch's part will prove unfruitful. Why? The simple fact is: Enoch would never have been so self-serving. Just because pyramidologists insist they have proof of the existence of this signature in the Enoch Circle—with its distinctive dimensions of 365.242—does not necessarily mean that this is so. To make such an assumption, one must first demonstrate that this was Enoch's specific intention, but clearly no such evidence exists. So rather than call it the Enoch Circle, they should call it the Christ Circle, because God's obvious intention in ending Enoch's earthly sojourn at that age was to convey a numerically-based timeline involving messianic truth, not to glorify this merely human aspect of Enoch's life.

The real reason this number is built into so many aspects of The Pyramid's design is because, true to his calling, Enoch was being faithful to God's purposes in revealing a singularly pivotal aspect of biblical truth. The concept of time—in terms of messianic history—is not merely a human contrivance; it was specifically ordained by the Creator. Without the Earth revolving around the Sun once every 365.242 days, there would never be this thing we humans experience as day turning into night. Without that, days would never turn into weeks, or weeks into months, or months into years; and without these, there would be no such thing as the passage of time. Without the passage of time—not to be confused with the perception of time—there could be no commencement or consummation of the "set times" of God, and without these "set times," instituted by the Lord of Time Himself, there could be no possibility of human redemption as it is revealed in Scripture.

This biblical reality is never made clearer than when Adam and Eve, facing the initial consequences of their garden exile, had to endure the harsh reality of the very first nightfall. Having known only perpetual light as a result of their luminous nature in Eden, this stark, new experience was more than they could bear. It took only one seemingly endless night of terror, swallowed up in utter blackness, before they were begging God the next day to hold back the Sun to keep the darkness from overtaking them again.[157]

In response to their terrified prayer, the Word of God visited them and said:

> "I wish I could accommodate you both, really I do, but if I did hold back the Sun, then the agreement I made with you (concerning My promise to rescue you after *five and a half* 'days') could never be fulfilled."
>
> "But why, Lord?" asked Adam.
>
> "Because without the Sun, there would be no more hours or days or years. Then, I'm afraid, you'd remain banished from the garden. You and everyone you loved would be plagued by endless disaster, and no salvation would reach any of you, *ever*."[158]

The next thing I hope to do, in offering this series of pivotal ideas, is provide evidence to prove that the heretofore hidden link between Enoch and The Great Five and a Half Days constitutes more than a passing remark located in *The Secrets of Enoch*. What I am referring to concerns Enoch's remark that our first parents resided in Eden for *five and a half* "hours," which then leads us to the text in *First Adam and Eve* where we discover that they were to be exiles for *five and a half* "days." As it turns out, to find such evidence, one need simply continue reading further in the books depicting the life and times of Adam and Eve, because in them there are, in fact, two more occurrences of the Lord informing mankind about the prophecy of the *five and a half* "days." The next time, however, God is speaking not to Adam but to Seth, his third son. In *The Second Book of Adam and Eve*, the following scene is recorded:

---

157 *First Adam and Eve* 26:2-6
158 Ibid. 26:9-10

As the days of Seth came to an end, he asked his sons to bring him an offering so that he might bring it before the Lord, and God accepted his offering and sent His blessing upon him and his children. Then He said to Seth, "At the end of The Great Five and a Half Days, which I told your father about, I'll send My Word to save you and your descendants."[159]

The next occurrence of the *five and a half* "day" prophecy is in the following scene:

Then Jared made an offering on the altar, just as Adam had commanded him… And God appeared to Jared at the altar, and blessed him and his children, according to the offering… Then, God revealed to him the promise that He had previously made to Adam: He explained to Jared the 5,500 years, and revealed the mystery of His coming upon the Earth… And Enoch kept the command of Jared, his father… It is this Enoch to whom many wonders occurred, and who also wrote a celebrated book; but all those wonders could not be contained here in this place.[160]

Three things may be surmised from the preceding text. First, God, after informing Seth of the *five and a half* "day" prophecy, did not give it to Seth's son, Enos, or his grandson, Cainan, or even his great-grandson, Mahalaleel. Instead, He waited four generations before reiterating this all-important prophecy, that is, until the time when Jared, the father of Enoch, had become the leader of the clan. Second, an emphasis is provided in the text that Enoch was faithful to the legacy of his father, which assumes the responsibility that comes from knowing about this pivotal prophecy, as well as his role in communicating it to subsequent generations. And third, this Enoch, as opposed to the one named as a descendant of Cain, was unmistakably the same man who had written about his wondrous experiences, presumably as a result of his face-to-face encounter with the Lord Himself.

To be sure, then, there are clear-cut connections between these various texts, all of which exist as necessary cogs in the wheels of an extended historical train. Having said all that, however, I would now like to convey an even more explicit way to demonstrate Enoch's awareness of this nearly forgotten prophecy found in both books of *Adam and Eve,* along with what can be inferred from *The Secrets of Enoch.* Or to put it in the form of a question: Is it possible to demonstrate Enoch's knowledge of The Great Five and a Half Day prophecy beyond that which is displayed in the written record of apocryphal literature? And if so, where would one look to find the evidence

159 *Second Adam and Eve* 12:2, 5-6
160 Ibid. 18:13-14; 19:1; 22:1-2

for such an awareness?

The reason for such an inquiry is because I am so acutely aware of the skepticism ingrained in most people who are reading all this for the very first time. Naturally, I would not blame them in the least for thinking that I had simply made up the so-called "connections" I believed I had found between various manuscripts. Maybe what I had discovered were actually connections that had been planted by well-intentioned historians who were hoping to embellish their own translations. As depressing as that sounds, one might never rule out such a tragic possibility.

Therefore, it behooves me to seek an antidote for just such a poison to truth. In this case, if our poison is rooted in ordinary language — something so necessary in typical communication — then all the more reason that I am obliged to offer a potential antidote in the form of a medium of communication that transcends language, that is to say, the mathematically-based message found in The Great Pyramid.

This is why it has been so vital to demonstrate that the God Who inspired the mathematics embedded in The Pyramid's dimensions — like *pi*, the solar year, and the Earth-Sun relationships — did not do so arbitrarily, as if those who discovered these numerical patterns had stumbled onto a mere sidebar of biblical revelation. And if establishing such patterns has been adequately done, then what I am about to reveal may not seem so far-fetched after all, and enduring the foregoing deluge of information will, in the end, have been worth it.

Doubly-Gifted Enoch

HAVING SAID ALL THAT, there remains the apparently insurmountable feat of stemming the tide that resists the restoration of lost wisdom once it has slipped from the scene. Never mind that it is right there in front of you, as obvious as the nose on your face, yet residing just below the threshold of public awareness. How does one go about getting people to see the connections between things that seem so obvious to some but so absurd to others?

What are we talking about here, anyway? After all, what could be that difficult about proving that the prophetic wisdom of Enoch, found in the books that bear his name, is so much more than pseudepigraphal in nature? We have all the necessary tools in our arsenal, do we not? We have the dramas that transcend interpretation. We have the language of mathematics. What more do we need? We have the ability to combine these two sides of the same coin; and what do we get?

What we get is a picture of the doubly-gifted Enoch, who, oddly enough, bears a remarkable resemblance to that two-faced Roman god Janus. As it turns out, this dual-natured Janus is depicted as having one face that is looking to the right and another, to the left, which, it is said, enables him to look into both the past and the future. Hence, the word *Janus* is the origin of the name for our month of January, which marks the point at which the previous year ends and the next one begins, and the first day of which we traditionally reminisce about the year just past and imagine the possibilities for the one that lies ahead.

What else is Janus known for? Well, he is, among other things, identified with gateways pertaining to space and time. Concerning space, he is a controller of doorways, bridges, and boundaries. Concerning time, he is associated with the Sun, the Moon, and the year; in one of his ancient temples, the hands of his statue were positioned to signify the number three hundred and sixty-five, said to symbolically express his mastery over time. And just like our doubly-gifted Enoch — equally fluent in word and stone alike — this two-faced Janus was said to possess a key that provided him access to Heaven. Accordingly, Janus symbolizes the transition from the past to the future, from one vision to another, from one Universe to the next.

Do any of the foregoing attributes sound familiar? If so, on which side of the fence do you sit? Are you the sort of person who dismisses such similarities as merely coincidental? Or, instead, do you believe — like the eighteenth-century Italian scholar Giambattista Vico believed — they could only be possible because the mythology of the one actually reflects the lost but not forgotten history of the other?

It is also significant to note that before this Roman identification between Janus and Enoch, the Greeks knew Enoch as Hermes, who was best known as the messenger of the gods. Additionally, he was considered a god of transitions and boundaries, acting not only as an intercessor between the natural and the Divine but as a conductor of souls into the afterlife as well. Interestingly enough, according to their mythology, the Greeks believed that Hermes was the only god who had been officially authorized to visit Heaven.

And before the Greeks, the Egyptians knew Enoch as Thoth, the god of all wisdom. E.A. Wallis Budge, the British Egyptologist who famously translated the 1895 version of *The Egyptian Book of the Dead*, said that Thoth was "the scribe of the gods, and as such was regarded as the inventor of all the arts and sciences known to the Egyptians. Some of his titles include 'lord of writing,' 'master of papyrus,' and 'maker of the palette and the ink-jar.' As the chronologer of Heaven and Earth, he became the god of the Moon, and as the reckoner of time, he obtained his name, Thoth, which is to say, the 'measurer.'"[161] Although best known for having invented writing, he was also credited by the Egyptians with instituting the 365-day calendar as opposed to the original 360-day version, as well as — take note of this, please — designing The Great Pyramid of Giza.

---

161 *The Egyptian Book of the Dead*, E.A. Wallis Budge, p. cxviii

So what does all this mean in terms of our trying to restore the status of Enoch's lost wisdom to public acceptance? It means that if the kinds of historical clues we have just outlined really do exert such unmistakable resonances from age to age, so that Enoch's attributes clearly crop up in the otherwise muddled mythology of the ancient world, then we have yet another example of the power of dramas that transcend interpretation. And although Enoch's contribution to the history of knowledge has become skewed over time, it means that the indelible nature of it is such that it is never really lost but is merely transmuted in the process of being conveyed from culture to culture. If so, then maybe our quest for historical certainty is not as hopeless as it might at first appear. In other words, restoring the so-called "lost" wisdom of Enoch is not — as so many have presumed to be a matter of searching for what is missing — as much as it is a case of interpreting that which is not missing at all but is merely hidden in plain sight. And if this is the case, then maybe the time has come to finally connect all the dots to this extended storyline. Time to see, finally, if this domino of ideas tumbles neatly toward a tidy ending or simply fizzles out midstream. Ready or not, here I go.

A System of "Fiveness"

FIRST, WE CONSTRUCTED a narrative chronicling God's promise to rescue Adam and Eve after *five and a half* of His "days," which reached an unexpected climax when Annas and Caiaphas confessed to Pilate that they had become convinced this promise of "days" was fulfilled in Jesus of Nazareth. However, because of the ongoing controversy over the potential for biblical mistranslations, we were forced to look for a unique way to verify such a prophetic timeline that does not involve the idiosyncrasies of human language. To that end, we began an investigation into the potential of mathematically-oriented messages contained in The Great Pyramid because it is known to contain the kind of prophetic timelines so often found in the biblical texts, both canonical and apocryphal. But instead of trying to decipher a series of numbers like *Bible*-code folks are prone to do, we took a different approach. Rather than bombard you with a mind-numbing numerical blitz, I tried to anchor the numerology of The Pyramid in terms that are more human. This, then, would explain my attempts to verify the existence of Enoch's fingerprints in its architectural design via such unmistakably human values as *pi*, the solar year, and the Earth-Sun relationships. All that remains is to connect the prophecy of The Great Five and a Half Days to both the man who stood face to face with the Lord of Time and to the pillar of testimony that bears the stamp of his authorship. How might we go about doing this?

Well, we already know that The Great Pyramid presumably depicts every major turning point in biblical history, from the Exodus of Israel to the Advent of Christ. Therefore, if we were to simply re-examine the work handed down by generations of pyramidologists, one might assume that if evidence for a *five and a half* "day" chronology exists it should quite naturally "speak for itself," as it were. And if this evidence is actually found, then the next question one might ask is: Why has no one ever detected such a pyramidal timeline of *five and a half* "days" before now? To which I would reply: It is certainly because no one has ever thought to look for it. Had they done so, they would have found that not only is there evidence for this timeline in The Pyramid, but—as with all biblical prophecies—there is also ample foreshadowing of it, which its measurements portray in microcosm. In other words, besides a prophetic chronology depicting this *five and a half* "day" period from Adam to Christ, there are numerous occurrences of the primary number that comprises this promise of "days." Accordingly, the most predominant numerical value to be found in the architectural design of The Pyramid just happens to be … the number *five*.

Again, I turn to my most eloquent allies for their views on this subject. According to Joseph A. Seiss, the numerical value of *five* is so "inherently characteristic" in the dimensions of The Great Pyramid's construction that "with this number, its multiples, powers, and geometric proportions, the number *five* speaks as loudly as stones can be made to speak."[162] In Seiss' view, the ubiquitous nature of the number *five* is no mere happenstance; it is the very basis of its existence. Said Seiss:

> From this, The Pyramid seems to have its name. Though different authors have sought to derive this word from the Greek, Arabic, and other sources, the evidence is rather that it came direct from the builders of the edifice and was meant to describe it in the common language then used in that country. The nearest to that language is Coptic, and in the ancient Coptic, *pyr* means "division," the same as *peres* in Daniel's interpretation of the handwriting on the wall; and *met* means "ten." And putting them together—*pyr-met*—we have the name of the structure.[163]

According to Adam Rutherford:

> There is one, and only one, number that is prominent in The Great Pyramid, and that number is *five*. C. Piazzi Smyth spoke of it as "the sacred number of The Pyramid." Septimus Mark wrote, "The number *five* is at the foundation of much of the teaching connected with The Pyramid." This, of course, should be understood to mean *five*, and also multiples of *five*. The Pyramid's sacred cubit itself is com-

---

162 *The Great Pyramid of Egypt: Miracle in Stone*, Joseph A. Seiss, pp. 27-28
163 Ibid. p. 28

prised of twenty-five pyramid inches, that is, *five* times *five* inches; and this inch is the *five* hundred millionth (500,000,000th) part of the Earth's axis of rotation...

The principal apartment, the King's Chamber, has one hundred stones in its walls, built in *five* courses. It stands upon the *fiftieth* course of masonry in The Pyramid. The King's Chamber is twenty sacred cubits long and ten wide. The north and south walls of the Queen's Chamber are respectively, *five* sacred cubits north and *five* sacred cubits south of The Pyramid's east-west axis. The axis of the Niche in the Queen's Chamber east wall is twenty-five inches south of The Pyramid's east-west axis.[164]

Returning to Seiss, he added:

Accordingly, a system of *"fiveness"* runs through The Great Pyramid and its measure references. Counting *five* times *five* courses of masonry from the base upwards, we are brought to the floor of the Queen's Chamber. The measurements of that chamber all answer to the standard of *five* times *five* pyramid inches. It is characterized by a deep sunken Niche in one of its walls, which Niche is three times *five* feet high, consisting of *five* strongly marked stories. The topmost is *five* times *five* inches across, and its inner edge is just *five* times *five* inches from the perpendicular center of the wall into which it is cut.[165]

The height of the King's Chamber is eleven point eighteen (11.18) cubits, which is itself the square root of one hundred and twenty-five, or *five* to the third power (5^3). The diagonal length of the roof of the chamber is twenty-two point thirty-six (22.36) cubits, which is both twice its height and the square root of *five* hundred. The diagonal line of the short wall is fifteen cubits. The diagonal length from the upper corner to the opposite lower corner is twenty-five cubits. And finally, the volume of the Open Coffer is one *fiftieth* that of the King's Chamber in which it resides. Insisted Seiss:

This *"fiveness"* could not have been an accident, and likewise corresponds with the arrangements of God, both in nature and revelation. Note the *"fiveness"* of termination to each limb of the human body, the *five* senses, the *five* books of Moses, the twice *five* precepts of the Decalogue.[166]

And just in case one is tempted to give in to the notion that all this so-

---

164 *Pyramidology: Book I*, Adam Rutherford, p. 150n
165 *The Great Pyramid of Egypt: Miracle in Stone*, Joseph A. Seiss, p. 28
166 Ibid. p. 28

called "symbolism" has nothing to do with the kind of symbolic truth portrayed in *The Bible*, one would do well to take note of the following. Known to any advanced student of Pyramidology is that C. Piazzi Smyth pioneered the idea that, based on Isaac Newton's evaluation of the sacred cubit, the dimensions of The Ark of the Covenant were such that they exhibit an uncanny similarity to those found displayed in the Open Coffer in the King's Chamber. (To read about how this conclusion was reached, read pages 347-53 and 395-400 of C. Piazzi Smyth's book *The Great Pyramid: Its Secrets and Mysteries Revealed*.)

Naturally, as with so many aspects involved with pyramidal computations, there is no end to the debate over the validity of the numerical values invoked to measure such dimensional relationships. More often than not, the final determination in accepting or rejecting such possibilities comes down to one's own *a priori* position. In other words, it comes down to which version of the sacred cubit one prefers to accept. Do you lean toward the one espoused by Isaac Newton and C. Piazzi Smyth, who decided on twenty-five inches? Or, instead, do you lean toward those determined by other standards, which put it at eighteen or twenty inches? Either way, whichever standard of measurement one prefers, it is noteworthy that *The Bible* states in no uncertain terms that The Ark of the Covenant was to be made with these specific dimensions: "Have them make an ark of acacia wood—two and a half cubits long, a cubit and a half wide, and a cubit and a half high."[167]

The importance of such dimensions, for the sake of our study, is the unadulterated fact that even a child can apprehend. Two and a half, plus one and a half, plus one and a half, equals how much? Hmmm, let me see. The answer is *five and a half*, right? Right. That said, if you are the type of person who can accept the idea that the Open Coffer in The Pyramid is dimensionally related to The Ark, then the fact that they both exhibit dimensions of *five and a half* sacred cubits is something you will not fail to notice. On the other hand, if you are the type of person who rejects the possibility, then at least you must pause to consider what even Annas and Caiaphas could not fail to appreciate. This numerical value of *five and a half* denotes a resounding signature that, more than any other, points to what was the hope of all Israel, which is the Christ Who was to come.[168]

Having established the number *five* as the most special number in the dimensions of The Pyramid, and its connection to *The Bible*, we turn next to examining its significance in scriptural terms. Interestingly enough, the number *five* is repeatedly associated with the grace of God. In his informative book *Number in Scripture*, E.W. Bullinger explained:

---

167 *Exodus* 25:10
168 *Nicodemus* 22:10-14

Grace means *favor*. But what kind of favor? Favor shown to the miserable is called *mercy*; favor shown to the poor is called *pity*; favor shown to the suffering is called *compassion*; favor to the obstinate is called *patience*; but favor shown to the unworthy is called *grace*. This is favor indeed — favor which is truly divine in its source and in its character, as it is spoken of in *Romans* 3:24, "being justified freely by His grace." The word here translated "freely" occurs again in *John* 15:25, and is translated "without a cause."

And so it was with Abram. There was no cause in him why God should have called him and chosen him. Therefore, when God established His covenant with Abram — though childless at the time — regarding His intention to multiply his descendants like the stars and the sand, He confirmed this promise by instructing him to offer up *five* sacrifices, that of a heifer, a goat, a ram, a dove, and a pigeon.[169]

It is remarkable, also, that afterwards, when God changed Abram's name to Abraham,[170] the change was made very simply, but very significantly (for there is no chance with God), by inserting into the middle of it the *fifth* letter of the Hebrew alphabet, "h" (*hey*), the symbol of the number *five*. All this was of grace.[171]

Three additional points can be inserted here regarding the role of the number *five* in the previous instances. First, when God established His covenant concerning Abram's descendants becoming like stars and sand, it was the *fifth* time in the canonical record that the Lord had revealed Himself to Abram. Second, when God added the *fifth* letter of the Hebrew alphabet to Abram's name, He did the same thing to Sarai's name by changing it to Sarah, an apparent coincidence overlooked even by Adam Rutherford, who otherwise noted the significance of Abram's name change as it pertains to the number *five* within the dimensions of The Great Pyramid.[172] Third, and most importantly, in the context of the prophecy of The Great Five and a Half Days, this moment of the renaming of Abram and Sarai takes on greater significance. Before one has been made aware of the revelatory nature of the number *five* in the overall scheme of things, the *five and a half* "day" timeline seemed skewed. What do I mean by that? Well, just think about the sequence with which we have become familiar: Enoch explained that Adam and Eve were in Eden for *five and a half* hours before they fell and were made

---

169 *Genesis* 15:9
170 Ibid. 17:5
171 *Number in Scripture: Its Supernatural Design and Spiritual Significance, Part II: Spiritual Significance, Five*, E.W. Bullinger
172 *Pyramidology: Book I*, Adam Rutherford, pp. 150-51n

to wander as exiles for *five and a half* "days." Then, no mention of it occurred in the pivotal tale of Abraham and Sarah, until the timeline culminated in the story of Pilate and Jesus. But now, in light of God's insertion of the letter 'h' into the names of Abraham and Sarah, one can better understand how this prophecy of the promise of grace—so enmeshed in this *five and a half* "day" schematic—impacted even the life of the father of faith.

In this way, we can see that this infusion of the letter 'h,' or *five*, represents a succinct midpoint in our total time frame of *five and a half* "days" from Adam to Christ. It also helps us to see how this renaming of Abraham and Sarah instituted a reworking in their lives. Just as Adam and Eve are memorialized as our first natural parents, Abraham and Sarah—by way of this association of the *"fiveness"* of grace—likewise creates in them the status of a second Adam and Eve. In other words, as a result of their acting upon God's call, Abraham and Sarah were directly responsible for the birthing of a new race of spiritual beings. Accordingly, the Apostle Paul's words, in his letter to the Romans, could be modified to adapt the roles of both Abraham and Sarah.

> So *they are* the *parents* of all who believe... Therefore, the promise comes by faith so that it may be by grace, and may be guaranteed to all of Abraham *and Sarah's spiritual* children ... to all those who have the faith of Abraham *and Sarah*... As it is written: I have made you a father *and a mother* of many nations. *They are* our *parents* in the sight of God, in Whom *they* believed—the God Who gives life to the dead, and calls into being the things that were not.[173] (*Italicized words* inserted by the author.)

Another noteworthy example of the number *five* occurs when the nation of Israel made their most famous journey under Moses. *The Bible* tells us: "The Children of Israel went up harnessed out of the land of Egypt."[174] But in the margin it says: They marched out in groups of *five*. The same idea is conveyed when it is said of the people: "You will cross over before your brothers in battle array."[175] According to *The Pulpit Commentary*, this means that they were to travel in divisions of *five*. Furthermore, the Tabernacle in the Wilderness had the number *five* as its all-pervading numerical value, displaying in nearly every one of its measurements this number or some multiple of it. Again to cite Bullinger at length:

> The Outer Court was one hundred cubits long and fifty cubits wide. On either side were twenty pillars, and along each end were ten pillars, or sixty in all; that is, *five* times twelve, or grace in govern-

---

173 *Romans* 4:11, 16-17
174 *Exodus* 13:18
175 *Joshua* 1:14

mental display before the world, twelve being the number of the Tribes of Israel.

The pillars that held up the curtains were *five* cubits apart and *five* cubits high, and the whole of the outer curtain was divided into squares of twenty-five cubits. Each pair of pillars thus supported an area of *five* squared (5^2) cubits of fine white linen, thus witnessing to the perfect grace by which alone God's people can witness for Him before the world... *Five* times *five* was also the measure of the Brazen Altar of Burnt Offering. This was the perfect answer of Christ to God's righteous requirements, and to what was required of man...

The building itself was ten cubits high, ten cubits wide, and thirty cubits long. Its length was divided into two unequal parts, the Holy Place being twenty cubits long; and the Holy of Holies, ten cubits, being therefore a perfect cube of ten cubits. It was formed of forty-eight boards, twenty on either side and eight at the end, the front being formed of a curtain hung on *five* pillars. These forty-eight boards, that is, three times four squared (4^2), or four times twelve, are significant of the nation as before God in the fullness of privilege on the Earth. The twenty boards on each side were held together by *five* bars passing through rings which were attached to them...

The Entrance Veils were three in number. The first was "the gate of the court," twenty cubits wide and *five* high, hung on *five* pillars. The second was "the door of the Tabernacle," ten cubits wide and ten high, hung like the gate of the court on *five* pillars. The third was "the beautiful veil," also ten cubits square, which divided the Holy Place from the Holy of Holies. One feature of these three veils is remarkable. The dimensions of the veil of the court and those of the Tabernacle were different, yet the *area* was the same. The former was twenty cubits by *five*, which equals one hundred cubits; the latter were ten cubits by ten, equaling one hundred cubits also. Thus, while there was only one gate, one door, one veil, they each typified Christ as the only door of entrance for all the blessings connected with salvation. But note that the "gate," which admitted access to the benefits of atonement, was wider and lower (twenty cubits wide, and *five* cubits high); while the "door" which admitted access to worship was both narrower and higher (ten cubits wide, and ten cubits high); thus saying to us, that not all who experience the blessings of atonement understand or appreciate the true nature of spiritual worship. The highest worship—admittance to the mercy-seat—was impossible for the Israelites, except in the person of their substitute—the high priest; for "the beautiful veil" barred their access. Yet, this "veil" was split in two the moment the true grace which came by Jesus Christ was perfectly manifested, and it was torn by the act of God in grace, for it was split "from the top to the bottom."[176]

A similar pattern of numerological symbolism can also be found in the construction of Solomon's Temple, the dimensions of each part being exactly doubled of those found in the Tabernacle in the Wilderness. Considering the lengths to which God went in driving home the point that the salvation of His people was a total act of grace on His part, one might gain a greater appreciation as to why this number *five* is so thoroughly encrypted in what has become known as *The Bible* in Stone.

The Five and a Half Days

HAVING ESTABLISHED a link between the repeated occurrences of this number *five*, in both word and stone, all that is left is to establish a similar link between The Great Pyramid and the more specific figure of *five and a half*. But remember, we are not looking for just any old appearance of this number in pyramidal form. We are looking for this number insofar as it relates to the period from the time that God announced His promise of "days" to Adam until the moment that Christ made His appearance to make good on that promise. To do that, we will return to those esteemed pyramidologists who, by way of a lifetime of scholarship, have bequeathed to posterity a comprehensive body of knowledge. First, we will take some time to examine the work of one of the most preeminent scholars of both The Great Pyramid and biblical chronology, Adam Rutherford.

Specifically, we will be looking at two separate works by Rutherford, the first aptly titled *Treatise on Bible Chronology,* and the second, *Pyramidology: Book III.* In both of these, Rutherford focuses on the very period in which we are interested—that of the time span from Adam to Christ. And interestingly enough, as if to make his point crystal clear, Rutherford duplicates himself in both books—word for word—in a statement that spans seven full pages. His unmistakable purpose is to demonstrate that The Pyramid confirms the specific date not only of the life of Adam on this Earth but also when Jesus, as the Second Adam, strode upon the stage of world history. Furthermore, Rutherford is not merely satisfied to confirm this timeline within the dimensions of The Pyramid, but he also insists on verifying it by way of the written record of *The Bible.*

Our initial hurdle, however, in confirming the existence of a *five and a half* "day" timeline from Adam to Christ is already well known to any mod-

---

176 *Number in Scripture: Its Supernatural Design and Spiritual Significance, Part II: Spiritual Significance, Five*, E.W. Bullinger

ern-day biblical chronologist. Since the mid-seventeenth century, it has been considered common knowledge, courtesy of Archbishop Ussher, that this period was quite different in length, which is to say, 4,000 years as opposed to being 5,500 years. Moreover, to complicate matters further still, this belief has become so entrenched in Christian thought that to believe otherwise is tantamount to heresy. Fortunately, for our sake, though, there is a way to ferret out the truth of the matter, if one is simply willing to trace the history of how we in modern times have come to receive the knowledge of what *The Bible* has to say about the sacred chronology of ages past.

Apart from Rutherford's contribution to this area, many esteemed biblical chronologists in the last one hundred and fifty plus years have shed a great deal of light on this subject, and for anyone who is interested to look, he or she will find numerous books on the subject. Among those who have added so much to this discussion are Nathan Rouse, Michael Russell, George Smith, and William Hales. In what certainly constitutes one of the great lost chapters of biblical history, there is a veritable mountain of evidence that suggests the findings of Ussher are completely at odds with the scriptural tradition that had been universally embraced for more than fifteen centuries, from pre-Christian times until the Reformation Era. Suffice it to say, however, I will only be able to provide a brief summary of their work in an effort to elucidate a better understanding of the glaring discrepancies that exist in the domain of such a critical subject—one which, I believe, has so much to say about God's faithfulness to Adam and his descendants.

And speaking of Adam, it is at this point that I feel it necessary to insert a critically important point concerning a distinction between his creation, as the father of mankind, and the creation of the Universe, in general. In fact, in all the various discussions concerning the multitudinous timelines, this just happens to be one of the most misunderstood aspects. I mean, really, do biblical chronologists who purport that the Scriptures depict anywhere from a four to six thousand year period from the Creation to Christ expect us to just dismiss all the geological and astronomical evidence of a Universe that clearly exceeds their claims by many millions of years? If so, how can any rational, intelligent person take any of this business seriously? After all, in today's scientific-savvy world even the average individual is doubtlessly aware of the overwhelming evidence afforded us by way of the geological and astronomical communities. Every museum in town displays its collection of dinosaur bones, while every night sky is teeming with countless stars. Considering the physical evidence of these prehistoric bones, then, together with the knowledge that the light from the stars has taken millions of years to get to us, one cannot possibly argue with the silent but eloquent testimony that the Universe is far older than any of these biblical chronologists seem to be telling us.

Notice, though, that I said this is what they *seem* to be telling us. The reason is because of the very important distinction of which I was alluding to earlier; and the distinction is this: The starting point for our timeline has a built-in theological conundrum. What does that mean? It means that, for as long as most people can remember, the creation of the Universe and the creation of Adam have been seen as simultaneous events as far as the traditional biblical rendition is concerned. *"The Bible* says," intone the vast majority of theologians, "in the beginning, God created the Heavens and the Earth, and then six days later, He created Adam and Eve." End of story. Therefore, any discussion concerning the period leading up to the Advent of Christ is presumed to commence from this moment when the creation of both the Universe and Adam occurred.

Unfortunately, this notion simply does not hold up to scrutiny when one takes the time to examine the linguistic origins of the *Genesis* text in question. So as not to entirely lose our train of thought at this juncture, I will not belabor the point, but for the record—according to more than a century and a half of scholarship to support it—evidence suggests that the events depicted in the first two verses of *Genesis* did not take place at the same time. That is to say, when the Scriptures declare, "in the beginning, God created the Heavens and the Earth, and the Earth was without form and void,"[177] the second verse can just as correctly be rendered, "and the Earth *became* a waste and a desolation." In other words, "in the beginning, God created the Heavens and the Earth," and then some kind of cataclysmic event—which I and others equate with the primordial casting down of Satan after his expulsion from Heaven—caused the Earth to *become* what it originally was not, which was "without form and void."

The implications of this possibility are far-reaching to say the least. If true, then the creation of the Universe and the subsequent creation of Adam can no longer be seen as concomitant events. Accordingly, biblical scholars postulate there is a vast gulf of time between verse one, when God first created the Universe, and verse two, when a cataclysm struck the Earth, which then forced the Lord to "re-create" the world after it had "become" a waste and a desolation. This, say scholars who espouse this theoretical model, would explain why God told Adam and Eve to "replenish" the Earth as opposed to telling them to "plenish" it. In theological terms, this is known as the "gap" theory, a philosophical tenant not unlike the one that helps to interpret the meaning of *Old Testament* passages referring to the work of Messiah. Prior to the unfolding of history, the Advent of Christ had always been thought to be a one-time event, that is, until the facts concerning the life and death of Jesus finally enabled mankind to perceive the manifold nature of His coming. Based on the premise of this "gap" theory, then, scholars have

---

177 *Genesis* 1:1-2

postulated the existence of a vast separation of time between the original creation of the Earth and its re-creation subsequent to the cataclysmic casting down of Satan. (For further details on the "gap" theory as it pertains to the creation story in *Genesis*, please refer to the book by Arthur C. Custance entitled *Without Form and Void*.)

But again, without getting bogged down in the finer points of this ongoing debate, keep in mind that when this work cites the beliefs of the various biblical chronologists throughout history, it is important to distinguish the fact that we are not referring to the creation of the world as our starting point for the period in question. Rather, we are referring to the creation of Adam on this Earth, and more specifically, not simply to his creation but to the moment when God promised him that He would be rescued after *five and a half* "days." This, quite apart from all of the theological debates about the "gap" theory, is critically important to hone in on, because, in fact, we are not in this particular case seeking to ascertain the age of the Universe as it is purported in *The Bible*. That, in terms of this present pursuit, does nothing to confirm or deny God's faithfulness to His promises, particularly as they pertain to the foundational verse found in *Second Corinthians* assuring us that all His promises are confirmed in the Advent of Christ.

Make no mistake; the timeline we are looking for is one that runs from the life of Adam to that of Christ's, and even when some biblical chronologist or historian refers to this timeline as being one which runs from the Creation to Christ — in the course of my reporting the historical record — do not confuse these two separate creation events as though they were one and the same just because this is what so many of the Church Fathers assumed. Fair enough? If so, we can return to Ussher.

It should be noted that when the esteemed archbishop determined the world was created on the 23rd day of October, in the year 4,004 B.C., he was using the Hebrew texts found in *Genesis* 5 and 11, together with numerous other passages from Scripture. The important thing to understand is that he arrived at this date using the genealogy of the antediluvian patriarchs found in the *King James* Version of *The Bible*. This, according to Adam Rutherford, lies at the heart of the discrepancy of our two time periods. This is because the younger Hebrew-based *Masoretic* Text, which provided the basis from which the *King James* translators produced their version, contained a genealogy with life spans that were different from the older Greek-based *Septuagint* Version. "When we say *Septuagint*," said Rutherford, "we are referring to the earlier *Alexandrine* Version of *The Septuagint*, not the *Sixtine* Text of it. The Greek *Septuagint* (LXX) is thus witness to a much earlier and purer form of *The Hebrew Bible* than is our *English Bible*."[178]

---

178 *Treatise on Bible Chronology*, Adam Rutherford, p. 197; *Pyramidology: Book III*, Adam Rutherford;, pp. 698-99

As a result of this tacit acceptance of the *Masoretic* Text by the *King James* translators, the time period from Adam to the Flood falls far short of what we would expect in our effort of confirming a *five and a half* thousand year period that extended to the Advent of Christ. In fact, as the *King James* Version has it, there are only sixteen hundred and sixty-five years from the time of Adam to that of the Flood, whereas in the *Septuagint* Version, there are two thousand, two hundred and fifty-six years for the same period—a difference of nearly six hundred years. So, considering the fact that most biblical chronologists—Rutherford included—date the occurrence of the Flood around 3,145 B.C., this addition of approximately six hundred years puts the creation of Adam around 5,407 B.C., surprisingly close to the date that we have been searching for, which is 5,500 B.C.

Just think: Had the *King James* Version reflected this lengthier period for the lives of the antediluvian patriarchs, it might have been much easier to locate a canonical confirmation for this prophecy of the *five and a half* "days." So why did the translators of the *Masoretic* Text differ to such an extent with those of the *Septuagint* Version? The answer might shock if not downright anger you. Rutherford cited the following:

> Down through the centuries till Christ's time, great precautions were taken to prevent tampering with the sacred Scriptures, but after the destruction of Jerusalem by Titus in 70 A.D., and still more so after the Diaspora of the Jews in 135 A.D., a great change took place. As Dr. Hales says, "After the first destruction of Jerusalem by Titus, the Jews were so oppressed by national calamities that they could think of nothing else for some time; but about the end of the first century of the Vulgar Era, they were roused to oppose the wonderful progress of Christianity. What principally excited their rage and vexation was that their own Scriptures were turned into artillery against them to prove that Jesus was indeed the Christ, from the days of the Apostles.[179] And the chronological aspect formed no small part of that bombardment, for there was a very widespread belief, indeed, it was almost universal among the Jews that just as man was created in the sixth 'day' of Creation, so the Messiah would come in the sixth 1,000-year 'day' of human history, for *a thousand years with God are but as one day.*"

As we have ascertained, Adam came to life in the year 5,407 B.C., consequently five thousand years were complete in 407 B.C. *The Old Testament*, therefore, contains human history covering a period of five thousand years (in round numbers), hence the Jewish historian Josephus says regarding his work *Antiquities*: "Those An-

---

179 *Acts* 18:28

tiquities contain the history of five thousand years, and are taken out of our sacred books but are translated by me into the Greek tongue."[180] The sixth "day" of a thousand years from the date of Adam thus began in 407 B.C., and so ended in 594 A.D., during which very "day" Christ came, as anticipated.

As every student of the history of *The Bible* knows, many copies were made, and many versions of Scripture, both Jewish and Christian, sprang into existence in the early centuries of the Christian Era, and considerable variation existed between the different texts. The Jewish scholars and rabbis, taking advantage of this confusion, and professing to bring out "authentic" texts, in reality, seized on the opportunity to corrupt the number of years in the genealogies of the early patriarchs of *Genesis* so as to make it appear that the sixth 1,000-year "day" had not yet arrived, and, therefore, Jesus could not be the Messiah. This fact is definitely recorded in history, for Ephrem the Syrian, who lived only three hundred years after Christ, wrote, "The Jews have subtracted six hundred years from the generations of Adam, Seth, etc., in order that their own books might not convict them concerning the coming of Christ; He having been predicted to appear for the deliverance of mankind after *five and a half* millennia."[181]

Just who is this individual by the name of Ephrem the Syrian? Was he alone among the Church Fathers to have held this view concerning the *five and a half* "day" timeline from Adam to Christ? What about the fact that he stated the coming of Christ would not simply occur *sometime* during the sixth "day" of human history but specifically after *five and a half* millennia? And most importantly, is there any evidence to indicate that this statement attributed to Ephrem constituted anything more than a passing remark?

Born in the city of Nisibis, Turkey in 306 A.D., Ephrem the Syrian was a man possessed of rare talents and gifts. Not only was he a prolific hymn writer, of which it is said that over four hundred of his hymns still exist to this day, but Ephrem also wrote biblical commentaries, homilies, prose, and biographies steeped in his imaginatively metaphorical style. His works were richly laden with the poetry of *The Bible* as well as the folk tales of the multicultural Roman world in which he lived. Universally praised, Ephrem is revered by both branches of Christianity. In the East, he is regarded as a Venerable Father; in the West, he has been proclaimed a Doctor of the Church. His various titles include the Harp of the Spirit, the Deacon of Edes-

---

180 *Against Apion*, Flavius Josephus, Book 1:1

181 *Treatise on Bible Chronology*, Adam Rutherford, pp. 194-95; *Pyramidology: Book III*, Adam Rutherford, pp. 695-97

sa, the Sun of the Syrians, and a Pillar of the Church. In short, this man was no bit player in the history of Christian thought, and when someone like that has something to say about *The Bible*, it would be wise to pay attention to what he has to say.

Some two centuries before Ephrem, this same view was articulated by Theophilus, the seventh bishop of Antioch in Syria from about 168 to 174 A.D. Theophilus was, said British theologian William Sanday, "one of the precursors of that group of writers who, from Irenaeus to Cyprian, not only broke the obscurity which rested on the earliest history of the Church, but alike in the East and in the West carried it to the front of literary imminence, and outdistanced all their heathen contemporaries."[182] Theophilus is also cited as being the first Christian chronologist, and it was in this vein that he outlined a detailed chronology from the creation of the world up to his present day; the result being that he estimated the time of Adam's creation at 5,510 B.C.

Whereas Theophilus worked out a detailed chronology based on the specific dates that he found in *The Bible*, a theologian soon after him, Hippolytus of Rome, sought to date Adam's creation within the framework of the allegorical implications of Scripture. Writing in what is believed to be the oldest surviving Christian commentary, he stated:

> The first appearance of our Lord in the flesh took place in Bethlehem, under Augustus, in the year 5,500... But someone may ask, "How will you prove to me that the Savior was born in the year 5,500?" That is an easy thing to learn, oh, man, because this all took place a long time ago in the wilderness, under Moses, concerning the Tabernacle, which constituted types and emblems of spiritual mysteries, in order that when the truth appeared in Christ in these Last Days you might be able to perceive that these things were fulfilled. For God said to Moses, "You will make The Ark of imperishable wood, and overlay it with pure gold, within and without, and you will make the length of it two and a half cubits, and the width, one and a half cubits, and the height, one and a half cubits," which when summed up measures *five and a half* cubits so that the 5,500 years might be signified thereby.[183]

Parenthetically, in regard to the dimensions of The Ark of the Covenant, I would like to take a slight detour so I can point out some things that have probably gone unnoticed so far. The first thing to consider is that Hippolytus was not the first man of the cloth to realize that the dimensions of The Ark

182 *Studies in Biblical and Patristic Criticism, Volume 1*, William Sanday, S.R. Driver, p. 90

183 *Commentary on Daniel*, Hippolytus of Rome, Fragment 2:4-5

provided a time-oriented clue to the Advent of Christ, although one might argue that he was the first to do so gladly. That's because, in one of the great ironies of biblical history, the first man to detect this dimensional connection between The Ark and Christ was in fact one of Jesus' most ardent adversaries, that is, Annas, the chief priest at Jerusalem.[184] Furthermore, Annas, unlike Hippolytus, did not make this inference from The Ark alone, but he did so by connecting it with a passage from Scripture that directly spoke of the 5,500-year chronology from Adam to Christ.

As the story goes: When Pontius Pilate demanded to know if the Jewish leaders who crucified Jesus had learned anything from their own Scriptures, Annas confessed to his bitter discovery. Stepping up to their most sacred text, Annas said, "In the first of *The Seventy Books*," the chief priest explained, "we found a conversation between Michael, the archangel, and Seth, the third son of Adam, in which Michael told Seth that the Christ was to come after 5,500 years."[185]

The reason I mention this here is because I would like to know if anyone reading this stopped to ask: To which book was Annas referring? The fact that it was referred to as *The Seventy Books* no doubt brings to mind *The Septuagint*, which itself comes from the Latin word for *seventy*; and particularly intriguing about this is an often-overlooked fact concerning the origin of the name *Septuagint* itself. To this day, tradition insists it was so named because — and this is what I find so intriguing — seventy scholars supposedly translated it. Oh, sorry, wait, not seventy scholars, it was seventy-*two* scholars, actually, who translated it, six scholars from each of the Twelve Tribes of Israel. So, the question remains: If seventy-two scholars translated it, what, exactly, would the harm have been in calling it *The Seventy-Two* as opposed to *The Seventy*? None, I imagine; though in mentioning this apparently minor discrepancy here, I must leave it for now so I can pick it back up in just a moment.

Now, this is not to say that I believe the book that Annas was referring to was *The Septuagint* just because the promise of "days" he discovered was found in the first of *The Seventy Books*. Because had he been reading from *The Septuagint* he would have found it in *Genesis*. But clearly this is not the case. So, from which book was he reading? What I would suggest, in light of such testimony, is that there must be an alternative to such a possibility; and more importantly, I would suggest this in order to demonstrate that this all-important prophecy of the *five and a half* "days" has a basis in the written word of Scripture as well as its counterpart in stone.

If, then, the promise of "days" that Annas was referring to was not in *The Septuagint*, where was it? Could there be another candidate for this so-

184 *Nicodemus* 22:12-13
185 Ibid. 22:11

called *Seventy Books* to which the chief priest was referring? As a matter of fact, yes, I believe there is. And the man who produced that work is someone who biblical historians say lived around five hundred years before Christ. His name was Ezra, and he just happens to be a man whose role in all of this is made all the more interesting because so many aspects of his life story conform to the age-old pattern of messianic figures. In other words, Ezra, the scribe, seems to be cut from the same cloth as the narrator of humanity's history, Enoch. In *The Second Book of Esdras*, we find:

> "The world is a dark place," Ezra said to God, "and its people have no light. Your Law has been destroyed by fire so that no one can know what You've done in the past or what You're planning to do in the future. Please send me your Holy Spirit so I can write down everything that has been done in this world from the beginning, everything that was written in Your Law. Then in the Last Days, people will be able to find the right way and obtain life if they desire it."
>
> So God answered, "Prepare a large number of writing tablets, Ezra... Then come here, and I'll light the lamp of understanding in your heart, and it will not go out until you've finished what you're supposed to write. When you've finished your work, you'll make some of it public, and you'll give the rest to the wise ones, who will keep it secret..."
>
> For forty days, ninety-four books were written, and after that, God, the Most High, said to me, "You are now to make public the first twenty-four books that you wrote so that everyone, whether they are worthy or not, may read them. But the last seventy books you wrote are to be held back and to be given only to those who are wise among your people."
>
> And I did so, in the seventh year, in the sixth week, after five thousand years of the Creation.[186]

So, what can we surmise from the preceding information? Several things, in fact. First, we see the allusions to the pattern set forth in Enoch's story: Because the knowledge of God's actions, past, present, and future, were no longer available—no doubt associated with the nationwide loss of Scripture during the Babylonian captivity—Ezra was commissioned to restore that knowledge. Second, this restoration of knowledge was said to be for the benefit of not only Ezra's generation but also a future generation, which will arise "in the Last Days." Third, this God-inspired knowledge that was given to Ezra was to be segregated, with some of it to be "made public," and some of it to be "kept secret." Fourth, this division between public and secret knowledge came with the stipulation that the first twen-

---

186 *Second Esdras* 14:21, 22, 24-27, 44-48

ty-four books were to be made public, while the remaining seventy books were "to be held back and given only to those who are wise among your people." And fifth, all this occurred at a point in history that Ezra described as being "after five thousand years of the Creation," which, according to biblical historians took place approximately five hundred years before Christ, thus providing our first corroborative testimony derived from a canonical text — or at least according to all non-Protestant Canons — concerning the *five and a half* "day" chronology.

That said, I would now like to hone in on the salient points in regard to the question of which book Annas found the passage that convinced him the Messiah would arrive after 5,500 years, and after doing so, I will then continue with our present train of thought regarding the testimony of the early Church concerning the chronology of *five and a half* millennia.

In this particular case, I would like to point out that in the seventy secret books of Ezra, we have, by far, the most obvious candidate for the work that Annas called *The Seventy Books*, a book that was described as being so enormous that it required the combined efforts of four men to carry it.[187] Clearly, this book was by no means an ordinary book, and as such was certainly not one that was being passed around from synagogue to synagogue. In other words, everything about this unusual book spoke of its clandestine nature, particularly in light of Annas' testimony as to his own ignorance of its contents, until such time as the peculiar events surrounding the resurrection of Jesus of Nazareth compelled him to examine the book more thoroughly.

Furthermore, the utmost regard with which this sacred book was held is most likely because of what we see cropping up, some two and a half centuries earlier, when *The Septuagint* was created. As so often happens in the history of the dissemination of influential ideas, the memory traces of Ezra's volume of *The Seventy Books* was so potent that the reports surrounding its creation eventually found itself woven into the legend concerning the allegedly miraculous creation of *The Septuagint*. This is all the more evident when one considers the otherwise inexplicable discrepancy, in that according to all historical accounts, seventy-two scholars produced it, not seventy; nevertheless the book is dubbed *The Seventy*, rather than *The Seventy-Two*. So why call it *The Septuagint*? They did so, I believe, because of the irresistible and overriding concern, which in this case was to lend credence to its formation, recalling the way Ezra's most secretive and therefore most precious books were formed, and all of it hearkening back further still, to that greatest of all scribes in the Hebrew pantheon, Enoch, and the special books he was inspired to write.

Finally, it is important to take note of two more things as we conclude this parenthesis. First, if Annas were in fact reading from the secret books

---

187 *Nicodemus* 22:2-3

of Ezra, it would explain both why the primordial account of Adam and the prophecy of the Great Five and a Half Days was not a matter of common knowledge, and how an awareness of this prophecy was transmitted to mankind, quite apart from the revelation conveyed by Moses via *Genesis*.

Returning now to the testimony of the early Church concerning the 5,500-year period from Adam to Christ, we find that another important figure among their ranks subscribed to it as well. His name was Julius Africanus, a Libyan historian and chronologist of the late second and early third century. While unheard of by most people, Africanus is highly regarded for his influence on other more well-known figures among later Church Fathers, most notably Eusebius. Concerning this period, he wrote:

> Why should I speak of the three myriad years of the Phoenicians or the follies of the Chaldeans with their forty-eight myriads? For the Jews, deriving their origin from the descendants of Abraham ... together with the truth by the spirit of Moses, have handed down to us, by their extant Hebrew histories, the number of 5,500 years as being the period up to the advent of the Word of Salvation that was announced to the world ... in the time of the Caesars.[188]

As a result of his work, this same chronology became firmly rooted in the Eastern Mediterranean world, which afterward placed the date of Creation at or about 5,500 B.C.

Significantly, Ephrem, Theophilus, Hippolytus, and Africanus were not the only ones among the early Church who professed the idea that Christ had been expected to arrive 5,500 years after Adam. Many Church Fathers, as well as a number of early Church historians, who all adhered to the reckoning of time depicted in *The Septuagint*, believed the Creation took place around 5,500 B.C. Based on their estimation derived from it, the following dates were adhered to: Clement of Alexandria (5,592 B.C.), Abulfaragius of Armenia (5,586 B.C.), Julius Hilarion (5,530 B.C.), Georgius Cedrenus (5,506 B.C.), Maximus Martyr (5,501 B.C.), Lactantius, Eutychus, Nicephorus, Gregory of Tours, and Georgius Syncellus (5,500 B.C.), Pandorus of Alexandria and Maximus the Confessor (5,493 B.C.), and Sulpicius Severus (5,469 B.C.). Accordingly, the Byzantine Calendar dated the creation of the world at 5,509 B.C., while in Ethiopia, it has been observed: "The most authentic ancient history of that country, according to James Bruce, is *The Chronicle of Axum*," which attests that "there is an interval of 5,500 years between the creation of the world and the birth of Christ."[189]

---

188 *The Extant Fragments of the Five Books of the Chronology of Julius Africanus: On the Mythical Chronology of the Egyptians and Chaldeans*, Julius Africanus, Fragment 1

189 *Encyclopedia Perthensis: Or, Universal Dictionary of the Arts, Sciences, and Literature, Volume 9*, John Brown, p. 91

So what can we surmise from the foregoing information? Primarily, that many of the most influential Christian theological minds, writing in an era not so far removed from the time of Jesus as we are today, were all in agreement as to this particular time frame of *five and a half* "days" from Adam to Christ. This evidence from the historical record, then, stands in stark contrast to the numerical system that provided the basis for Ussher's calculations, a fact which when fully appreciated clearly undermines any merit thus far given to his chronological claims. Notwithstanding our modern-day ignorance concerning these facts of history, they have not gone unnoticed by others. In his 1856 book, entitled *A Dissertation of Sacred Chronology*, Nathan Rouse stated in no uncertain terms:

> We cannot but express our regret that ... the demonstrably erroneous and absurd system of Archbishop Ussher is still permitted to retain its place in the margin of our *Bible*, and to be taught to the youth of our country. We should despise a man who would at the present day undertake to teach the Ptolemaic system of astronomy, and yet our pulpits and schools are perpetually disgraced by inculcating a manifestly corrupt rabbinical system of scriptural chronology...
>
> The Ussherian chronology ... is inconsistent not only with itself but likewise with all antiquity, both Jewish and Christian... And yet, although we have had the good sense to renounce an erroneous system of astronomy, we doggedly cling to a false system of biblical chronology, and are almost disposed to charge the man with heresy who presumes to call our falsehood into question. It is to be hoped that the time is not too distant when Protestant communities will wipe this disreputable blot from their escutcheon, and when our pulpits and schools will no longer lend their influence to the propagation of such a pernicious untruth.[190]

Needless to say, however, in the more than one hundred and fifty years since Rouse wrote his book, the typical Christian is still no more aware of the preceding sentiments than when these words were first penned. The simple fact remains that most people who have investigated the subject of biblical chronology are still under the impression that the only correct view is the one that has been handed down to us by Archbishop Ussher, which has been singularly revered ever since it was first offered to an unsuspecting public in 1650.

But if the false chronology of the *Hebrew Masoretic* Version of *The Bible* was dismissed in favor of the Greek *Septuagint* Version as early as the eighth century of the Christian Era, what could have happened between that time and the mid-seventeenth century to allow for such a radical shift in our un-

---

190 *A Dissertation on Sacred Chronology*, Nathan Rouse, pp. 51-52

derstanding of biblical chronology? If someone whose name became synonymous with admiration and respect—that is, one Venerable Bede—failed to
impose his view concerning a 4,000-year time frame, who did succeed? The
answer, like any that a vigorous historical investigation has to offer, is one
that turns out to be another of the great ironies of history. And though this
shift came in conjunction with the effort of a single individual, unlike the
effort of Bede, who was specifically trying to bring about this change, this
man was in no way, shape, or form trying to undermine the chronology of
the Greek *Septuagint*.

In fact, this shift in theological thinking did not come as a direct result
of any specific act made by this one man but was merely an outgrowth of a
movement that he instigated. What is undoubtedly the most important advancement in human civilization, this revolution in thought is unsurpassed
in terms of its enlightenment and edification of the human race; and the
movement I am referring to is the Reformation. Yet, ironically, for all the
good that this uniquely positive force in history accomplished, there was
a peculiar downside to it as well, although certainly one that could never
have been anticipated by its founding father, Martin Luther. In this case,
the unanticipated downside occurred as a result of the inevitable backlash
that came in response to all things Roman Catholic, a backlash involving the
rejection of anything seen as even remotely connected to Papal influence.
Concerning this ill-fated turn of events in the history of biblical chronology,
Rouse had this to say:

> Notwithstanding the attempt of Venerable Bede, the *Septuagint*
> chronology prevailed down to the time of the Reformation, and
> during this entire period, there is no instance upon record of any
> church, in either the East or the West, having adopted the rabbinical
> corruptions of the Hebrew. The Protestant reformers, however, did,
> in this respect, what no Christian church, even in the darkest ages,
> had ever done. They adopted the chronological corruptions of the
> Jewish rabbis.
>
> On this point Bishop Russell remarks: "It has not escaped ob-
> servation that the prejudices against the Roman Church, which ani-
> mated the disciples of Luther, were allowed to mix deeply with their
> investigations into this intricate science. The Protestants, aware that
> the Papal communion followed the computation of *The Septuagint*,
> exerted all their learning in order to prove that the chronology of *The
> Hebrew Bible* possessed a higher authority than could be claimed for
> the most approved version of the Scriptures. And overlooking the
> convincing evidence that is supplied by the writings of the ancient
> Jews, as well as the Christian Fathers during the first four centuries,
> they took part with the Talmudists and modern rabbis, against both

the Eastern and Western Churches, and maintained that the Messiah appeared upon the Earth at the end of the fourth millennium."[191]

So, whereas the human spirit won a great victory against the forces of tyranny in the wake of the Reformation, the unexpected casualty in this war of ideology just happened to impact the future of mankind's understanding of this most critical facet of God's control over history. Writing about the same time as Rouse, George Smith confirmed this same idea:

> Up to that period, the authority of the Greek *Septuagint*, and the unanimous consent of the Church Fathers, were still found to regulate public opinion with respect to the age of the world. But the reformers were easily induced to consider the extended chronology as one of the errors handed down by Rome, and, therefore, when Archbishop Ussher, in his great impartiality for rabbinical literature, adopted the Masorite numbers, the Reformed Church eagerly caught at the change, and from that time the so-called "Hebrew verity" was defended with as much zeal as if the entire truth of revelation depended on that system of numbers.[192]

And with the fateful decision to substitute the version of *The Bible* that had been accepted by every Christian church from the time of Christ to the Reformation with this — in the view of the reformers — non-Catholic version, the door was opened wide for a new generation of scriptural chronologists. No wonder that men like James Ussher and John Lightfoot, well-intentioned as I am sure they were, would, as a result of referring to the *Masoretic* Text, deduce that the Creation occurred just 4,000 years prior to the Advent of Christ as opposed to the previously accepted period of 5,500 years.

Having therefore established the preceding facts of biblical history, the only question that remains is: What evidence is there to suggest that Ephrem's fourth-century reference to the *five and a half* millennia from Adam to Christ was anything more than a passing remark? To answer that, we now turn to another piece of ancient literature that most *Bible* students are unfamiliar with — one that purports to represent a compendium of events from the Creation to the birth of Jesus. More importantly, this work is attributed to none other than Ephrem the Syrian. Entitled *The Cave of Treasures*, it presents this history in six chapters, corresponding to the six days of creation, in which the first five chapters each depict a period of one thousand years, with the final chapter depicting a period of five hundred years. In other words, this Syriac text — that naturally is besieged by scholastic skepticism

191 *A Dissertation on Sacred Chronology*, Nathan Rouse, p. 22
192 *The Patriarchal Age: The History and Religion of Mankind from the Creation to the Death of Isaac*, George Smith, p. 40

as to its genuine Ephremic authorship—just happens to depict a biblically-inspired timeline that spans 5,500 years from Adam to Christ. An excerpt from the last chapter, dubbed a Chronological Statement, reads as follows:

> Understand now and see, my brother Nemesius, that in the days of Jared, in his fortieth year, the first thousand years came to an end. In the six hundredth year of Noah's life, the second thousand years came to an end. In the seventy-fourth year of Reu, the third thousand years came to an end. In the twenty-sixth year of Ehud's life, the fourth thousand years came to an end. In the second year of Cyrus' reign, the fifth thousand years came to an end. And in the five hundredth year of the sixth thousand years, Christ was born in human form.[193]

In the following way, then, one can see that the comment attributed to Ephrem the Syrian, suggesting a messianic timeline of 5,500 years, was certainly no passing remark. Quite to the contrary, it became the basis of Ephrem's voluminous work in which he meticulously chronicled "the succession of the families from Adam to Christ," no small feat as one can imagine.

But just because Ephrem, and other Church Fathers like him, gave credence to this timeline of *five and a half* millennia, what evidence is there to indicate a link between it and the *five and a half* "days" found in the document that forms the basis of the present narrative in *The Book of Days*? To locate such a link, one need simply turn to the preface of the English translation of *The Cave of Treasures*, produced by E.A. Wallis Budge, who wrote:

> There is no doubt whatsoever that the writer of *The Cave of Treasures* borrowed largely from *The Book of Adam and Eve* ... where God promised more than once to Adam that after *five and a half* days—i.e. 5,500 years—He would send a Redeemer into the world Who would save both Adam and his descendants from the destruction which his sin in Paradise had incurred.[194]

Moreover, Budge confirmed the literary link between the two texts in his recounting of the rediscovery of *The Cave of Treasures*, in which he stated:

> The famous author of *The Catalogue of Oriental Manuscripts* in the Vatican Library, one Giuseppe Assemani, described a Syriac manuscript containing a series of apocryphal works ... which contained the history of a period of 5,500 years, i.e. from the creation of Adam

---

193 *The Cave of Treasures: The Book of the Succession of the Generations*, Ephrem the Syrian, Fol. 43b, col. 1

194 *The Book of the Cave of Treasures: A History of the Patriarchs and the Kings, their Successors, from the Creation to the Crucifixion of Christ*, E.A. Wallis Budge, pp. 7, 10

to the birth of Christ, and that it was a historical chronicle based upon the Scriptures... But no attempt was made to publish the Syriac text; in fact, little attention was paid to it until August Dillmann, the nineteenth-century German Orientalist, began to study *The Book of Adam and Eve* in connection with it... And then he noticed that the contents of whole sections of *The Cave of Treasures* in Syriac and *The Book of Adam and Eve* in Ethiopic were identical.[195]

Therefore, from Rutherford and Ephrem to Rouse and Budge, one can trace a clear connection concerning the historical roots of this prophecy of The Great Five and a Half Days. No longer can the river of this *day*-oriented timeline—found in such universally accepted texts as *The Septuagint*—be seen as existing apart from its headwaters flowing from those previously marginalized books like *Adam and Eve*. Now that it has been exhumed from the depths of apocryphal obscurity, this *five and a half* "day" prophecy can no longer be disregarded as a fanciful tale left over from some bygone era. It is time, then, to restore it to its rightful place in Christological thought, just as the God of *The Bible* originally intended—as integral as that primordial prophecy, which speaks of the seed of the woman being bruised by the seed of the serpent, which, in turn, is ultimately crushed in the very process of its ill-advised bruising.[196]

The Eye of Faith

WITH ALL THE FOREGOING in mind, the only thing left is to connect this *five and a half* "day" timeline, so firmly rooted in the written record of Scripture—both canonical and apocryphal—to that marvelous megalith, *The Bible in Stone*. And the reason for this is two-fold. First, as has been previously stated, one reason is because there are still far too many who stubbornly cling to the view that any contradictions to their traditional interpretation of Scripture are merely by-products of mistranslations that have been handed down from age to age. Therefore, in answer to such objections, we will attempt to offer an antidote, which by its very nature precludes any errors in translation. This answer, then, like all that are conveyed via the geometry of The Great Pyramid, will be one that is conveyed entirely by way of the universal language of mathematics. As such, a message of this sort will be the same today as it was when this ancient testimony of geometric wisdom was originally constructed.

And second, in the process of connecting the numerical value of *five and a half* in The Pyramid with such texts as *Adam and Eve, Secrets of Enoch,*

---

195 *The Book of the Cave of Treasures: A History of the Patriarchs and the Kings, their Successors, from the Creation to the Crucifixion of Christ*, E.A. Wallis Budge, pp. 13-14
196 *Genesis* 3:15

and *Nicodemus*, we will also be elevating these works to a status above and beyond that which has thus far denigrated them to the crude level of *pseude-pigrapha*. In other words, even if biblical scholars are willing to entertain the potential contribution of these texts from a purely literary and anecdotal perspective, they still only do so with the caveat that they were written long after the texts themselves imply. As such, anyone who would dare suggest that the message contained in them could have any basis in *bona fide* biblical truth would certainly find themselves at odds with the prevailing status quo. But—I repeat—by connecting this all-important numerical value with both The Great Pyramid and the written texts in question, one goes a long way in providing a much sounder argument for their great antiquity. This is not to say that previous attempts to date these manuscripts holds no merit; please do not misunderstand me here. What I am suggesting, though, is that by demonstrating a connectivity between stone and word alike concerning this number *five and a half*, which is evidently so integral to the central messianic timeline of Scripture, we find ourselves on much more secure ground in arguing that these later texts are undoubtedly based on other source material from an earlier period—such as Ezra's seventy secret books—that far exceeds previously accepted historical limits.

To that end, let us review: In our effort to demonstrate a correspondence between *The Bible* and its counterpart in stone, we first traced the origin of the prophecy of The Great Five and a Half Days as it is depicted in *Adam and Eve, Secrets of Enoch*, and *Nicodemus*. We then proceeded to analyze the "who," "how," and "why" of the construction of The Great Pyramid of Giza. In the process, it was determined by every known criterion of authorship that Enoch, the seventh patriarch from Adam, is the only person in history capable of designing the prophetic implications that are purportedly contained in its geometric features. Additionally, he is known to have had an association with the kind of "construction crew" who alone could build such a structure, that is, the Watchers, who were both endowed with superhuman strength and divinely commissioned to communicate their wisdom to humanity. Together, these essential ingredients provided us with the following conclusions. One, Enoch was the architect of The Great Pyramid. Two, the Watchers provided the angelic "muscle power," as it were, required in The Pyramid's otherworldly construction. And three, it was built according to God's express purposes, as per *The Book of Jubilees*, "in order that they, *the Watchers*, should instruct mankind, *by way of The Great Pyramid's geometric design*, and that they should execute judgment and uprightness, *as a result of the prophetic message revealed in it*."[197]

Finally, after having rescued the prophecy of The Great Five and a Half Days from the mists of time and establishing that Enoch and the Watchers

---

197 *Jubilees* 4:15

were commissioned to incorporate their God-inspired wisdom within the geometry of The Pyramid, we turned our attention to the final phase of our quest. In a nutshell: If all the prophetic timelines depicting messianic history are conveyed via the dimensions of The Great Pyramid's architecture, then there is every reason to believe that this foundational prophecy — this promise of "days" — should also be found there. We have now seen the extent to which the number *five* is thoroughly embedded into The Pyramid's schematics; therefore, considering the ubiquitous nature of this number, it should not be too difficult to locate the number *five and a half*, if one looks for it in the proper place, right? Should we then expect to find it buried within a series of complex computations, as is the case of the numerical value of 365.242? Should we look for it as part of a geometric relationship, such as the one that reveals the factor of *pi*? As a matter of fact, no. One need not look nearly as hard as one might expect to find such a significant numerical value. So where do we find it? And just as importantly, if it really is so significant, then why has no one discovered it yet?

As it turns out, the answer to the last question is even more difficult to answer than the actual locating of the *five and a half* "day" timeline, because, like so much of the numerological significance built into the design of The Pyramid, there are no "neon signs," so to speak, pointing the way to such things. Discoveries of this sort are simply the by-product of serendipitous circumstances. That they are made at all is a testament, rather, to the genius of the designers of The Great Pyramid as opposed to those who grab hold of the train that is the whole history of what has been discovered in its marvelous construction. Just as *The Bible* is a document whose contents are hidden in plain sight, so, too, the divine wisdom embodied in The Pyramid, though hidden to the undiscerning, is still there for all to see, if only to those who pursue it with the eye of faith. Of this kind of apprehension of truth, Ephrem the Syrian had much to say. Sebastian Brock, in his study on the life of Ephrem entitled *The Luminous Eye*, said this:

> When Ephrem explores the infinite number of symbols and types in nature and Scripture, we must be constantly aware that, although human understanding of them is essentially fluid and variable, what they all point to is an objective reality that Ephrem calls "Truth." Furthermore, the presence in the types and symbols of what he calls the "hidden power," or "meaning," lends to them some sort of inner objective significance of reality, which is different from that outer reality, which the scientific observer would call objective.[198]

Said Ephrem:

---

198 *The Luminous Eye: The Spiritual World Vision of Saint Ephrem the Syrian*, Sebastian Brock, p. 55

Lord, Your symbols are everywhere, yet You are hidden from everywhere.

Though Your symbol is On-High, yet the height does not perceive that You are.

Though Your symbol is in the depths, it does not comprehend
Who You are.

Though Your symbol is in the sea, You are hidden from the sea.

Though Your symbol is on dry land, it is not aware of what You
are.

Blessed is the Hidden One shining out![199]

Truth according to God's intention, then, paradoxically contains two
separate yet insoluble components, whether in terms of Scripture or, in this
case, The Great Pyramid. In other words, truth has both a surface meaning
that is obvious to most people, and a deeper meaning that is understood by
only a few. As Brock explained it:

Types and symbols are to be found everywhere simply as a result
of the world having been created by God; they are pointers to His
existence and creative activity... But they are only observable by the
eye of faith; and the clearer that eye is, the more the symbols will
become visible, and each individual symbol will also become more
meaningful.[200]

Yet this idea is certainly not new to anyone who has read any of this so
far. Repetition, after all, has constituted a major component to my approach
throughout this work, and this is no time to depart from such tried-and-true
methods. Admittedly, though, I did not invent the concept myself. To tell
you the truth, I stole it; or, rather, I would like to think I borrowed it. In fact,
one of the most obvious clues that a single mind is behind both *The Bible* and
The Great Pyramid is this overwhelming repetition of theme, character, and
style. Scripture is methodically redundant in its use of types, which inevitably move from the vaguely general to the highly specific, that is, from the
lesser messianic figures such as Elijah and Jonah, who set the stage for the
greater messianic figures like John the Baptist and Jesus of Nazareth. Likewise, The Pyramid exhibits a similar method of redundancy, in this case the
repetition of the number *five*, which, in turn, sets the stage for the appearance of *five and a half*.

So keeping in mind that the symbolic truth of The Pyramid, like that of
The Bible, is only discernible to those who approach it with the eye of faith,
we may proceed in our attempt to connect the *five and a half* "days" in stone

---

199 *Faith*, Ephrem the Syrian, 4:9
200 *The Luminous Eye: The Spiritual World Vision of Saint Ephrem the Syrian*, Sebastian Brock, p. 56

with that which is found in word. To reiterate: Do we find it buried within a series of complex computations or as part of a geometric relationship? Again, I say no. Believe it or not, we "see" this *five and a half* "day" timeline from Adam to Christ every time we look at The Great Pyramid. Let me say that again for anyone who might think I just misspoke: In every picture you have ever seen of the exterior of The Pyramid, sitting so majestically upon the Giza plateau, you were actually staring straight at the very timeline that we have been seeking. That is, you have looked at it without realizing that what stood before you contained "more than the eye could see." In other words, like so much of what is revealed symbolically in The Pyramid, the knowledge it contains is hidden right before your eyes. Let me explain what I mean by that.

Whenever one looks at a standard image of The Great Pyramid, the first thing one sees rising from the desert floor is a rocky edifice composed of four triangular planes, which all converge at its pinnacle several hundred feet above ground. And what does one see at the summit of this magnificent Pyramid? Does it have a point like every other pyramid around it? No, it does not. Unique among the pyramids of Egypt, this greatest one of all has no capstone, no "crown," as it were, at its peak. But why? To this day, no one can say for sure. Some argue that it was placed there but, like its original outer casing stones of polished limestone, was removed in an act of vandalism. Some claim that it was never built in the first place, while others insist that it was built but, because it was flawed in its workmanship, was never set in place. The only thing we can be sure of today is that it is missing and has been for as long as anyone can remember. Is that the end of the story, then? Of course not; but as one can imagine, only an explanation that offers a decidedly biblical view would be of any consolation to this author. Fortunately, when one looks to the many esteemed pyramidologists, there is much that has been said to connect the meaning of this missing capstone and *The Bible*, which The Pyramid has obviously been intended to symbolize.

To a man, this missing capstone is interpreted as representing Christ, Who spoke of Himself as being the "Chief Cornerstone that was rejected by the builders."[201] The Apostle Peter confirmed this idea when he testified before the Sanhedrin, saying, "Jesus is the stone that you builders rejected, which has become the Cornerstone."[202] In this, Peter was echoing the words of the psalmist, who wrote concerning this Rejected One: "The Lord has done this, and it is marvelous in our eyes."[203] Elsewhere, Peter continued

---

201 *Matthew* 21:42
202 *Acts* 4:11
203 *Psalm* 118:23

this same thinking, which speaks not only of Jesus as the Chief Cornerstone but also of believers in Christ becoming like Him to a lesser degree. As stones gathered by the purposeful hand of a Master Builder:

> You come to Him, the Living Stone — rejected by humans but chosen by God and precious to Him. You also, like living stones, are being built into a spiritual house to be a holy priesthood, offering spiritual sacrifices acceptable to God through Jesus Christ. For in the Scripture it says, "See, I lay a stone in Zion, a chosen and precious cornerstone, and the one who trusts in Him will never be put to shame."[204]

Said the Apostle Paul:

> Consequently, you are no longer foreigners and strangers but fellow citizens with God's people and also members of His household, built on the foundation of the apostles and prophets, with Christ Jesus as the Chief Cornerstone. In Him, the whole building is joined together and rises to become a holy temple in the Lord, and in Him, you, too, are being built together to become a dwelling in which God lives by His Spirit.[205]

In this way, one could not possibly articulate a more perfect analogy of what is being expressed via this idea of Christ as the "missing capstone" atop The Great Pyramid — a "holy priesthood," who as "living stones," rise up to constitute the "spiritual house" of which Jesus, holding the entire edifice together, is the "Chief Cornerstone." Again, I turn to the eloquence of Seiss, who said this about the preceding verses of Scripture:

> All these are great central passages of the divine word, and not one of them can be properly interpreted without The Pyramid, whose light alone brings out their full significance and beauty... Common architecture furnishes no preeminent cornerstone. There is no chief cornerstone without The Pyramid. That alone has ... a cornerstone, uniquely and indisputably the chief...
>
> The shape of it is altogether peculiar. It is *five*-sided and *five*-pointed... It is itself a perfect pyramid, the original of the edifice which it completes and adorns... Every other stone in all the mighty construction stands in it, and has place with reference to it, and is touched by its weight and influence, as well as sheltered under its lines, and honored and perfected by its presence. It is indeed the "all in all" of the whole edifice. To its angles is "all the building fitly

---

204 *First Peter* 2:4-6
205 *Ephesians* 2:19-22

framed together." And in it, every part and particle that belongs to the structure, from foundation to capstone, has its bond of perfectness, its shelter, and its crown.

About such imagery there should be no question. In all the richness of the Scriptures, there is not a more luminous, expressive, and comprehensive picture of Christ — in Himself, in His experiences, in His relations to His friends or foes, in His office and place in all the dispensations of God toward our race — than that which is given in these texts when studied in the light of The Great Pyramid.[206]

From Adam to Christ

HAVING ESTABLISHED that the summit of The Great Pyramid is symbolic of Christ, we can return to locating this *five and a half* "day" timeline to which I have been alluding. To reiterate: Not only is Jesus represented by this missing capstone, but, based on an interpretation from *The Bible*, the entire structure beneath its summit represents the "House of God," made up of "living stones," which are all "fitly framed together and sheltered under its lines." Therefore, if Christ represents the summit of this grand edifice, and the stones that comprise it represent those who make up His body, then who might represent the foundation of this marvelous megalith? Who else but Adam, that is, the father of mankind?

Again, as I previously stated: Whenever someone looks at the exterior of The Great Pyramid, they are actually seeing the *five and a half* "day" timeline from Adam to Christ that we have been seeking. How can we be sure of this? The certainty lies in what is well known to every student of Pyramidology, that the height of The Pyramid has long been determined to be 5,449 pyramid inches. Yet to my knowledge, this particular dimension has never been understood beyond the fact that it bears an uncanny relationship to the biblical passage in *The Book of Isaiah*, to which pyramidologists point as proof of The Pyramid's divine origins. Whereas Egyptologists insist that The Great Pyramid, like every other pyramid in Egypt, was built simply as a royal funerary heap, pyramidologists vehemently deny this assertion; and to prove their case, they offer up the existence of the all-important verse in *The Bible*:

> In that day, there will be an altar to the Lord in the midst of Egypt, and a pillar of God at its border. It will become a sign and a witness to the Lord of Hosts in the land of Egypt, for they'll cry to God because of the oppressors, and He'll send them a Savior and a Champion to deliver them.[207]

---

206 *The Great Pyramid of Egypt: Miracle in Stone*, Joseph A. Seiss, pp. 125-28
207 *Isaiah* 19:19-20

Called the "Great Pyramid Text of Scripture," these two verses contain thirty Hebrew words, each letter of which contains a corresponding numerical value. Ironically, when one "adds up" all of the words contained in this *Isaiah* passage, the sum total is 5,449, which, as we just stated, constitutes the distance from The Pyramid's base to its summit. Moreover, in light of our present search for a 5,500 year timeline, this numerical value of 5,449 pyramid inches bears a striking similarity to that time frame, even more so than Rutherford's dating of 5,407 years from Adam to Christ.

Still, one might legitimately ask: What evidence is there that this number depicting The Pyramid's height has anything to do with the *five and a half* "day" timeline that you are talking about? As usual, the best way I know to answer such a question is not to simply look for a one-dimensional response. By that I mean I will attempt to provide an answer that, in accordance to the pattern of both the Scriptures and The Pyramid, is so sufficiently redundant that there could be no other way of looking at it.

To begin with, in attempting to demonstrate that The Pyramid's height represents a timeline distinctly messianic in nature, one should take notice of three important facts. First, not only is The Great Pyramid 5,449 pyramid inches tall, but it is also built up of 203 courses of masonry, a fact which will come into play a little later in our discussion. Second, this exterior measurement of 5,449 pyramid inches does not simply occur once, but it can be found there a second time. And third, the numerical figure of 5,449 can also be located as a measurement within the interior passages of The Pyramid. Together, this tripartite repetition substantially reinforces this number's importance and thus its potential for supporting our claim that The Pyramid's height unmistakably represents a timeline with messianic implications.

Our initial clue that this dimension of 5,449 represents a prophetic — and therefore messianic — chronology comes to us by way of its association with the previously mentioned "Great Pyramid Text of Scripture." Not only is there a correspondence between the numerical value of the *Isaiah* verses and the height of The Pyramid, say pyramidologists, but the total length of the downward passageway also produces a similar measurement of 5,449 pyramid inches. And, mind you, this downward passageway includes the universally acknowledged starting point of the entire timeline of prophetic dates, which are all subsequently revealed in every other point within The Pyramid. In other words, no proponent of The Pyramid's prophetic chronology would dismiss, for an instant, the correctness in seeing this downward passageway as portraying a time-oriented numerical value — one that corresponds precisely with the same number that represents its height.

The next clue concerning the importance of the number 5,449 comes to us when we return our attention to those peculiar "air shafts," which run diagonally from both the King's and Queen's Chambers up to, and toward, the structure's exterior, respectively. Ever since investigators first turned their attention to them, there has been no end to the speculation over their true purpose. Some point to the more mundane assumption that they were designed to provide a perfectly regulated atmosphere for future generations who would require an adequate air supply while investigating its interior. Others—who point to the fact that the shafts from the Queen's Chamber stop short at both ends—lean toward an esoteric interpretation, insisting that their role has more to do with spiritual or astronomical concerns.

Yet whichever direction one leans, a mathematical significance does leap out when one takes the time to look. In his book *The Great Pyramid Decoded*, Peter Lemesurier points to a series of unique dimensional facts, that is, four specific measurements, which are all supremely pertinent to our present inquiry. Two of these measurements we have just discussed, which is, the height of The Great Pyramid is 5,449 pyramid inches, and the total floor-line length of the lower passageway also equals 5,449 pyramid inches. The other two measurements to which Lemesurier refers have only been alluded to so far.

The first measurement involves the combined heights where the shafts leading from the Queen's Chamber would, if extended, penetrate The Pyramid's exterior, which together equal 5,449 pyramid inches. In other words, the shaft leading toward the north face of The Pyramid intersects the exterior at a vertical height of 2,724.5 pyramid inches, while the shaft leading toward the south face does so at the same height, which when added up comes to 5,449 pyramid inches. The other measurement involves the two shafts leading from the King's Chamber, both of which actually do penetrate The Pyramid's exterior, at the 101st and 102nd level of masonry, north and south faces respectively, which when taken together add up to 203 courses. This figure, as you may recall, just happens to equal the height of The Pyramid in terms of its total courses of masonry. As for the significance of such apparent coincidences, Lemesurier said:

> Taking these four measurements together, it becomes clear that The Pyramid's architect wished to emphasize that this number, which represents its height, was of some overriding importance, and that he, therefore, deliberately included the above four references to it in his design.[208]

Again, considering the numerically-oriented information in The Pyramid, what else could the designer have intended by this conspicuous repetition if not to emphasize that, just as the downward passageway represents a messianic timeline, the height of The Pyramid also represents a chronology

---

208 *The Great Pyramid Decoded*, Peter Lemesurier, p. 380

of similar significance? In this case, it bears an uncanny relationship to the 5,500-year prophecy that we have encountered throughout the apocryphal record and early church history. Together with Justin Martyr's second-century reference to *Nicodemus* — a.k.a. *The Acts of Pontius Pilate* — we have yet another way to undermine claims that such texts date to no earlier than the seventh century of the Christian Era. And if this is so, then we are on even firmer ground that this very influential work is based on much earlier texts that really have been lost to history. The reason for this is because just as the reoccurring dimensions in The Pyramid reinforce an awareness of its divinely-inspired message, it seems equally certain that the recurrence of this number *five and a half* in the texts of *Adam and Eve*, *Secrets of Enoch*, and *Nicodemus* should also be understood in the context of this same conspicuous repetition — a "pattern with a purpose," as it were. In other words, just as The Pyramid calls attention to itself through its repeated use of the number *five and a half* — in its height, together with the dimensions of the Open Coffer in the King's Chamber, which in turn corresponds to the *five and a half* sacred cubits of The Ark of the Covenant — it should be just as obvious that the apocryphal texts have been inspired by the same author and with the same purpose of conveying the most central messianic timeline in biblical history.

Finally, there is still one more interesting way at discovering the number *five and a half* in the height of The Great Pyramid, which comes via a revealing web-based article dedicated to the numerical value known as *phi*, or the number 1.618 — not to be confused with *pi* — sometimes called the "golden number," the "golden ratio," or the "divine proportion." According to the site's author, Gary Meisner:

> This "golden ratio" is unique in its mathematical properties and pervasive in its appearance throughout nature... Most everyone learned about *pi* in school, but few curriculums included *phi*, perhaps for the very reason that grasping all its manifestations often takes one beyond the academic realm of the spiritual just by the simple fact that *phi* unveils an unusually frequent constant of design that applies to so many aspects of life...
>
> The positions and proportions of the key elements of many, if not most, animals are based on *phi*. Examples include the body and wing sections of insects, the spiral of sea shells, and the position of the dorsal fins on porpoises. Even the spirals of human DNA embody *phi* proportions... More intriguing yet is the extensive appearance of *phi* throughout the human form, in the face, body, fingers, teeth, and the impact that this has on our perceptions of human beauty... It seems that *phi* is hard-wired into our consciousness as a guide to beauty...

With all the unique mathematical properties of *phi*, and its appearance throughout creation, it is little wonder that mankind would not only take notice of this number and the "golden ratio" that it creates but also use it to capture the beauty and harmony of nature in our own creations in art, architecture, and other areas of design. In some cases, mankind's application of *phi* is undeniable. In other cases, it is still the subject of debate. The Great Pyramid of Giza appears to embody the "golden ratio" in the dimensions of its base, height, and hypotenuse, but its state of ruin and the absence of any mention of *phi* in ancient Egyptian writings make it difficult to prove conclusively that this was by design...

The description of this "golden ratio" as the "divine proportion" is perhaps fitting because it is seen by many as a door to a deeper understanding of beauty and spirituality, unveiling a hidden harmony, or connectedness, in so much of what we see. That's an incredible role for a single number to play, but then again this one number has played an incredible role in human history and in the foundations of life itself. The line between its mathematical and mystical aspects is thus not easily drawn. *Phi* does not appear explicitly in *The Bible*, yet we find that the dimensions given by God to Noah for the Ark, and to Moses for The Ark of the Covenant, both reflect a 5 to 3 proportion.[209]

It just so happens that this five-to-three ratio built into Noah's Ark, The Ark of the Covenant, and The Great Pyramid produces a numerical value of 1.666, while *phi* equals 1.618, a difference of just .048. Furthermore, having established a clear connection between these three divinely-inspired objects and the universal constant of *phi*, Meisner added the next point so pertinent to our investigation:

> In addition to the relationships of The Pyramid's geometry to *phi* and *pi*, it is also possible that The Pyramid was constructed using a completely different approach that simply produced the *phi* (and *pi*) relationships... Another possibility is that The Great Pyramid is based on another method, known as the *seked*. The *seked* is a measure of slope, or gradient. It is based on the Egyptian system of measure in which one cubit equals seven "palms," and one "palm" equals four "digits." The theory is that The Great Pyramid is based on the application of a gradient of *five and a half sekeds*... The slope of a pyramid created with *sekeds* would be 51.84 degrees, while that of a pyramid based on *phi* is 51.83 degrees.[210]

209 *Phi: 1.618, The Golden Number: Golden Ratio Overview*, Gary Meisner
210 Ibid.

It is important here to understand that according to most pyramidolo-gists the gradient angle of The Pyramid has been found to be 51.51 degrees. So depending on your opinion of what was motivating The Pyramid's archi-tect in deciding on its angle of construction — whether it was *pi*, *phi*, the *seked*, or some other as-yet-unknown factor — the difference between these three numbers is far too slim to have been the result of mere coincidence, and in the end, one is left to ponder the same thing that Meisner has: "The question remains, though, as to why *five and a half* would be chosen over some other number for the gradient. What was more appealing about *five and a half* rath-er than simply using a gradient based on five or six?"[211]

Certainly by now, anyone who is aware of the *Septuagint* chronology, the apocryphal record, and the testimony of the Church Fathers, will in-stantly see the irony in such an apparently innocuous question as that posed by Meisner. To anyone following our present inquiry, however, the answer might seem purely academic, especially in light of one simple but unmis-takable fact. Not only is the number *five and a half* found in the angle of The Great Pyramid, but this angle also creates a pyramidal structure which itself attains a height bearing the same numerical value of *five and a half*.

Through a Glass Darkly

AT THIS POINT IN demonstrating the various ways that the number *five and a half* is incorporated in the dimensions of The Pyramid, I would like to take some time to deal with one of the more difficult aspects concerning its design features. The difficulty I am referring to involves certain discrepan-cies that have arisen in the process of measuring the exterior of this admit-tedly enigmatic megalith. Specifically, I wish to focus on one of the previous points made by Meisner concerning The Pyramid's possible incorporation of *phi* and the *seked*. "The Great Pyramid of Giza," he said, "appears to em-body the 'golden ratio' in the dimensions of its base, height, and hypote-nuse, but its state of ruin ... makes it difficult to prove conclusively that this was by design."

Due to the great antiquity of this grand edifice — the only extant struc-ture among history's renowned Seven Wonders of the World — it is unfortu-nate that ever since it was stripped of its protective outer casing of polished limestone The Pyramid has had to endure what any other man-made build-ing is subject to as a result of centuries of erosion and subsidence. In short, any exterior measurements that have been made of the structure, which re-veal the dimensional relationships built into it, are inevitably impaired to a certain degree because the stones wear away and settle. As a result of such structural changes, one is forced to incorporate these discrepancies into a

---

211 *Phi: 1.618, The Golden Number: Golden Ratio Overview*, Gary Meisner

modified view of what the actual dimensions might have been when the original builders finished their completed work. This inevitably leads one to a philosophical crossroad in determining the meaning of such dimensional implications, particularly when it comes to such numerical values as *pi*, *phi*, and the *seked*, which certainly do seem to be built into The Pyramid's dimensions.

I, too, am often challenged by all the various modes of pyramidal interpretations. However, I have also come to the conclusion that just because one is repeatedly confronted by conflicting data, one must never succumb to the temptation to dismiss the whole affair into the realm of myth and legend. After all, we do not throw *The Bible* out the window simply because we encounter vagaries and ambiguities when trying to penetrate its mysteries. So why would we dismiss the findings of generations of pyramidologists simply because, like its counterpart in written form, there were discrepancies to be found amongst their ranks? No, when one becomes inundated with conflicting interpretations that both scholars and laypersons offer in their defense, our proper response should be one that is similar to that famous band of blind men who are all individually interacting with the proverbial elephant. In other words, we must simply accept the fact that we, as finite human beings, can never know the totality of truth, whether in scriptural or megalithic form, and being fully aware of this, we must never cave in to the inevitable frustration that arises when one attempts to ascertain the unsearchable riches of divine revelation. As has been observed by many an astute theologian, "It is as blasphemous to define God as it is to deny Him."

Still, you may be asking yourself: What is the point of all the preceding back and forth points of your discussion? First, you assembled your four dimensional facts, each corroborating the idea that the height of The Great Pyramid not only represents a 5,449-year timeline of messianic events, but that this numerical value also bears a striking resemblance to the timeline of The Great Five and a Half Days from Adam to Christ. Next, you introduced evidence that demonstrated The Pyramid's apparent incorporation of the "golden ratio," a geometric dimension that is alluded to in the construction of both Noah's Ark and Moses' Ark of the Covenant. And finally, on top of all that, you showed how a unique method of construction gave The Great Pyramid a gradient angle that demonstrated a geometric design of *five and a half sekeds*. What more do you need, you may be wondering? Why all the fuss about structural changes that have interfered with mankind's ability to measure the exterior of The Pyramid with absolute accuracy?

I mention all this because, while in the process of trying to connect the prophetic implications of Enoch's Pillar with those of apocryphal literature, I came across a different measurement for The Pyramid's height to which other pyramidologists have referred. What is more, this different measurement, which they claimed to represent its height, came even closer than the previous one. It was at that point that I came to a crossroad. Originally, I had been fairly satisfied with the fact that most pyramidologists held the view that The Pyramid's height was 5,449 pyramid inches, a figure quite close to that of 5,500. But notice how I said that I was "fairly satisfied." That is, I was until I, quite unexpectedly, came across this other measurement that came even closer. What was I to do, then, with all the data that had been previously gathered concerning the 5,449? Should I simply "sweep it under the rug" in favor of this new figure? How might I explain such an about-face?

But, alas, before I do anything rash, let me remind you—and in doing so, me as well—that one thing should never be forgotten while in the throes of pursuing the answers to such mind-boggling mysteries. When one considers the many obstacles involved in interpreting the prophetic timelines in Scripture, our greatest hurdle is that we all suffer from the irrevocable condition of "being human." Still, though this humanness means that we have been disconnected from the divine presence, God has deigned to rescue us from this fallen state. But in order to make good on this rescue effort—and this is the crux of my reminder—God has apparently chosen to invoke a process in which we humans are only gradually, and by varying degrees, rescued from the spiritual slavery we inherited from our first parents. In other words, we humans are to be rescued only in due time, and only through an incremental process of receiving God's word that involves many centuries, many generations, many encounters.

With this harsh reality in mind, then, one must always remember that when we humans receive this prophetic knowledge, only God understands entirely what that entails, while we, as mere participants in this process, are always "looking through a glass, darkly."[212] As a result, we can never fully ascertain the big picture from the divine perspective, any more than an insect can understand what has happened to it, when out of the kindness of some human heart it has been rescued from some impending calamity, and instead of being squashed, it is rescued, relocated, and released, unharmed.

Again, you may be wondering: What has all this got to do with the "price of tea in China?" And again, I will reiterate. What have we been doing this whole chapter? We have been tracking the nature of prophetic timelines, both in Scripture and stone. In the process, we encountered the inevitable difficulties inherent in such a daunting task, embarked upon by humans who can only hope for a glimpse into the vastness of God's control over history. Furthermore, we have attempted to outline, to the best of our ability, the history of how we humans have collectively come to understand these prophetic timelines—whether in *The Bible* or The Pyramid—and how we can cooperate in this divinely-inspired rescue effort. That is to say, we

---

212 *First Corinthians* 13:12

have sought to ascertain the "times and seasons" of the Lord's intention to make good on His promise to Adam, according to a plan of salvation that can be anticipated. In line with this revelatory expectation is that the Scriptures depict the creation of Adam on the sixth day, which then led students of prophecy to expect the coming of Messiah to occur in the sixth "day" of God's prophetic history.

As a result, one of the earliest Church Fathers—Ephrem the Syrian— even went so far as to chronicle the history of God's people according to a 5,500-year timeline from Adam to Christ. Then, having established a correspondence between The Great Five and a Half Day prophecy and the writings of the Church Fathers, we sought to connect this timeline to such texts as *Adam and Eve*, *Secrets of Enoch*, and *Nicodemus*, as well as the megalith that bears Enoch's authorship. Through various pyramidologists, such as Rutherford and Lemesurier, we discovered a dimensional connection with The Great Five and a Half Days of apocryphal literature with the various prophetic timelines in The Pyramid, that is to say, among others, its height of 5,449 pyramid inches, a figure not exactly that of 5,500 but one that was very close.

It was then that I was forced to confront one last hurdle in the process of hunting for a more precise connection of the numerical figure that we have been seeking, because, in fact, other pyramidologists—most notably, Rodolfo Benavides—have published their own findings about their approach to measuring The Pyramid's exterior. To my surprise, I found that they were claiming the height of The Great Pyramid was slightly higher than that which was previously believed. What is more, the findings of these pyramidologists were even more telling in view of the search established in this work. Instead of finding the present-day height of The Pyramid to be 5,449 inches, they have found it to be 5,496 pyramid inches, just *four* inches short of 5,500.[213] It was this unexpected discovery that then led me down the most recent leg of our journey, where we took the time to ponder mankind's convoluted attempts to measure The Pyramid, considering that—more than any other feature—its exterior was so vulnerable to change caused by weather and subsistence.

The main reason for my withholding this latest discovery of the height of The Pyramid at 5,496 inches, as opposed to that of 5,449, was because, like most people who grapple with its mysteries, I became so overwhelmed with conflicting data that I simply did not know which "peg to hang my hat on," so to speak. The most obvious problem in discussing any given dimension of The Pyramid naturally arises from the fact that unless one possesses the ways and means to personally go to Egypt to measure the structure, one is forever left to accept the findings of others who have accomplished such a

---

213 *Dramatic Prophecies of the Great Pyramid*, Rodolfo Benavides, p. 123

Herculean feat. To date, history records only a handful of individuals who have done so; among them are C. Piazzi Smyth, Flinders Petrie, David Davidson, and Adam Rutherford. Consequently, the only choice that one is left with is to work with the measurements that have been handed down to posterity, and for better or for worse, it is this database of numerical values that has been analyzed, speculated upon, and thus debated over ever since.

So, even if one is inclined to accept the possibility that The Pyramid's builders incorporated *pi, phi*, or the *seked* into its construction, or that the lengths and angles of the interior passageways reveal a timeline of messianic events, all this potential "meaning" must still be seen in the "context" with which all forms of communication are understood. In other words, any meaning derived from such mathematical modes of communication should never be considered the final word on the subject. Make no mistake, however, this does not happen only with mathematical meaning; the same thing occurs with linguistic messages — whether they are delivered in oral or written form. As such, no message can ever be "proven" to mean just one thing and one thing alone. In this, it is just as we cited earlier in this chapter: Truth is always multilayered in content. That is to say, truth has both a surface meaning, which is obvious to most people, and a deeper meaning, which is only understood by a few. Thus, the hard, cold facts of any form of communication is that *numbers*, just like *words*, contain, by their very nature, more than a single potential meaning. As a result, the content of any given message — in this case, a mathematical one — will always convey different meanings to different people, depending on the perceived context with which that message is received.

Signposts

I WOULD NOW LIKE to propose a formula that might help to interpret all the conflicting data when analyzing the dimensions of The Great Pyramid. However, before I do, I would like to review some of the numbers that have been introduced so far. In no particular order, then, pyramidologists insist on the following: That the height and base of The Great Pyramid of Giza reveal, to a striking degree, the same relationship with which any given circle has to its diameter and circumference. In this way, the builders, they say, purposefully intended to convey that they possessed an awareness of such mathematical values as *pi, phi,* and/or the *seked*. But in order to do this — and herein lies the rub — these pyramidologists employ several different heights of The Pyramid, which they each propose to be the correct one.

First, they point out that, because The Pyramid does not have a capstone at its peak, they have decided to utilize a measurement to that point, which is 5,449 pyramid inches high. However, other pyramidologists insist that the more accurate measurement to said point is 5,496 pyramid inches. Next, in the interest of both fairness and thoroughness, one must take into consideration that there are at least two other accepted heights of The Pyramid that one must consider. Why? This is because, without a capstone, there is yet another dimension of The Great Pyramid that has to be included, which has been coined its "actual height," a numerical value that requires projecting a line along the same angle of The Pyramid to an imaginary point where all four "lines" eventually converge. This, they say, produces an "apex point," which provides us with the so-called "actual height" of The Great Pyramid.

Why is all the foregoing information important? As it turns out, what most people do not understand is that many of the dimensional relationships that pyramidologists find so compelling are actually produced by using this projected height and not the present-day height of The Pyramid without the capstone in place. Therefore, in order to ascertain the value of *pi*, *phi*, or the *seked* within the dimensions of The Great Pyramid, one is generally doing so by way of a numerical value that represents this "actual height," which, by virtue of the logistical difficulties in acquiring this measurement, is such that it changes from investigator to investigator. Accordingly, such esteemed pyramidologists as Adam Rutherford have deemed that this "actual height" of The Pyramid is 5,831 pyramid inches, while others, like Meisner, believe it to be 5,767 pyramid inches. If this is the case, then how can we be sure of anything when it comes to discerning the true meaning of any of these so-called "dimensional" relationships? If no one can even agree on these foundational figures, then certainly no meaning can be ascertained at all, right? To which I would respond, as I so often do: You think? This, then, leads me to introducing the aforementioned formula for interpreting such conflicting bits of data.

For just a moment, imagine that you are going on a journey, and on this journey, you have a roadmap. Then, let us say, your starting point is Los Angeles, California, and this journey you are about to embark upon is going to take you, for the very first time, to a place called Las Vegas, Nevada. In addition to having this roadmap, you have also received advice from some of your friends who have already made the same trip. So together with your map and some advice, you now are going to try and figure out exactly how long it will take you to make this journey to Las Vegas while traveling there in your car. This way you can decide when you should leave so that you will be able to arrive and check into your hotel at just the right time. What would you expect the map to tell you in the process of determining a path to your given location? How much of the advice that you received from your friends would you consider in order to get there as fast as possible? And how might you incorporate all this information into your attempt to find this magical City of Lights located somewhere in the middle of a vast landscape called the Nevada Desert?

Naturally, the first thing you would do is give the map a good looking over. Using it, you would see exactly which roads to take that would get you from Los Angeles to Las Vegas. You might even highlight what you considered the best route, and maybe even toss in a nice sightseeing spot along the way. Then, armed with this planned route, together with a careful consideration of the advice you had received from friends, you would come up with an approximate time of arrival. So, to the best of your ability, you might make an educated guess: Based on the route you had chosen, which includes a one hour stop for brunch, and, assuming that you will be traveling an average of, say, seventy miles an hour on the highway, you should arrive in Las Vegas in about five and a half hours. Accordingly, since you have been told that check-in time for your hotel is one o'clock in the afternoon, you decide to leave Los Angeles at precisely seven-thirty in the morning.

Therefore, assuming that you should be arriving to your destination some five and a half hours after your departure, you proceed with your journey as planned. But lo and behold, after taking all the planned roads, finishing your one hour brunch right on time, and moving to the final leg of your journey at exactly your predicted speed, you find that you did not arrive to your destination point after five and a half hours. In fact, you pulled into town after just five and one quarter hours. So what did you do? Well naturally, you kept right on driving because, based on everything you had understood to be true, you deduced that you must not "be there" yet. The map ... your friends' advice ... your average speed of travel ... together, all of it precisely predicted the location of this golden city in the desert, so *ipso facto*, this could not possibly be the place you were looking for. Well, would not that be your reaction, too? No? Of course not, because any dumb fool would be able to tell they were in the City of Lights when they have arrived, even if it was only a quarter to one in the afternoon. It does not require a Ph.D. in geography to figure out something so self-evident.

Why, then, would anyone expect the timelines in The Great Pyramid to be any less ambiguous than the roadmap in the previous illustration? And why would anyone expect that the interpretations applied to these timelines to be any less idiosyncratic then our friends' advice? After all, the numerical values in The Pyramid are just like the milestones on a roadmap. The designated role of a milestone is to indicate to travelers on a highway how far along they are in their journey. They are signposts to let you know that you are still on the right path. However, they are not always perfectly measured out from point to point; yet they do still perform their specified purpose. The same thing holds true for the numerical values found in The Great Pyramid.

Now, just in case anyone thinks that I am being footloose and fancy-free with my methodology for coping with the discrepancies arising from a study of The Pyramid, I would like to point out that a similar method of interpretation is already being employed in the sacrosanct realm of *Bible* prophecy. Let me take a moment to explain, and in doing so, we will finally come to a swift and merciful end in this our own eventful journey.

By Design

PREVIOUSLY in this work, we brought up the subject of the Seventy Weeks of Daniel, which happens to be one of the most famous prophetic timelines in all of Scripture. But just because so many biblical scholars point to it as a roadmap from which to interpret historical events does not mean that the passages comprising this timeline are not themselves fraught with ambiguities and discrepancies. Unfortunately — or fortunately, depending on your attention span — we will not be able to go into detail regarding the well-documented intricacies contained in the book attributed to the prophet Daniel. Suffice it to say, however, because this portion of Scripture contains such an important timeline in terms of God's overall plan, it does merit whatever time we can devote to it. Said John F. Walvoord, long-time president of Dallas Theological Seminary:

> Although other major prophets received detailed information concerning the nations and God's program for salvation, Daniel alone was given the comprehensive program for both the Gentiles ... and Israel, as recorded in *Daniel* 9:24-27. Because of the comprehensive and structural nature of Daniel's prophecies for both the Gentiles and Israel, the study of *Daniel*, and especially this chapter, is the key to understanding the prophetic Scriptures.[214]

Yet for all its importance in regard to understanding the prophetic meaning of *The Bible*, the prophecies in *The Book of Daniel* are probably the most difficult passages for theologians to interpret. In fact, the only other book in Scripture more difficult to interpret is *The Book of Revelation*, which is why *Daniel* is so often referred to as its *Old Testament* counterpart. Yet for all of its ambiguities and discrepancies, this vital book has never been excised from the Canon. Part of the problem that occurs in dealing with the prophecies in *Daniel*, particularly as it is found in the ninth chapter, is that — apart from its extended usage of mystical symbolism — it incorporates two chronological factors that are clearly as difficult to decipher as any of those contained in The Great Pyramid.

First, *The Book of Daniel* tells us, "seventy weeks of years have been determined upon the people of Israel and its capital, Jerusalem."[215] This, say

---

214 *Daniel: The Key to Prophetic Revelation, Chapter Nine, The Prophecy of the Seventy Weeks*, John F. Walvoord
215 *Daniel* 9:24

theologians, speaks of a unique timeline of historical events depicting God's intervention in the lives of His people, but unfortunately, these same theologians have never been able to come to any consensus as to the exact meaning and time span of these so-called seventy "weeks," because the word which we translate into English as "weeks" is actually a Hebrew word that simply means *sevens*, which does not necessarily specify seven years. Nevertheless, such an interpretation does seem to be inferred, especially when seen in the context of the usage of the prophet Jeremiah—whom Daniel had been studying and from whom he was receiving his initial inspiration in this matter—when the aforementioned prophet spoke of seventy years of bondage that the southern kingdom of Judah was to endure. Second, this timeline of human events, which is said to encompass an initial phase of sixty-nine "weeks" of years, is said to begin with "the announcement to restore and rebuild Jerusalem," and that its duration will last "until Messiah, the Prince, will be cut off but not for Himself."[216] That is to say, according to most theologians, there will be a period comprised of sixty-nine years multiplied by seven, or four hundred and eighty-three years, from the commandment to rebuild Jerusalem until such time as Christ was to be crucified on Calvary. There is just one problem with tracking this timeline—quite separate from any disagreement over the nature of these "weeks" of years—and that has to do with the discrepancies over the actual date of this announcement to restore and rebuild Jerusalem. According to biblical historians, there are no less than four separate decrees to rebuild that are recorded in Scripture, all of which are said to be potential qualifiers for such a designation.

Just imagine, then, the frustration of anyone living in the time of Christ who was trying to determine the "set time" of the appearance of their long-awaited Messiah, what with so much confusion over Daniel's meaning of the phrase seventy "sevens," and what supposedly qualified as "the announcement to restore and rebuild." In many ways, these semantical and chronological quandaries are exactly the same kinds of stumbling blocks that have plagued advocates of Pyramidology ever since its inception. But just like our traveler making that hypothetical journey to the City of Lights, anyone who had personally come face to face with the Light of the World would have had no trouble realizing that the day of His arrival had come, despite all the inherent ambiguities in the signposts they encountered in the prophecies of *Daniel*.

So why, you may ask, does God even bother inspiring prophets to foretell the coming of messianic events if they are so difficult to interpret? Certainly, if God is all-knowing, then He must realize that the prophecies contained in Scripture are laden with more twists and turns than an Agatha Christie mystery. Why does He even bother? Fortunately, for our sake, the

---

216 Ibid. 9:25-26

answer to such an obvious question is nowhere near as baffling as those that pertain to the specific mysteries buried in either the Scriptures or The Pyramid. In a nutshell: The reason that God's prophetic word is fraught with an apparently impenetrable web of ambiguity is because it was done this way precisely by design. Can I say this again for those who think I might have misspoken? I repeat: *The Bible* is a constant source of mystery — just like its counterpart, The Great Pyramid — because that is exactly the way God wants it. In this, it is just as Jesus described when His disciples asked Him why He spent so much time teaching in parables. He told them:

> The secret of the Kingdom of God has been given to you, but to those on the outside, everything is said in parables so that: "They may see but never perceive, and hear but never understand; otherwise they might turn and be forgiven."[217]

Simply put, prophecy, in any form, has never been intended by God as a tool to predict the future *per se*. In fact, the God of *The Bible* summarily condemns prognostication in general. The failure in every case, in misunderstanding the prophetic future depicted in the various scriptural and megalithic chronologies, always rests squarely on the shoulders of those who attempt to predict the future for the sake of their own human purposes, however well-intentioned those purposes may seem. Just as in the case of biblical prophecy, where one is forced to examine historical events as a touchstone to confirm the veracity of prophetic utterances, it should be remembered that the so-called "predicted" events portrayed in The Pyramid must also conform to this same methodology. In other words, the prediction of future events must always be evaluated, and re-evaluated, in light of the actual facts of history. Therefore, one must always resist the urge to predict the future in order to satisfy proof seekers and be satisfied to let history "fill in the blanks," so to speak, just as historians have always had to do when analyzing biblical prophecies.

All this, then, should be remembered when attempting to apprehend the prophetic wisdom that has been so marvelously encrypted in *The Bible* and The Pyramid, because in failing to do so, one might find themselves as thoroughly frustrated as that long list of fortune hunters who are forever vexed by the impossible intricacies that shut them out. But to those who are willing to enter in as little children, they have God's assurance that they will see and perceive, and hear and understand all the wondrous grandeur that has been held in store just for them.

This principle is never more evident than with mankind's understanding of the prophecy of The Great Five and a Half Days — in terms of Scripture and stone alike. Whereas this extended time frame made it virtually

---

217 *Mark* 4:11-12

impossible to anticipate its fulfillment to generations prior to the Advent of Christ, hindsight made it possible to recognize this historical fact once it occurred. And in verifying the Lord's faithfulness to His word as it pertains to the Incarnation, mankind can then rest assured that all the promises of God can be counted on as well. In this way, one can better see the flaw in Archbishop Ussher's chronology of just 4,000 years from Adam to Christ, in that it does nothing to confirm the faithfulness of the Lord, because never once in the biblical record, either canonical or apocryphal, has it ever been recorded that God promised to rescue mankind after four "days." But *if*— and this is the crux of this entire work — *if* it can be shown that Christ strode upon the stage of world history after *five and a half* "days," then it clearly demonstrates the faithfulness of God to an onlooking world.

After all, who really cares if The Pyramid predicts the Exodus of Israel, or the invention of the printing press, or the age of Reformation? What purpose, if any, could there be in that? That is to say, what does it profit anyone in the present age? The only purpose, it seems to me, is to verify a chain of events that are all themselves mere echoes of a much larger event. By themselves, the events that the great explorers and philosophers claim that The Pyramid's prophetic chronology depict appear somewhat meaningful, I grant you. Yet in isolation they utterly pale in comparison to the greater scheme of things. As individual ticks on the clock of history, they represent interesting sidebars in the pantheon of human achievements, but seen in the context of that long-awaited moment, when that clock would finally chime the completion of those *five and a half* "days," the events depicted by way of The Pyramid's interior and exterior dimensions prove to be quite significant after all. Then, and only then, does their fulfillment, as echoes of prophetic truth, find true meaning and purpose; and in doing so, God's hidden hand in history is ultimately revealed for all to see, and thus confirmed once and for all time.

Of Talismans and Timelines

This Extended Puzzle

NOW FOR THE final sequence in this work. All along, the purpose of this work has been clearly stated – to reveal a startling proof of God's control and faithfulness. To do this, it was essential to first build a secure foundation, one that has been provided by way of investigating some of the most neglected chapters of biblical history. But considering the tremendous amount of resistance to such a non-traditional rendition of said history, we also took the time to examine the historical and scriptural validity of these freshly resurrected chapters.

In our opening analyses, we examined how certain books have been unjustly marginalized due to the stigma of their being labeled "apocryphal." In the process of validating these stories, we saw the extent to which they can be harmonized with the canonical texts of *The Bible*. It was during this process that we introduced such topics as the prophecy of The Great Five and a Half Days, which we discovered would provide a central thread from which this present narrative would be woven. Next, we sought to confirm the validity of the timeline of The Great Five and a Half Day prophecy outside the realm of apocryphal literature by turning to the most famous of all megalithic monuments, The Great Pyramid of Giza. There, while investigating the way that this *five and a half* "day" timeline is depicted in the dimensions of The Pyramid, we uncovered a great many facts that most history books have neglected to report. It was then that we saw how The Pyramid's prophetic chronology is uniquely mirrored in the chronology of *The Septuagint Bible*, which, as we discovered, actually provided the basis for the early Church's view of a 5,500-year period from Adam to Christ. Moreover, we saw how widely held this view was by reviewing the much-neglected testimony of many of the most influential early Church Fathers and historians – men like Hippolytus of Rome, Ephrem the Syrian, and Julius Africanus.

Thus, having satisfied ourselves with locating a firm historical foundation for this 5,500-year prophetic timeline, we continued to hone in on the various ways that this numerical value of *five and a half* was built into the geometric design of The Great Pyramid. It was then that we were confronted with a series of uncanny numerical nuances that seemed to offer the very evidence that we were seeking.

The first thing one was struck by was the way in which the dimensions of The Pyramid's Open Coffer in the King's Chamber bore a striking similarity to those of The Ark of the Covenant, which as it so happens was built—according to God's instructions to Moses—using the dimensions of *five and a half* sacred cubits. Subsequent to discovering this dimensional relationship, pyramidologists have ever since interpreted this to mean that the Open Coffer, like The Ark itself, is a type of the Incarnation of Christ. Another way this number *five and a half* was located in the dimensions of The Pyramid came in the wake of researchers having determined, through various ways and means, its height to be—within a mere four inches—5,500 pyramid inches. And finally, this same numerical value was found to be incorporated in the geometry of The Great Pyramid while examining one of the potential design methods used in its construction. Known as the *seked* method, this particular choice of The Pyramid's builders just happened to require the incorporation of the numerical value of *five and a half sekeds* – not five, not six, but *five and a half*, and as it turns out, using this angle of *five and a half sekeds* produces a pyramidal structure with the same height as the one sitting on the plateau of Giza.

Therefore, in light of this string of uncanny connections—that is, between the repeated occurrence of this number *five and a half*, in *The Septuagint Bible*, The Great Pyramid, and The Ark of the Covenant, and its obvious relation to that nearly forgotten promise of "days" – one can no longer entertain the possibility that it could all be a product of sheer coincidence. Rather, seen together as a continuum, these occurrences must be understood as one more clue in demonstrating the extent to which the God of *The Bible* is truly the Lord of Time. In this case, what we have is the God of Set Times, Who revealed there would be an "appointed time." That is to say, there was a specific time period, which began when the Word of God told Adam that He would rescue him and his descendants, and which ended 5,500 years later when, "in the fullness of time,"[218] that same Word put on flesh and blood, thereby "confirming all the promises of God"[219] in that single act.

Having thus revealed the hidden link that connects the promise of "days" with *The Septuagint Bible*, The Great Pyramid of Giza, and The Ark of the Covenant, it is now time to weave two more of Christendom's most sacred artifacts into our tapestry of talismans and timelines: The Spear of Destiny and The Shroud of Turin. Let me demonstrate how this can be done.

Another Impossible Possibility

SO FAR, we have narrowed in on several ideas in our attempt to validate the truth found in the present work. We have witnessed a peculiar and persistent connectivity in things that have all, until now, been seen as so many random points on the biblical map—the prophecy of The Great Five and a

---

218 *Galatians* 4:4
219 *Second Corinthians* 1:20

Half Days, *The Septuagint*, The Ark, and The Pyramid. No doubt to skeptics such occurrences represent nothing more than poetic nonsense. However, to those who are inclined to believe that *The Bible* is more than poetry, they come together in a way that no mortal mind could possibly conceive. Together, they form a matrix of ineffable wonder. To the eye of faith, what is hidden to most is clearly discernible. Therefore, to those who might appreciate yet another impossible possibility, I offer the following.

At the long-awaited culmination of The Great Five and a Half Days, a man stood at the foot of the cross of Jesus. The name of that man—a Roman centurion standing guard at the crucifixion—is never revealed in canonical Scripture. Legend has it that his name was Longinus. Naturally, the source for this legend just happens to be the apocryphal record—in both *The Gospel of Nicodemus* and *The Letters of Herod and Pilate*. Though unnamed in *The New Testament*, he is said to be the man who, gazing upon the Crucified One, declared, "This Man really was the Son of God."[220]

However, what is recorded in the received text is that the Jewish leaders demanded that Pilate hasten an end to the crucifixion in order to prevent the bodies of Jesus and the two thieves from remaining there into the evening. As the gospel record reveals:

> The soldiers therefore came and broke the legs of the first man who had been crucified with Jesus, and then those of the other. But when they came to Jesus and found that He was already dead, they did not break His legs. Instead, one of the soldiers pierced Jesus' side with a spear, producing a sudden flow of blood and water.[221]

At this point *The Bible* inserts an intriguing sidebar, one that John, the gospel writer, included for the sake of posterity, as if the casual observer might otherwise overlook the previous verses.

> The man who saw it has given testimony, and his testimony is true. He knows that he tells the truth, and he testifies so you may also believe. These things happened so that the Scripture would be fulfilled: "Not one of His bones will be broken,"[222] and as it says elsewhere: "They'll look upon Him Whom they have pierced."[223]

The thing to notice so far, in terms of this final piece of our puzzle, is this piercing of the side of Jesus on the cross, at which point both blood and water flowed from the wound. Several important things emerge from this event: First, there was the Roman centurion who, having been ordered to

---

220 *Matthew* 27:54; *Mark* 15:39
221 *John* 19:31-34
222 *Exodus* 12:46; *Numbers* 9:12; *Psalm* 34:20
223 *Zechariah* 12:10

hasten the death of Jesus, found Him already dead, thus eliminating the need to break His legs. Then there came the subsequent piercing of the side of Christ at the hands of this centurion, and the torrent of blood and water from the wound. And finally, in that moment, a battle-hardened centurion, who presumably worshiped only the gods and goddesses of Rome, did a complete about-face, and uttered, in an apparent epiphany, that he was gazing upon the true visage of the Son of God.

Ever since that fateful event, a unique legend sprang up regarding the centurion's spear, which speaks of the kind of miraculous power attributed to none other than the risen Christ Himself. This, in turn, leads us to ask: How did The Spear that spilled the blood of Christ become imbued with such power? And what, exactly, is the story behind its miraculous power that could explain this kind of God-inspired effectualness?

The Very Finger of Destiny

CERTAINLY ONE OF the most provocative takes concerning The Spear comes to us by way of a book by Trevor Ravenscroft, entitled *The Spear of Destiny*. According to Ravenscroft, there is ample evidence to confirm that this spear, throughout its history, became associated with miraculous power. Concerning the centurion and his spear, he wrote:

> It was said that, for a moment in time, he had held the destiny of mankind in his hands. The spear, with which he had pierced the side of Christ, became one of the great treasures of Christendom, and a unique legend attached itself to this weapon, gaining strength with the passing of the centuries, that whoever possessed it and understood the powers it served, held the destiny of the world in his hands for good or evil.[224]

For that reason, Longinus' spear came to be known as The Spear of Destiny. Passing from hand to hand, and generation to generation, The Spear was said to have been held in possession by nearly every emperor of Western Europe, all of whom believed that it imparted to them the power they sought to affect world history. Ravenscroft continued:

> Constantine the Great, one of the world's most enigmatic figures, claimed he was guided through providence when holding The Spear of Longinus at the epoch-making battle on the Milvian Bridge outside Rome. This battle settled the rulership of the Roman Empire and led directly to the proclamation of Christianity as the official religion of Rome... In his old age, when building the new Rome in Constantinople — a bastion which would withstand all assaults for

---

224 *The Spear of Destiny*, Trevor Ravenscroft, p. xii

a thousand years—Constantine carried The Spear in front of him when treading out the boundaries of the site of the new city, saying, "I follow in the steps of Him Who I see walking ahead of me."

The Spear had played a conspicuous role through the centuries of the gradual decline of the Roman Empire, both in resisting the invasions from the North and East and in converting the Barbarians to the new Faith and the Roman cause... Men like Theodosius who tamed the Goths with it in 385 A.D., Alaric the Bold, the savage convert to Christianity, who claimed The Spear after he sacked Rome in 410 A.D. ... and the mighty Visigoth, Theodoric, who rallied Gaul with The Spear, and turned back the ferocious Attila the Hun in 452 A.D....

In the eight and ninth centuries, The Spear had continued to be the very pivot of the historical process. For instance, the mystical talisman had become an actual weapon in the hands of the Frankish general Charles Martel, the Hammer, when he led his army to gain a miraculous victory over the massed forces of the Arabs at Poitiers in 732 A.D. Defeat would have meant that the whole of Western Europe would have succumbed to the rule and religion of Islam.

In 800 A.D. Charlemagne, the first Holy Roman emperor, founded his whole dynasty on the possession of The Spear and its legend of world-historic destiny—a legend which attracted the greatest scholars in all of Europe to serve the civilizing power of the Frankish cause...

Altogether, forty-five emperors have claimed The Spear of Destiny as their possession, between the coronation in Rome of Charlemagne and the fall of the old German Empire, exactly a thousand years later. And what a pageantry of power and majesty it was! The Spear had passed like the very finger of destiny through the millennium, forever creating new patterns of fate which had, again and again, changed the entire history of Europe.[225]

Yet, alas, as much as history has galvanized this notion that whoever possesses The Spear of Destiny will control the fate of humanity, there is another aspect to the legends that suggests there is a dark side attached to it as well. In other words, just as there has been a decidedly upside to possessing The Spear, a menacing downside reveals that not a few of their glory-seeking owners got far more than they bargained for. On no less than four separate occasions throughout its history, The Spear has not only imbued its owners with great power, but it has also brought them a swift and untimely end.

---

225 *The Spear of Destiny*, Trevor Ravenscroft, pp. 14-17

As victorious as he was while maintaining control of The Spear, Theodoric found that one false move could reverse its power. While leading a heroic cavalry charge, the Visigoth king accidentally dropped The Spear, and after falling from his horse, he was trampled to death in the crush of his troop's horses that were following him into battle. And though his allies rose above this tragedy and won the victory, this single battle proved to be the final such military operation that would ever be undertaken by the Western Roman Empire.

Throughout his illustrious life, Charlemagne never let The Spear out of his sight, even going so far as to sleep with it, but one day he accidentally dropped it as he returned from his last victorious campaign. If not so obvious to Charlemagne himself, those closest to him saw it as a terrible omen of things to come, not only for him but for his kingdom as well. Subsequently, the last years of Charlemagne's reign were filled with many difficulties, and in the end the Frankish king would die a disheartened man, bitterly disappointed at all the hopes and dreams he never saw come to fruition.

Frederick Barbarossa, the twelfth-century Holy Roman emperor, is widely regarded as one of the greatest rulers of the Medieval Era, primarily because of his uncanny skills in battlefield tactics and political maneuvering, which made him seem almost superhuman in relation to those around him. What is less known to history, however, is the conspicuous role that The Spear of Destiny played in the illustrious life and ignominious death of Frederick. Having inherited The Spear from previous emperors, like Henry the Fowler and Otto the Great, Barbarossa managed to unite his kingdom by walking a fine line between war and diplomacy.

Sadly, though, all of that ended one fateful day, in 1190, when Frederick, upon instituting the Third Crusade to Jerusalem, met his untimely end. After initial successes in two battles, the German king was proceeding through southern Turkey, where he and his army were in the process of traversing a bridge. Impatient to join his son on the other side, Barbarossa decided to bypass the bridge and cross the stream on horseback. Much to his surprise, the current was stronger than he had anticipated, and hindered by the weight of his armor, he was drowned when his horse collapsed in the undertow. As one historian poignantly noted, "As he was crossing the stream, the Holy Lance fell from his hand at the very moment of his death."[226]

But by far the most famous example of the consequences of losing control of The Spear comes to us in the case of a man who idolized Barbarossa, a man who dreamed of one day wielding his own irresistible power to reunite the splintered realms of the German Empire, just as the legendary king had done before him. That man was Adolf Hitler.

---

226 *Secrets of the Holy Lance: The Spear of Destiny in History and Legend*, Jerry E. Smith and George Piccard, p. 201

What Sort of Madness?

AS A WAYWARD YOUTH in Vienna, Austria, Adolf Hitler intensely sought a meaningful direction for his life. According to those who knew him at the time, he was a man strangely driven by a determined self-awareness that he was destined for greatness, and that this greatness somehow involved his future role in returning Germany to her former days of glory. Said Ravenscroft: "Many hours were spent every day in the Hof Library studying Nordic and Teutonic mythology and folklore, and reading broadly in German history, literature, and philosophy."[227] As a result of his research, Hitler became convinced that:

> With the passing of time, humanity had entered a kind of canyon of sleep so that former golden ages, in which man had enjoyed a magical relationship with the Universe, had been forgotten, the only evidence of such sublime conditions lying hidden in myths and legends in which nobody any longer believed.[228]

This, for Hitler, was the key that unlocked the mystery of how his beloved Germany had fallen into such a pathetic state of political impotency and spiritual confusion. All that remained was to discover the appropriate antidote for such a hopeless condition.

Then one day while Hitler visited the Hapsburg Treasure House, he believed that he had finally come face to face with the answer he had been seeking and, along with that discovery, the very means with which he would achieve his world-historic destiny. For it was at that time that he first encountered The Spear, there amongst the regalia of the Hapsburg Dynasty. Initially, Hitler had paid little attention to the ancient spearhead as it lay inconspicuously upon a red velvet dais, sitting with the official Hapsburg crown, scepters, and jeweled ornaments. That is, until he overheard a tour guide telling his entourage about the significance of what was in front of them. As Hitler recalled: "And then I heard the words which were to change the rest of my life: 'There is a legend associated with this Spear that whoever claims it, and solves its secrets, holds the destiny of the world in his hands for good or evil.'"[229] Hitler later recounted seeing The Spear for the first time:

> I knew with immediacy that this was an important moment in my life. And yet I could not divine why an outwardly Christian symbol should make such an impression... The Spear appeared to be some sort of magical medium of revelation, for it brought the world of

---

227 *The Spear of Destiny*, Trevor Ravenscroft, p. 5
228 Ibid. pp. 26-27
229 Ibid. p. 7

ideas into such close and living perspective that human imagination became more real than the world of sense. I felt as though I myself had held it in my hands before in some earlier century of history — that I myself had once claimed it as my talisman of power and held the destiny of the world in my hands. Yet how could this be? What sort of madness was this that was invading my mind and creating such turmoil in my breast?[230]

Spurred on by this chance encounter, Hitler proceeded to turn his acute powers of inquiry to determining if The Spear in the Hapsburg Treasure House was real or not. After ruling out several other candidates that laid claim to being the true Spear of Longinus, Hitler became convinced that this one, cloistered amidst the imperial regalia of the Hapsburgs, was the genuine article. His next step was to trace its path from past to present. Ravenscroft described his efforts:

Hitler spent three days in his first tentative researches into the history of The Spear of Longinus. Perhaps he felt a tingling in his spine as he strode across the library to pull out from the shelves the works of the great German philosopher Hegel, for it seemed to him that the men who had claimed The Spear throughout history and fulfilled its legend fitted into Hegel's description of world-historic heroes — "heroes who carry out the will of the world spirit, the very plan of providence..."

Hitler became utterly fascinated with the passage of The Spear throughout the era in which all his childhood heroes had lived. He found to his astonishment and delight that the great German figures who had filled his youthful dreams had held The Spear as the holy aspiration of their ambitions, their talisman of power... men like Otto the Great, who had lived illustrious lives of world-historic significance.[231]

But of all the emperors who had laid claim to The Spear of Destiny, the one that "excited Hitler's imagination most of all was Frederick Barbarossa."[232] Said Ravenscroft:

Here, indeed, was a German of incomparable greatness! Barbarossa ... had the qualities of a monarch Hitler could really admire ... chivalry, courage, unlimited energy, great joy in battle, love of adventure, startling initiative, and, above all, a certain harshness, which gave him the ability to both frighten and charm at the same time.

---

230 *The Spear of Destiny*, Trevor Ravenscroft, pp. 8-9
231 Ibid. pp. 16, 18
232 Ibid. p. 17

Frederick Barbarossa, who fancied he could re-establish the Roman Empire without the Roman legions, had conquered all Italy, proving himself supreme even over the Roman Pontiff himself.[233]

With discoveries such as these, Adolf Hitler had all the assurance he would ever need, and so he began his impassioned quest to take possession of The Spear of Longinus as his very own.

The year 1933 saw Hitler and his National Socialist German Workers Party ascend to power over all of Germany. One of his first acts in his bid for world conquest was to instigate a *coup d'état* in his original homeland of Austria. In 1934, on Hitler's direct orders, S.S. assassins murdered Engelbert Dollfuss, the Austrian president, but much to Hitler's chagrin, the *coup* failed to materialize. Furious, he turned to S.S. Chief Heinrich Himmler for answers.

More than anyone else in the Nazi hierarchy, Heinrich Himmler was attuned to Hitler's otherworldly aspirations, which meant that whenever he was called upon to provide a solution, it surely called for unorthodox methods. Unbeknownst to most observers at the time, the S.S. was not just a military organization that Himmler had created as Hitler's bodyguard; it was also a quasi-religious order, one in which its members were expected to dedicate their lives in absolute submission, much in the same way that the Jesuits had once served the Pope. In this case, however, the leader of this new pseudo-pagan state religion just happened to be Adolf Hitler; and Himmler was his ever-obedient Loyola.

Jumping into action, Himmler, who was also convinced of the occult power of The Spear of Destiny, had an exact replica of it made—in lieu of securing the real one—and set about restoring the seventeenth-century Wewelsburg Castle in the Austrian Alps, specifically meant to enshrine a knowledge and history of The Spear. In what was certainly the world's first "theme park," each room in the castle was decorated in honor of those who had throughout the centuries claimed the hallowed Spear as their own. Naturally, a room for Hitler was built—if he had ever been so inclined to go there—down to the smallest detail, to recreate the by-gone days of his beloved twelfth-century hero, Frederick Barbarossa.

Finally, in 1938, Hitler's dream of world conquest began to bear fruit, when the Nazis rolled, unopposed, into Austria and were greeted with overwhelming enthusiasm by the unsuspecting population. Upon seizing power there, Hitler wasted no time in giving the order to grab the real Spear from the Hapsburg Treasure House, at which point it was transported, along with the rest of the imperial regalia, to Saint Catherine's Church in Nuremberg. Now the proud possessor of The Spear of Longinus, after so many years

---

233 *The Spear of Destiny*, Trevor Ravenscroft, p. 17

of yearning for it, Adolf Hitler turned all his efforts into making use of its legendary powers.

After having so easily annexed Austria, while in possession of a mere replica of the famed spear, Adolf Hitler, with the genuine article in hand, ordered his Nazi juggernaut into action. Before long, the ferocious German forces had proceeded to roll through most of Europe with their seemingly unstoppable Lightning War machine. Like tumbling dominoes, country after country fell before Hitler's indomitable troops, commanded by his equally indomitable will to power, and for one brief moment in time, the world held its collective breath, as Hitler seemed poised to make good on the legend of world-historic domination that had fueled the myth of the power of this strange artifact for nearly two thousand years.

Absolute Power

AS HISTORY ELOQUENTLY records, the reign of terror orchestrated by Hitler fortunately did not last nearly as long as the Supreme Leader of the Holy Roman Empire had hoped for. Like all tyrants before him, his days were numbered. But why, exactly, did Hitler fail in his bid for world conquest once he took possession of The Spear? Was the object he stole from the Hapsburg Treasure House a fake, as many historians have suggested? Or, if The Spear really was the one that pierced the side of Christ, what might explain the reversal of fortune that ultimately spoiled Hitler's plan? To answer such enigmas, we again find ourselves revisiting the apocryphal record.

Before Hitler exerted his will upon the stage of world history, there was the equally insatiable Nimrod, the grandson of Noah, whom *The Bible* says led one of history's most infamous rebellions at the Tower of Babel. And like Hitler after him, legend has it that Nimrod's meteoric rise to power was not merely the result of one man's indomitable "will to power." In fact, what can be determined by examining *The Book of Jasher* is that Nimrod was aided and abetted by way of perhaps the most enigmatic of all sacred artifacts: Adam's garment, which was given to him by his father, Cush, after he had stolen it from Noah.

It is said that through the instrumentality of that sacred garment Noah had exerted an uncanny influence over the animal kingdom in securing their cooperation in entering the Ark. In this activity, Noah faithfully served God's purposes, and as a result of his righteous intentions, his life in conjunction with that garment was blessed. As for why this garment was said to exude such miraculous powers will be discussed in just a bit, but for now we will focus on its role in Nimrod's life.

What of Nimrod and his usage of the garment, then? According to *Jasher*, Nimrod did not begin his adventure in defiance of God. Contrary to popular opinion, he initially followed in the footsteps of his righteous forefather, Noah, as the apocryphal record clearly states:

> Nimrod became strong when he put on that garment because God gave him might and strength. He was a powerful hunter in the Earth, and he built altars where he offered the animals he had hunted before the Lord... And the Lord delivered all the enemies of his family into his hands, and God prospered Nimrod in his battles, and he reigned upon the Earth.
>
> Therefore, a saying became popular in those days. When a man had been trained for battle, it was said to him: "As God has done for Nimrod, the mighty hunter who succeeded in all his battles and rescued his family from their enemies, so may God do the same for you."[234]

Therefore, it appears that as long as Nimrod honored God and His purposes, he was revered as the "mighty hunter before the Lord."[235] But in contrast to the lifelong blessing that Noah experienced, he was only blessed, in concert with that garment, at the beginning of his life. Eventually, the power that accrued to him by way of this ancient talisman caused Nimrod to make the age-old mistake of turning away from God and turning toward self. As it is written:

> And Nimrod reigned in the Earth over all the sons of Noah, and they were all under his power and counsel, but Nimrod did not continue in the ways of the Lord... He made idols of wood and stone, and bowed down to them in rebellion against the Lord. Not only that, but he also began to teach his subjects to do the same thing.[236]

In short, Nimrod turned away from serving the God-ordained purpose that Adam's garment was intended to convey. No longer was it being honored as the "shadow" that it was, of the Redeemer Whose coming would restore order to a crestfallen Universe, and as history subsequently records, when Nimrod's pride triggered his decision to defy the Lord and use the power of the garment for his own selfish purposes, at that moment he was forever changed. In this, Nimrod's incorporation of Adam's garment presents us with a phenomenon much akin to what we encountered when observing God's usage of the types of Christ. This time, however, it appears to be a type of Anti-Christ. So that just as Enoch and his role as a divine mediator serves as a type of Jesus, Who was the Ultimate Mediator, in this instance, Nimrod and his role as would-be world conqueror serves as a type

---

234 *Jasher* 7:30, 32-33
235 *Genesis* 10:9
236 *Jasher* 7:45-47

of Adolf Hitler, who was himself the ultimate would-be conqueror.

Ironically, like Constantine, Charlemagne, and Barbarossa before him, Hitler for a brief moment in time actually found himself attuned to the potential of The Spear to wield its world-changing power. That is to say, as long as the Supreme Commander of Germany sought to reinvigorate the nation in a way similar to the well-intentioned — although imperialistic — actions of the aforementioned European emperors, Hitler did seem invincible. Yet, like Nimrod before him, having become corrupted by the power that comes in the wake of wielding these divinely-inspired talismans, Hitler, too, was defeated as a result of his own inward turning to self.

In the end, just as all those who have risen and fallen in their brief stints of world-historic domination, Adolf Hitler succumbed to the dark side of the power of The Spear of Destiny. As is so often cited: Power corrupts and absolute power corrupts absolutely. Never is this truer than in the case of anyone who dares wield the power of this ancient talisman that has for more than two thousand years shaped and reshaped the face of history, to both the benefit and detriment of mankind.

The Fickle Nature

THE SUMMER OF 1941 saw the launching of what was to be Hitler's dagger in the heart of Mother Russia: *Operation Barbarossa*, aptly named for the Supreme Commander's beloved idol, Frederick. For all intents and purposes, what should have followed seemed obvious to all who looked in awe at the unrivaled superiority of Germany's military might. After all, in two short years, the Nazis' Lightning War machine had defeated and occupied most of Europe. Between 1939 and 1941, the German Empire had gobbled up Czechoslovakia, Poland, Denmark, Luxembourg, France, Yugoslavia, Greece, and Norway. The combined might of the Nazis then proceeded to turn its fury upon a reeling Great Britain to the north and a teetering Soviet Union to the east. It appeared to the whole world as if Hitler might actually prove unstoppable. At the time, though, very few people had the slightest notion that the real secret to the Nazis' seemingly invincible war machine had nothing to do with military hardware. Very few, actually — until long after the war's end — would ever come to know that the most technologically advanced society in the world had unreservedly tapped into the most otherworldly of phenomena.

Just like Barbarossa before him, with The Spear of Destiny firmly in his control, Hitler seemed almost superhuman in his ability to strike fear into the hearts of his enemies, both in his uncanny use of military strategy and political maneuvering. Ironically, though, it turned out that Hitler's mysterious gift actually opened the door for the eventual fall of his vaunted war machine. For every fantastic victory won by the Axis regime, just as many inexplicable blunders would undermine the German advance. As legendary as are Hitler's lightning victories in Czechoslovakia and Poland, there are also accounts of an intensely superstitious Hitler who delayed his V-2 rocket program because he dreamed that such an aerial attack would rain fire down from Heaven, not only on his sworn enemies but on his beloved pan-Germanic Empire as well.

So, just as Nimrod discovered the truth about the fickle nature of the powers he had harnessed in possessing Adam's garment, Hitler likewise found himself at a loss when he chose not to manifest the power of The Spear in the spirit with which it was intended. In this, Hitler came face to face with the true nature of this double-edged Universe of ours, as it has clearly been ordained by God. In other words, nothing exists that is wholly good or wholly evil. This is well known not just to philosophers but to everyone. How many times, for example, have you heard that guns or fire are not evil, in and of themselves? Only those who use or misuse them make them so. Naturally, the same holds true for objects of an otherworldly nature, as well as those of a worldly nature.

In this way, history has confirmed just such an interpretation concerning the power of The Spear. Again and again, the same individuals who have blessed the world through its power have also been cursed by it when they lost sight of its true purpose as ordained by the One Whose blood it spilled. This is why, even before the final shot that ended the European conflict was fired, Adolf Hitler's real defeat occurred when he, too, was no longer willing to yield to the same purposes that initially motivated such world-historic figures as Constantine, Charlemagne, and Barbarossa. How ironic, then, that most military historians consider Hitler's ill-conceived decision to invade Russia, codenamed: *Barbarossa*, to be the turning point of the war. What for Hitler was to be his greatest stroke of military genius led, instead, to the Nazis' worst defeat at the Battle of Stalingrad, in the winter of '42, just one year after the zenith of Hitler's power. After their disastrous defeat at Stalingrad, the Nazis would never recover, and as a result of redeploying a large portion of their western troops to fill the vacuum in the East, Germany's enemies wasted no time in marshaling their forces for the 1944 D-Day invasion at Normandy, France. It was truly the beginning of the end.

An Insatiable Lust

THE YEAR 2015 MARKED the seventieth anniversary of the end of the war in Europe and the Hitler-inspired regime that was unleashed upon an unsuspecting world. Like all tragic figures, Hitler, even in death, still provokes a tremendous amount of controversy. Did he really commit suicide, as most historians insist? Or did he fake his death and flee to South America, like so many other expatriated Nazis? Several things are certain in an attempt to answer such mysteries. If Hitler did not commit suicide, he would hardly have been in any condition to traipse off to Buenos Ares or some other such destination, considering the sheer number of forces surrounding him at the time and his well-documented physical condition after so many attempts on his life by his own generals. One has only to remember Hitler's battered body after he was nearly killed in a bomb-blast in July of '44 while attending a staff meeting. In any case, the threat of Hitler, whether as a result of suicide or some other form of exiting his Berlin bunker, April 30, 1945 marks the end of the European war as most people understand it.

The reason this date is so important is because it happens to be the day that an American Army lieutenant by the name of Walter Horn was supposedly digging through the battered remains of a building in Nuremberg that had recently been leveled in an Allied aerial attack. And just as there is an ongoing debate concerning the ultimate end of the Nazi's Supreme Commander, there is a similar debate as to exactly when this American lieutenant found what he found. Nevertheless, to anyone who has been following the string of events as they are depicted in this work, it may not seem so open to discussion, because according to most accounts, the lieutenant found The Spear of Destiny, which had been hidden in the basement of that building in the hopes that it might not fall into the hands of the advancing enemy. But as luck would have it — or should I say, providence — found it he did.

By one account, the time and date of its recovery was said to be 3:00 PM on the 30th of April in that fateful year of 1945.[237] Why is that so significant? Well, it happens to be significant because anyone who believes in the mystical power of The Spear of Destiny would doubtlessly find it interesting that it was recovered at this exact moment, which, according to another account, occurred just one half hour prior to Hitler's suicide.[238] In other words, The Spear's most recent claimant had it removed from his control, and by way of some uncanny sense of loss and defeat, the will to power seems to have been summarily yanked from its earthen vessel. So, having been deprived of his very heart and soul, Hitler, like the soulless zombie that he had become, utterly succumbed to the dark side of the legend of The Spear, and in response, the demonic spirit that it had conjured up finished the job in the quintessential act of surrender, thereby destroying the human vessel that it had until then filled with an insatiable lust for world domination. And in that final, inevitable act of suicide, Adolf Hitler, in death, finally came to grips with the true meaning of The Spear's power in a way that he could never have done in life.

---

237 *Last Days of the Third Reich, Part Three*, Walther Johann von Löpp (Compiler)
238 *World War II in Europe: The Death of Hitler*; The History Place

The Tie That Binds

AS WE WIND DOWN our inquiry into whether The Spear of Destiny has ever been associated with the kind of miraculous power that we see in such sacred artifacts as Adam's garment, this leads us to ask: If The Spear does exhibit such power, what is God trying to reveal via this symbolic meaning?

Like so many mysteries of *The Bible*, what is not made clear in the canonical record is made crystal clear in the parabiblical record. There we begin to see what might imbue extraordinary significance to mere clothing. There we find a definitive answer to the obvious question concerning Adam's garment: What could be so special about a simple loincloth?

In *First Adam and Eve*, we discover that God instructed the first couple where they could find something to cover their nakedness. The Lord told them: "There you will find skins of sheep that were left after lions ate the carcasses. Take them and make garments for yourselves, and clothe yourselves with them."[239] But Satan overheard God telling Adam about the sheepskins, and — consumed by his hatred of these humans — raced ahead of the couple, hoping to destroy the garments before they could use them as they had been instructed. Fortunately, as the story goes, the Word of God — or rather the pre-incarnate Jesus — bound the devil in chains before he could carry out his plan so that when Adam and Eve arrived they got their first real look at the hideous creature they had only previously encountered in the guise of the elegant serpent.[240]

Gazing upon the sheepskins that lay at his feet, Adam was the first person in history to experience an insight into the true meaning of what theologians would many centuries later come to label as "vicarious substitute," a term that referred to the death of Christ as an atonement for the sins of the people of God. According to *First Adam and Eve*:

> Standing over the sheepskins, Adam stood and stared blankly down at them for several moments.
>
> "What's wrong now, Adam?" asked Eve.
>
> "I'm sad thinking about how we got these skins, that's all."
>
> "Sad, why?"
>
> "I'm sad because these skins have come from owners who have died, and when we put them on, we'll be wearing emblems of their death."
>
> "And someday," continued Eve, beginning to realize what he was saying, "we'll die just like they did, won't we?"[241]

---

239 *First Adam and Eve* 50:7
240 Ibid. 51:2-5
241 Ibid. 52:2

The significance of these sheepskin garments, then, lies in the fact that God was conveying a truth not only to them but to every one of the descendants of that first couple as well — to all of us, in fact. These sheepskins, which were the result of an attack by a lion, represented the first "type" in history that was to foreshadow the sacrificial death of the Lamb of God, Jesus, Who was slain before the foundation of the world.[242] And as God allowed evil men, compelled by the devil, to shed the blood of His Son,[243] it was a roaring lion, as a type of Satan, which killed the sheep that provided the first adequate covering of its kind for fallen humanity — sheepskins, which came as a result of the shed blood of their owners.

This same idea of Satan as a roaring lion is perfectly illustrated by E.W. Bullinger in his groundbreaking study entitled *The Witness of the Stars*, where he pointed to the significance of the constellation of Orion as typifying the conquering Hero of Heaven. As is well known to any biblical scholar, this constellation is mentioned three times in Scripture — twice by Job and once by Amos.[244] Both men, in no uncertain terms, proclaim that Orion was created by God, and, according to Bullinger, the purpose revealed in such a creative act was to corroborate the truth as it is portrayed in God's written word. In this case, Orion — the brightest constellation to be found in the night sky — is a mighty warrior who holds in his left hand the head of his vanquished prey, a lion's head.

Just who is this conquering hero, one might ask? The names of the stars that comprise this impressive constellation, said Bullinger, provide us with the necessary clues. In the raised foot of this figure is the star *Rigel*, which means "the foot that crushes." One of the stars in Orion's belt — the most famous among this trio of lights — is called *Al Nitak*, which means "the wounded One." Another star in his right leg is called *Saiph*, which means "bruised," the same Hebrew word found in the primordial prophecy of the Redeemer described in the first book of *The Bible*.[245] "And the Lord said to the serpent: 'Because you've done this thing, I'll create hostility between you and the woman, between your children and her children; he will crush your head, and you will *bruise* his heel.'"[246] Here we have a perfect illustration of none other than Jesus Christ, in a dual role as both the Suffering Servant and Conquering Hero. Having crushed His enemy, while in the act of being bruised Himself, He triumphantly holds aloft the head of his ancient foe, that is, Satan, who is forever seeking his next victim — in this case, the sheep killed by a lion that provided Adam's garment.

---

242 *Revelation* 5:6, 12; 13:8

243 *First Peter* 5:8

244 *Job* 9:9; 38:31; *Amos* 5:8

245 *The Witness of the Stars*, E.W. Bullinger, pp. 124-27

246 *Genesis* 3:14-15

No wonder that Adam's sheepskin garment, as it was handed down from generation to generation, became such a remarkable source of divine power. It provided the initial step in the reconciliation between God and Adam after the tragic expulsion and alienation of that first couple. It enabled Noah to tame the animals so that they not only cooperated in their entering the Ark but also were temporarily freed from their adversarial nature while confined in it. Next, it was stolen from Noah by his son Ham, who undoubtedly took advantage of the fact that his father was passed out, dead drunk, in his tent. This, in turn, would explain why Noah pronounced such a harsh punishment on Ham; not because he merely peeped and tattled on him but because he stole such a prized artifact—one that Noah knew would never again be used for the God-ordained purpose for which it had been originally provided. And finally, once in Ham's possession, the garment was handed down to his grandson Nimrod, who found in it a virtually limitless source of power prior to his inward turn to self that ultimately weakened its efficacy, even though he wore it on his person until the day of his death.

All this brings us to the next series of questions that again only the apocryphal record is able to answer; and the questions are these: What happened to Adam's garment after Nimrod had it? Did he pass it on to one of his sons like his father before him? How was it that Esau, apparently following in the tradition of Nimrod, became such a powerful hunter? And finally: Why did Esau so carelessly forfeit the birthright blessing of Abraham when it would have bestowed untold wealth and power on him? One need only continue reading further in *Jasher* to find the answers. With these answers, one comes face to face with some very important clues en route to our attempt to solving the ancient mysteries that we are presently investigating. According to *Jasher*:

> At that time, Esau, after the death of Abraham, often went out hunting in the fields. Around the same time, Nimrod, king of Babel, who was also known as Amraphel,[247] was in the habit of hunting during the coolest part of the day, accompanied by his most powerful warriors. As he did, Nimrod would see that Esau was also hunting in the same fields, and, over the course of time, the king of Babel grew jealous of the grandson of Abraham.
>
> One day while Esau was hunting, he spotted Nimrod wandering through the wilderness with two of his bodyguards. At the time, Esau could see that the rest of Nimrod's warriors were yet a great distance from the king, all heading in different directions, each in search of their own prey. So concealing himself there in the bushes, Esau began to stalk Nimrod as though he were hunting a wild ani-

247 compare with *Genesis* 14:1, 9

mal, and because Nimrod and his men had no idea they were being stalked, they eventually wandered right into the place where Esau was hiding.

Without warning, Esau lunged from behind the bush, sword drawn, and ran toward Nimrod intent on engaging him in hand-to-hand combat. Furiously, Esau slashed at Nimrod and his two body-guards, and in mere moments he beheaded the king of Babel and hacked the bodyguards to death. And when the rest of Nimrod's warriors heard their cries from a distance, they came running to find out what had happened.

From a distance, Esau could see Nimrod's men running toward him, so he grabbed the valuable garment of Nimrod, which had en-abled him to subdue an entire kingdom and, as quickly as he could, ran home with the garment securely in his grasp.

Arriving home, exhausted and still shaken from the thrill of bat-tle, he found his brother Jacob cooking a delicious meal and hungri-ly sat down next to him.[248]

It is at this crucial stage that the canonical record states that the fam-ished Esau sold his birthright at the cunning behest of his brother. What tra-dition does not point out, though, is why he made such a reckless, foolhardy decision. We are simply expected to accept the age-old tripe that because Esau was such a profane person he simply had no respect for such spiritual matters. However, considering the additional testimony of the apocryphal record, this view is forever altered. Far from seeing Esau as one who was incapable of appreciating the value of the family blessing, the picture that *Jasher* presents to us is definitely one of a very ambitious man.

In fact, Esau is portrayed as someone who was so rabidly ambitious that he was willing to take on the might of the most powerful man of the age. Once he had managed to kill Nimrod and rob him of the talisman that had enabled him to subjugate the entire world, he simply had no further need of the birthright of men like Abraham and Isaac. Certainly, these were not men who Esau aspired to emulate. These men were not known as world conquer-ors but as lovers of the kind of world that a benevolent God was attempting to establish, a God Who, above all, called men to offer their goods and ser-vices as a means of blessing humanity. In other words, however much the patriarchal blessing offered a man like Esau in terms of wealth and power it was still one that was implicitly meant to be shared and thus, in his view, squandered upon a pathetic, needy world. In contrast, the promise that Ad-am's garment held out to Esau was one of unmitigated fame and fortune. No wonder that Esau was suddenly so willing to trade away something that

---

248 *Jasher* 27:1-11

had previously been seen as a thing of value but in light of his newfound situation was only useful for filling his empty belly. In this, the canonical record is quite correct in describing Esau as a profane and foolish man with no depth of spiritual understanding. It simply misses the mark when it comes to revealing the specific underlying motive for such a rash decision on Esau's part.

Still, I can hear the grumblings of some who are asking, "But if what you say is true, then why did Moses leave this part of the story out when he wrote *Genesis*?" To which I reply: "Of course that kind of selective revelation is already explained in Scripture, particularly when it comes to what Jesus said." Based on the divine intention of His teaching via parables, God has caused many of His deepest truths to be hidden away until some future date when mankind is finally ready to hear them again, like the man in the parable of buried treasure who, after having discovered the truth, then reburies it.[249]

Similarly, this kind of omission has also plagued generations of people who wrestle with whether *The Bible* can be trusted as a valid source of truth, when we are told the sons of Adam and Eve had children, but *Genesis* never bothers to explain to whom those children were born? As a result, anyone who claims to believe in the truth of Scripture is left hanging their heads in want of an adequate explanation. But as usual, all that one needs to do is to look to the parabiblical literature to find the most obvious answer. In *The First Book of Adam and Eve,* we find that both Cain and Abel had twin sisters, by the name of Luluwa and Aklia, respectively, and it was those sisters who would provide history's first grandchildren.[250]

So, as for the story of Adam's garment being left out of the *Genesis* record: Was it an unconscious decision on the part of Moses to delete this all-important connection? Or was it an inspired decision willed upon him by the Holy Spirit? No one, I believe, will ever know for sure. Suffice it to say, that considering God's cosmic game of hide-and-seek it is a truth that deserves the attention of anyone fortunate enough to be confronted by it once it has resurfaced. The real tragedy is when people receive such enlightening forms of truth but fail to appreciate them, just as when old wineskins are filled with new wine but are incapable of containing it. Sadly, like those proverbial old wineskins, instead of embracing the newness of fresh truth from God's word, their minds figuratively burst because of their rigidity of thought.[251]

Still, I can hear others say, "Maybe Moses didn't record the part about Adam's garment because God wanted to suppress the knowledge of such

249 *Matthew* 13:44
250 *First Adam and Eve* 74:5-6; 75:11-12
251 *Matthew* 9:17; *Mark* 2:22; *Luke* 5:37

things so people would no longer expect divine power in mere objects but in Him alone. After all, since Jesus came along, stuff like that just doesn't happen anymore, right?" To which I would reply in typical style: "You think?"

Famous throughout the history of Christendom are numerous legends that would suggest otherwise. One example of this is found in a collection of letters exchanged between Herod Antipas and Pontius Pilate, in a document entitled *The Death of Pilate, who Condemned Jesus*. In it, there is an interesting story that refers to a famous object that has over time permutated into a variety of forms, all of them, however, involving a single element—that of an image of Christ. As the story goes: A woman named Veronica—or Berenice, depending on your language frame—encountered Jesus during His travels throughout Judea. Then at some point during their conversation, Veronica acquired a picture of the face of Christ on canvas, or as depicted in other versions, either a handkerchief or a cloth.[252]

Later in this same account, Veronica was met by an emissary of Tiberius Caesar sent to Jerusalem seeking the assistance of a man who had allegedly been healing the sick by merely speaking to them, namely Jesus. The reason this emissary had been sent there was because Caesar had fallen gravely ill, and because the emperor was unable to find a cure from his Roman physicians, he had been driven by desperation to seek help through any means possible. When Veronica told the emissary that she possessed a painting of Jesus, he suggested that they travel to Rome, whereupon presenting the image to Caesar he was miraculously healed from his disease. Pretty farfetched, right? I mean, really, how can anybody believe something as ridiculous as that? This story is nowhere in the Biblical Canon, so naturally it must be treated with grave suspicion.

But wait. What if there are similar examples in the received text of the Church? Would that suffice to deter one's skepticism? Then consider this: Such an incident can be found; and not just one but at least two. One of them has to do with ordinary articles of clothing that merely came into contact with the skin of the Apostle Paul, and from that point onward they supposedly took on healing properties. "Now God worked unusual miracles by the hand of Paul so that even handkerchiefs or aprons were brought from his body to the sick, and the diseases left them and the evil spirits went out of them."[253]

So, as in the case of Adam's sheepskin garment—which clearly conveyed spiritual power over the forces of nature—Veronica's painting and Paul's handkerchief were said to have contained similar properties.

Then, there is an even more important example of this in *The Bible*, one that involves none other than Jesus Himself. Certainly, you are aware of the

252 e.g., The Shroud of Turin
253 *Acts* 19:11-12

story of Jesus' seamless robe, are you not? No? Well, let me tell you about it then. See how it compares with the stories of Adam's garment, Veronica's painting, and Paul's handkerchief, and when you have heard it, you decide if such things are still sanctioned by the God of canonical Scripture. Said John:

> When the soldiers crucified Jesus, they took his clothes, dividing them into four shares, one for each of them, with the undergarment remaining. This garment was seamless, woven in one piece from top to bottom. "Let's not tear it," they said to one another. "Let's decide by lot who will get it."
>
> It happened this way so that the Scripture might be fulfilled, which said, "They divided my garments among them, and cast lots for my clothing." So this is what the soldiers did.[254]

Now, in telling the story of Jesus' seamless robe, I would like to add a sidebar. Just in case the reader thinks that we are dabbling in nonessential matters here, let me assure them of one simple fact. Although the discussion of such things as garments, paintings, handkerchiefs, and robes may not seem like legitimate subjects for the serious *Bible* student, they are subjects of great importance to the writers of Holy Writ, no matter how much the darkened mind of humanity tries to trivialize them. Case in point is a passage in *The Gospel of John* regarding the crucifixion of Jesus. In fact, it contains a reference to one of the most profoundly mournful psalms ever penned by King David, called a man after God's own heart. Later, it intrudes into John's Gospel as a brief insertion, but its implications far outweigh its brevity, as anyone who loves the Scriptures will attest. It does this through the uncanny way in which words that were spoken in *The Old Testament* are spoken again by One Who inhabits the world of *The New Testament*. As it turns out, by speaking these words afresh, the old words are imbued with new meaning, creating startling, unexpected connections between past and present. The twenty-second psalm of David's, then, which has Jesus breathing new life into his words, is so marvelous that the discerning reader will be astonished by its sheer poignancy. And I mention it here to lend credence to the overall importance to the words being quoted, because, in point of fact, so much of this remarkable psalm could have been spoken by Jesus, yet all but two verses are lifted out of it.

As Jesus hung on the cross, poised between Heaven and Hell, the haunting words of David flowed through Him like a rippling wave in time. Before Jesus quoted the words, no one in history could have ever anticipated them being spoken that way, because no one at the time understood the extent to which the lowly Nazarene really was the word of God made flesh. Only

---

254 *John* 19:23-24

then would it be revealed how inseparable were the past and the present, as the words of messianic figures like Enoch, Moses, and David found their ultimate expression in the mouth of Jesus, and never more poignantly than in the final moments before His death on the cross. A thousand years before Jesus would echo his words, King David lamented:

> My God, my God. Why have You forsaken me? Why do You remain so distant? Why do You ignore my cries for help? My enemies surround me like a herd of bulls; fierce bulls of Bashan have hemmed me in. Like roaring lions attacking their prey, they come at me with open mouths. My life is poured out like water; all my bones are out of joint. My heart is like wax, melting within me. My strength has dried up like baked clay. My tongue sticks to the roof of my mouth. You have laid me in the dust and left me for dead. My enemies surround me like a pack of dogs; an evil gang closes in on me. They've pierced my hands and feet. I can count every bone in my body. My enemies stare at me and gloat. They divide my clothes amongst themselves and throw dice for my garments.[255]

Only later, in the tumultuous events of the crucifixion, would the poetry of the psalmist take on the flesh and blood of actual history. As David mourned his plight as the hunted king of Israel prior to his eventual rise to the throne, Jesus would fulfill His own destiny in a similar manner, though in His case through death and resurrection. But en route to His ultimate exaltation, Jesus famously sighed, "My God, My God, why have You forsaken Me?"[256] And during His humiliation on the cross, the Roman soldiers gambled to see who would win His seamless robe.

But whatever became of this seamless robe of Jesus? Was it lost to history after those fateful days following the crucifixion? If the canonical record were our only source for such inquiries, then, yes, it would appear that it did. But how could something so important in the minds of the biblical authors simply vanish without a trace? Fortunately, for the sake of those who love the truth when they hear it, there is another source to be had concerning the history of Jesus' robe. In *The Death of Pilate*, the story is told how, in the days following Caesar's healing by way of the painting of Christ, Pontius Pilate was brought to Rome to be interrogated about his role in the crucifixion of Jesus. Continuing in the apocryphal record, we read:

> So Pilate was apprehended by order of Tiberius Caesar, and brought to Rome. When Caesar heard he had arrived in the city, he was so overwhelmed by an unquenchable fury that he demanded that the

---

255 *Psalm* 22:1; 12-18
256 *Matthew* 27:46; *John* 19:24

governor be brought before him right away.

Now Pilate brought the seamless robe of Jesus with him, and he wore it when he appeared before the emperor. And as soon as Tiberius saw Pilate, all his anger subsided, and he rose to warmly greet him. He was unable to speak harshly to him about anything. Before Pilate's arrival, Caesar had been furious, but in his presence, he acted gently.

Dismissing Pilate from the room, Caesar became enraged again, chastising himself for not expressing his anger. So he ordered to have him brought back in, swearing that Pilate was nothing but a child of death, unfit to live, but when he saw him again, he instantly greeted him with kindness, laying aside all his fury. Everyone there was quite astonished, as was Tiberius.

Eventually though — either by divine suggestion or persuasion by some Christian — Caesar had Pilate stripped of his robe and quickly the original fury of his mind returned. As the emperor pondered what was happening, someone explained to him that Pilate had been wearing the seamless robe of the Lord Jesus.[257]

What can one surmise from all of the aforementioned examples? First, we have Adam's garment, which not only procured divine favor for him and his wife but subsequently bestowed awesome powers upon Noah, Nimrod, and Esau after them. Then there is Veronica's painting of Jesus that brought healing power even to Tiberius Caesar, followed by Paul's handkerchief that brought healing to those who came into contact with it. And finally, there is Jesus' seamless robe and with it the uncanny power that was imparted to Pilate, who wore it with such dramatic results in the presence of the Roman emperor. Seen separately, as they have been for so many centuries, these various accounts lay about — like scattered jewels — without a proper context, without rhyme or reason, but seen together, in relation to the canonical texts, they coalesce to solidify and substantiate one's overall faith in *The Bible* as a whole. Seen as points on a continuum, the garment, the painting, the handkerchief, and the robe present a string of unlikely but powerful connections, which, to the discerning, clearly reveal God's hidden hand in history.

Of course, anyone familiar with *The Bible* knows full well that, from cover to cover, it is, and always has been, a book of miracles. The ultimate question we are trying to ascertain here, however, is not whether or not miracles are possible. Even much of today's scientific way of thinking lends credence to the possibility of the miraculous, the fantastic, the magical, led by such luminaries as English physicist and science fiction writer Arthur C. Clarke,

---

257 *The Death of Pilate, who Condemned Jesus*

who famously stated, "Any sufficiently advanced technology is indistin-
guishable from magic."[258] According to this worldview, the only thing that
distinguishes the natural from the supernatural is one of perspective, not in
anything that is inherent to nature itself. Therefore, it is best to keep in mind
that anyone who urges the spiritually-oriented person to abandon their faith
in biblical utterances on the grounds that no one was there to prove any of
it really happened would do just as well to urge the scientifically-oriented
person to abandon their faith in Big Bang utterances on the same grounds.
On the other hand, it is important to realize that someone does not need to
shake hands with Abraham Lincoln or George Washington any more than
they would Jesus of Nazareth or John the Baptist to prove that they existed.
Historical certainty — which is what we are after here — is not comprised so
much of scientific empiricism as it is of consistent patterns of eyewitness
testimony, much in the same way that the legal proceedings of any court of
law rest upon the overwhelming evidence of eyewitness testimony as much
as it does on the evidence of DNA testing.

So what does any of this have to do with the preceding assortment of
talismans of power? The importance of it lies in the all-important question:
What do all these objects have in common? The most obvious answer appears to be "*power*." But this association, in and of itself, seems to reveal
nothing to genuine students of *The Bible*. No, what we are looking for here
is more at: What is the nature of this power that all these items seem to
possess? Or more specifically: What is the common principle that connects
the power that emanates from these objects? Let us take a look, one by one.

First, we have Adam's garment, which as we have seen came from
sheep that were killed by a lion. From this one can surmise God intended to
convey a message to Adam and his descendants, that is to say, only through
the shed blood of another is there adequate appeasement of sin — the root
cause of spiritual alienation — in the divine view. The garment, then, clearly
typifies the sacrifice of Jesus as the Lamb of God. The same can also be said
of the painting of Christ that Veronica presented to Caesar. This event took
place after the crucifixion, and as such the healing powers it bestowed upon
the Roman emperor can be seen as a function of the efficacy of the shed
blood of the Savior. Likewise, Paul was a minister of the risen Jesus, Whom
He chose as "one born out of due time," endowing him with an extraordinary gift of healing as witnessed by the unique virtues of a handkerchief
that had simply come into contact with his skin.

And finally, we see the same thing happening in regard to the seamless robe of Jesus, which was worn by Pilate with such powerful results
in the presence of Caesar. Just like Adam, Noah, and Nimrod before him,
Pilate possessed a talisman that provided its wearer with a power that nul-

---

258 *Profiles of the Future*, Arthur C. Clarke

lified the potency of his adversary, in the same way that the wrath of God is quenched by the sacrifice of His Son. For one brief moment, Pilate stood before the furious emperor of Rome as a type of all mankind who stand guilty before the righteously indignant Emperor of the Universe, but because he had been wearing Jesus' seamless robe he was "covered by the skins," as it were, of the Lamb of God. As such, the wrath of the emperor was momentarily appeased. As long as Pilate wore it, Caesar was gripped not by unquenchable fury but by boundless compassion for this pitiful man who had been manipulated by forces — both human and divine — beyond his wildest imagination. But as soon as he was stripped of the robe, the emperor's anger was unleashed once again.

So the underlying principle that binds all these talismans of power together is the sacrifice of Christ, the Lamb of God Who gave His life as a propitiation for sin and thus as a vicarious substitute for the sake of mankind. In this way, the very thing that Jesus predicted is revealed in all its splendor. Then some of the scribes and Pharisees answered, saying, "Teacher, we want to see a sign from You." So He said to them, "An evil and adulterous generation seeks a sign, but no sign will be given to it except the sign of the prophet Jonah. For as Jonah was in the belly of the whale for three full days, so the Son of Man will be in the heart of the Earth."[259]

Upon first reading this passage, one might surmise that Jesus is saying that no matter how much you ask for a sign from Heaven, you are never going to get one. But far from refusing their request, what He was saying was that whenever God reveals Himself, as He so often does, the sign that He is performing has the sole purpose of typifying the death and resurrection of Jesus, of which Jonah in the belly of the whale is the primary example. According to this view, each and every one of the talismans of power we have examined so far conform to this paramount function, just as Cinderella's foot perfectly fits into the proverbial glass slipper.

As it turns out, then, the tie that binds all these talismans of power is the sacrifice of Christ Who gave His life as a vicarious substitute for the redemption of humanity. Therefore, if there is any truth to the legends concerning the power that emanates from the Spear of Longinus, then certainly it must do so because it is just as intimately associated with the death and resurrection of Christ.

That said, let us take a moment to see how The Spear of Destiny conveys the divinely-inspired message that we are seeking. Actually, such an inquiry produces two very important points. The first has already been revealed in countless essays on the meaning of The Spear. The second, however, will concern something I believe has never been previously cited. Admittedly, the first way in which The Spear of Longinus exemplifies the sacrifice of

---

259 *Matthew* 12:39-40; *Luke* 11:29-30

Christ is that it played a pivotal role in confirming the messianic claims of Jesus. As the story goes: When Pilate's soldiers were sent to break the legs of that trio of crucified men, the two thieves on either side of Christ did have their legs broken in order to hasten their deaths, but when the soldiers came to Jesus, they found Him already dead. It was then that Longinus made his fateful move in piercing the side of Jesus with his spear, thereby confirming the words of the prophets: "These things happened so that the Scripture would be fulfilled: 'Not one of His bones will be broken,'[260] and as it says elsewhere: 'They'll look upon Him Whom they have pierced.'"[261]

It is important to note here that what Longinus did was nothing more than what was already typical of Roman soldiers on the battlefield. Soldiers routinely pierced the rib cages of their fallen enemies to make sure that the dead men were not merely faking their deaths in order to escape later with their lives. Certainly, such a practice seems obvious enough. If the man lying there was really a corpse, it would not react, and it certainly would not bleed. In the case of Jesus, however, something quite unusual occurred. When Longinus pierced His ribcage with the blade of his spear, the expired Christ did not react. In this, what had happened was quite in line with what one would expect from a corpse. However, what was totally unexpected was that, in contrast to a lifeless body, this particular corpse did bleed, and not just blood exited the wound but water also. In this peculiar phenomenon, biblical scholars are quick to see a spiritual meaning. This flow of blood, they say, represents the price that Jesus paid as a ransom for mankind's redemption, while the flow of water depicts the advent of the Holy Spirit that was unleashed upon the world as a result of the efficacy of His sacrifice.

Therefore, if this were all that could be said of what The Spear accomplished in the hand of Longinus, this would certainly have been enough to imbue it with the kind of otherworldly significance with which it has ever since been associated. But is that all there is to the "story"? Is this the only way in which this sacred relic of Christendom speaks of the purposes of God in Christ? Well, according to the typical biblical historian, the answer to that question is yes. That is, until now.

Assurance Sufficient

HERE WE COME to the next way in which The Spear of Destiny tells its story concerning the death and resurrection of Christ. However, as I have done in the past, I must qualify what I am about to say with several key points en route. At the beginning of this chapter, our main goal was to present a series

260 *Exodus* 12:46; *Numbers* 9:12; *Psalm* 34:20
261 *Zechariah* 12:10

of ideas that have admittedly been outside the "mainstream" in terms of the general flow of biblical history. However, by no means has this work been expected to be evaluated apart from the traditional books of *The Bible* as we know them today. Still, you may be asking: What is the point in looking at extra-biblical texts when we are perfectly happy with the ones we already have? To which I would respond by saying that as long as there are such things as doubt and skepticism, there will always be a need to counterbalance the tendency to dismiss any biblical texts that assume their starting point with the miraculous and otherworldly. In other words, in the process of analyzing the nature of biblical texts—both canonical and non-canonical—it behooves the saints to take every opportunity to bolster their faith in a God Who has clearly demonstrated His desire to infiltrate the stream of human history.

In opposition, then, to this tendency to discredit any biblical text that reports an event of a miraculous and otherworldly nature, we have attempted to verify the events found in this work by approaching them in an entirely unique way. The reason for this approach is because the search for historical certainty is typically plagued by a myriad of obvious difficulties, the least of which being the classic argument against the human capacity for the attainment of any "truth" beyond one's own personal experience. As such, there stands at one extreme the view that nothing can be definitively ascertained about history. Voltaire articulated this point of view when he said, "Doubt is not a pleasant thing, but certainty is absurd."[262] On the other end of the spectrum, there exists at least a modicum of hope. Said John Stuart Mill, "There is no such thing as absolute certainty, but there is assurance sufficient for the purposes of human life."[263]

This is why we have repeatedly examined these narratives in light of the latter view. That is to say, while absolute historical certainty is not possible because of our inability to witness said facts of history for ourselves, we, at least, by way of a comprehensive approach to history, can arrive at an "assurance sufficient for the purposes of life." Of course, this will always be the case whether one is attempting to verify the historical certainty of events that took place last year, or last millennium, for that matter.

In this instance, our present pursuit involves the way in which the alleged Spear of Longinus, otherwise known as The Spear of Destiny, reveals an important truth about the death and resurrection of Christ. So far, we have dealt with its apparent role throughout the history of Western Europe, particularly as it pertains to the legend that whoever laid claim to The Spear would in some unique way control the destiny of mankind. This we have done despite the insistence by most historians that it can never be fully de-

---

262 *Voltaire in His Letters*, Voltaire, p. 232
263 *On Liberty*, John Stuart Mill, p. 40

termined that The Spear handed down throughout the centuries was actually the genuine artifact. Naturally, such a question can never be proven beyond a shadow of a doubt. In the end, all that is ever ascertainable is whether or not history has sufficiently conformed to the so-called "myth." By that criteria, at least, it does seem certain that the world-shaping events of history have confirmed the validity of such a claim—again, quite apart from verifying that it is the actual weapon that pierced the side of Christ, or that this historical impact was accomplished by way of some as-yet-undefined mystical force. All that is left now is to determine the "how" in which it reveals the story of Christ's death and resurrection.

First and foremost, as we have already noted, without the action of the dutiful centurion, the long-anticipated prophecy of the Messiah might have gone unfulfilled. But upon seeing Longinus pierce the side of the expired Jesus, the Roman soldiers' mission to hasten the Nazarene's death was thwarted. Thus, "not a single bone of His body was broken," just as the Scriptures had duly anticipated.

In the context of this work, however, I promised there was an added dimension concerning The Spear of Destiny in relation to the work of Christ—one that until now has been totally overlooked. In this, it turns out to be exactly as I have previously detailed concerning The Great Pyramid of Giza. Ever since the pioneering work of Robert Menzies opened the door to a new way of interpreting its geometric design, discovery after discovery has gradually unveiled the various messianic timelines contained in this greatest wonder of the world. Similarly, in light of the evidence outlined in the last chapter, one can now see that the numerical value of *five and a half* (i.e., 5,500)—something that was originally thought to be found only in apocryphal literature and early church history—can also be found within the geometry of The Great Pyramid.

So what, exactly, is this added dimension concerning The Spear of Destiny, that is to say, one which bears such a striking similarity to that which we recently discovered in The Great Pyramid? Well, in answering that we come face to face with yet another example of this ubiquitous numerical value of *five and a half*. In this special number, so pregnant with prophetic overtones, we discovered the ultimate timeline of divine redemption, from Adam to Christ, and from Enoch to Moses. Therefore, when one stumbles onto another occurrence of this same number, and this re-occurrence just happens to involve another icon of Christian history, one must undoubtedly marvel at the odds that it could prove to be merely a product of sheer coincidence.

More importantly, whereas biblical historians may question the extent to which the garment of Adam or The Spear of Destiny represent the story of Christ, even the most rabid of agnostics can see how this next icon relates to

it. The sacred object I am referring to, and to which I will subsequently connect to the legend of The Spear of Longinus, is none other than The Shroud
of Turin, the alleged burial cloth of Jesus of Nazareth.

A Curious Crossroad

BUT NOTICE HOW I said, the *alleged* burial cloth of Jesus. Why? I say alleged because like The Great Pyramid of Giza and The Spear of Longinus,
I do not claim to be able to prove—in the traditional sense of that word—
the validity of whether any of these things are "real," any more than I can
"prove" whether or not Jesus rose from the dead. And do not misunderstand me when I say this concerning the resurrection of Christ. Naturally,
as a Christian author who has been writing a book like this, I do believe in
the historical certainty that Jesus rose from the dead. Like the Apostle Paul,
I firmly believe that without the resurrection of Christ everything in *The
Bible* is utterly meaningless; without it, "our faith is useless."[264] Rather, what
I mean to say is, I have neither made, nor do I plan to make, any attempt
to lay claim to such things as the "reality" of The Pyramid or The Spear or,
in this case, The Shroud in—I repeat—the traditional sense. In many other
books, written by far more adventurous souls than mine, this has already
been managed with a far greater degree of proficiency than I am capable of.

To read the most elucidating and comprehensive arguments for the authenticity of The Turin Shroud, one need only turn to the works of British
author Ian Wilson. In a series of books like *The Blood and the Shroud: New Evidence That the World's Most Sacred Relic Is Real* and *The Shroud: The 2,000-Year-
Old Mystery Solved*, Wilson scrutinizes every challenge of those who insist—
by invoking such scientific bulwarks as carbon-14 dating—that The Shroud
dates back to no later than the thirteenth century A.D. Yet according to Wilson and numerous other supporters of The Shroud's genuineness, even this
so-called "evidence" as to its medieval origins still fails to account for the
fact that the mysterious image on The Shroud bears an uncanny similarity
to a "negative" photographic plate. According to Wilson:

> What can be said with absolute confidence is that The Shroud's
> lifelike photographic negative derives from no modern-day photo
> graphic trick. The hidden "photograph," whatever its origin, is a
> fact of The Shroud that has to be faced by The Shroud's detractors
> just as fairly and squarely as its supporters must face the results
> from the radiocarbon dating.[265]

---

264 *First Corinthians* 15:14
265 *The Blood and the Shroud: New Evidence That the World's Most Sacred Relic Is
Real*, Ian Wilson, p. 19

In other words, even if The Shroud can be scientifically "proven" to date from the Medieval Era, it still does nothing to explain how someone artificially imprinted an image that clearly no one in that time period had the knowledge or expertise to create. So try as they might, all the naysayers in the world have yet to undermine the conviction of true believers in such ineffable objects as The Shroud of Turin.

Still, as I have already stated, my purpose throughout this entire volume has been altogether different from those who simply offer up various pros and cons in their arguments for authenticity. What I do claim to offer is an original approach to understanding each and every one of these sacred things, from Adam's garment to Jesus' seamless robe, from The Pyramid of Giza to The Spear of Destiny. In short, what I am offering is an approach that "transcends language," whereas language inevitably loses something in the process of translation and mistranslation. What I am offering is an approach that "transcends the scientific method," whereas science, by its very nature, is incapable of surmounting the limitations of time and space. That is to say, what I offer is a new way to "see" the same old things, a new way to "connect" the same old dots, to view things with a completely original understanding of all that has, for so very long, been hidden in plain sight.

Having said that, I submit that the following discussion regarding the alleged facts surrounding The Shroud of Turin—just like those pertaining to the prophecy of The Great Five and a Half Days, The Great Pyramid, and The Spear of Destiny—will not be offered as intellectual or scientific "proofs" as such. Rather, what I will do is offer a new way of approaching the same old stuff, and via this original presentation, you, the reader, will come to your own inevitable conclusion. Yet, ironically, this conclusion will have the same authority as anything that could have been provided by either of the aforementioned pursuits simply by virtue of the fact that most knowledge is communicated without anyone ever experiencing said facts for themselves. In other words, truth is, and always will be, in the "eye of the beholder." But unlike most authors, I choose not to try and convince anyone of facts *per se*. Instead, what I have done, and will continue to do, is offer a unique way to interpret the so-called "facts."

In this, what I am doing is much akin to what any public defender or prosecuting attorney does when they address a jury in a courtroom. Naturally, the jury is incapable of going back in time to witness a given crime in person. So what is left for a trial lawyer to do? Why, naturally, all that they can do is to "paint a picture," so to speak, utilizing whatever elements of "truth" that can be organized and presented by the various advocates, in the form of either eyewitness testimony or physical evidence.

In this case, I am attempting to advocate ways to validate the fact that God has not only revealed His prophetic timeline of The Great Five and a

Half Days in apocryphal literature, but that He has also planted it through-out the entire landscape of human experience. To that end, I have attempted to paint a brand-new picture with this possibility in mind — of The Ark of the Covenant, of The Great Pyramid of Giza, and of *The Septuagint Bible*. And now, this attempt to paint a new picture regarding the *five and a half* "days" of redemptive history brings us finally to a curious crossroad, where this same numerical value has been found to occur not only in relation to The Spear of Destiny but is intimately tied to The Shroud of Turin as well.

What does that mean? How does this number, which has invaded the thinking of the builders of The Ark and The Pyramid, and the writers of *The Septuagint Bible*, connect to The Spear? And likewise: How does this num-ber, so imbued with symbolic meaning and sacred significance, connect to The Shroud? Again, my answer — as it oddly turns out — is *not* that it per-tains to "this one" in some way or "that one" in another but rather that the same answer *connects them both*.

If that sounds strange, then one can only imagine my difficulty in lead-ing up to offering it. In an interesting twist, this connection of the numerical value of *five and a half* with both The Spear and The Shroud — which in turn binds them to the other sacred things in our list — actually parallels what we have already encountered throughout the apocryphal record. After all, what made the phenomenon of the *five and a half* "day" prophecy so compelling was not simply that it had found its way into the story of Adam and Eve, but that it also been woven into the stories of Enoch and Pilate. In other words, its genuine power emanated from its unexpected connectivity from story to story to story, that is, from *Adam and Eve* to *Enoch* to *Nicodemus* — first with God's promise to Adam, then Enoch's reference to Adam's time in Eden, and finally with Christ's descent to Hades, where He made good on this promise to return Adam to Paradise. As separate elements standing alone, they existed as discordant notes scattered across time, but brought together into a continuous sequence of events, they took on an entirely new meaning — striking a "new chord," if you will — which burst forth as a result of someone simply connecting the dots of prophetic history that had been lying dormant all along, just waiting to be connected this way.

Now, we have come to the conclusion of another sequence of events, similarly discordant, yet similarly destined to one day be connected and rephrased. Like Adam's garment, Veronica's painting, and Jesus' seamless robe — all deriving their mystical power from their association with the death and resurrection of Christ — Longinus' spear, likewise, has exhibited its own uncanny power to sway the course of human history, hence its renowned designation as The Spear of Destiny. But why? Was it simply because it was used to fulfill the prophecies that no bone of the Messiah would be broken, and that they would look upon Him Whom they had pierced? If that were all that could be said of this famed talisman that would undoubtedly have sufficed. However, as it turns out, there is more to the "story" after all, because according to the evidence uniquely revealed in the haunting image of The Shroud of Turin, the spear that was thrust into the side of Jesus did not, as most have assumed, do its piercing without guidance from the hand of the Lord of Time Himself. What does that mean?

In a nutshell, it means that the story from which The Spear of Destiny derives its meaning—that is, the way it typifies the death and resurrection of Christ—comes from the fact that when Longinus thrust his spear into Jesus' side, it pierced His right rib cage between the *fifth and sixth* rib. Thus, in one fell swoop, this piercing not only confirmed the messianic dimension of Christ's dying on the cross, but it also brought into sharp focus the story that would forever imbue The Spear of Destiny and The Shroud of Turin with their otherworldly potential. And in this single, elegant act of piercing, The Spear and The Shroud uniquely combined to reveal—to any who cares to notice—yet another way in which the God of Set Times is conveying His truth concerning the primordial promise to Adam that when He finally would rescue mankind He would do so, right on time, after *five and a half* "days."

The Heart of the Mystery

FOR THOSE OF you who put all the pieces together on your own, you are now in possession of a tremendous insight that no one can ever disassemble or explain away. For those of you who have not yet connected these things in your mind, I offer the following summation to help clarify the matter.

Already well known to theologians and historians alike is the fact that *The Septuagint Bible* contains a chronology that depicts a genealogy from Adam to Christ that spans a period of 5,500 years. However, what most of them fail to recognize is why this is so. And if ever asked why, they would certainly admit that they had never even bothered to ask such an apparently meaningless question, considering they were perfectly satisfied with the chronology handed down to them from post-Reformation times, that is, the 4,000-year chronology devised by the esteemed Archbishop Ussher. But as one has seen from our earlier historical review concerning this grand blunder, this chronology was seriously flawed from its inception. What is worse, it not only presents yet another contradiction to fuel the never-ending controversy over the validity of biblical translations, but it also undermines any attempt that the word of God might offer mankind in the way of demonstrating His faithfulness to His promises. If, however, one looks to the chronology espoused by *The Septuagint*, this obstacle collapses like a veritable house of cards. More importantly, by embracing the 5,500-year

chronology of *The Septuagint*, one is all the more open to the potential significance of this all-important numerical value of *five and a half*, which, as we
have seen, so often finds itself at the heart of this mystery. This simple but
obvious fact, then, should never be overestimated, because once this reality
becomes fixed in one's mind, a whole series of truths concerning God's control and faithfulness begins to tumble into place.

Like So Many Dominoes

FROM REPEATED references to the number *five and a half*, we have the exact
period of time that would mark the fulfillment of God's promise to rescue
Adam and his descendants, as it is depicted in both *The Septuagint* and the
apocryphal literature, followed by its recurrence in The Ark, The Spear, The
Shroud, and The Great Pyramid. From this, we have even greater confidence
that—even if biblical scholars are convinced that narratives like *The First
Book of Adam and Eve* and *The Secrets of Enoch* are products of post-Christian
times, and *The Gospel of Nicodemus*, that of the Medieval Era—these texts
are doubtlessly by-products of much earlier manuscripts whose origins far
exceed traditional assumptions. From this, we also have a much more acute
awareness of the symbolic meaning presented to us by way of the dimensions of The Ark of the Covenant, which theologians naturally see as signi-
fying all that the Advent of Christ holds in store for humanity. This, in turn,
confirms the numeric significance of the dimensions of the Open Coffer in
the King's Chamber of The Great Pyramid, which all pyramidologists insist
presents us with a prophetic type of Christ.

Additionally, it explains the conspicuous redundancy of the number *five*
throughout the dimensions of The Pyramid, causing pyramidologists to declare that it is the most important number in all of its marvelous geometry.
This is further cemented by the fact that both the angle of the Pyramid's
slopes and its height correspond to this same numerical value in its dimensions, which, to those who are convinced of its prophetic meaning, points
to the very moment in history when the long-awaited Christ would arrive.
And from this, we discover the most overlooked connection of all—so that
we now see the world's two most famous Christian artifacts in a brand-new
light—in that The Spear testifies to the blood of the Savior it spilled, and The
Shroud, to the miraculous nature of Christ's resurrection from the dead.

Like so many tumbling dominoes, then, one thing leads to another, each
thing unifies the other, and together they translate into exactly the kind of
message that this entire work has endeavored to illustrate. On one hand, it
is a message that is hidden in plain sight, available to some, obvious to the
eye of faith, while at the same time remaining concealed to others, veiled
to the eye of doubt. And on the other hand, it is a message of universal dimensions, that is to say, a message that is communicated by way of God's

all-encompassing language of the ages—a message of dramatic significance that transcends all interpretation.

Therefore, to those who look with discerning hearts and minds, the message of divine grace embodied in all these sacred dimensions can be clearly understood, in any language spoken the world over and throughout all time. Whether that language is linguistically- or mathematically-based, the message remains the same: God really is in control of every facet of human history; and because the Lord kept His promise to rescue Adam, right on time, exactly as He promised, we, who are all children of Adam, can rest assured that our future is secure in the knowledge that He will be just as faithful to *all of His promises* that pertain to us.

BOOK THREE

*In theology ... from time to time, there are drastic changes...
A new view of man, world, and God begins to prevail in the
theological community, where the whole and its details
appear in a different light.*

Hans Küng, *Paradigm Change in Theology*

The Next Paradigm Shift

A Different Way of Seeing

WHILE MOST people still might find it hard to accept the validity of the lost books, lost chronologies, and lost truths detailed here, they would be more inclined to do so if a clear-cut connection could be made between them and those things they already associate with mainstream biblical truths—things like The Ark of the Covenant and *The Septuagint Bible*. And, quite frankly, to expect otherwise would be the height of folly on my part, especially considering the fact that part of the enigma surrounding these lost truths have actually occurred as a direct result of God's own desire to withhold a knowledge of these things until the time when a future generation was destined to rediscover them.

Therefore, keep in mind, I have no objection to the general reluctance of most Christians in this; in fact, knowing what I know about the unfolding drama of God's hidden hand in history, I gladly accept a healthy dose of skepticism. The only thing I do find intolerable, though, is the stubborn unwillingness on the part of any so-called "truth-seeker" to at least open their minds to the possibility that *if*—and this is a very important *if* here—*if* a sound biblical basis for them can be adequately demonstrated.

After all, it is no great secret that the hardest part of relating to the controversial subject matter contained in this work—subjects like scriptural interpretation, biblical chronology, and religious artifacts—is overcoming the psychological hurdles that are the result of a lifetime of skepticism and doubt. But the greatest tragedy of all would be if, once the validity of these lost books, chronologies, and truths was sufficiently demonstrated, the evidence was disregarded and dismissed simply because certain books and chronologies had not been included in the modern Canon.

In terms of the entire span of human history, however, this is certainly nothing new. In ages past, nearly every generation has been confronted with one such dilemma or another, whereby what was once thought to be "the truth and nothing but the truth" was challenged, then rocked to its core, and finally overturned by the next "paradigm shift." A term coined by American physicist Thomas Kuhn, in 1962, paradigm shift refers to a fundamental change that occurs in the basic ideology of science—a change that opens up entirely new vistas of perception that would never have been considered valid until that moment in time. Originally applied only to scientific thinking, this term has since evolved to the point that it is also used to describe changes in numerous non-scientific models or perceptions. Accordingly, the Swiss theologian and author Hans Küng has applied Kuhn's theory of change to the history of human awareness so that for Küng a paradigm shift is what occurred with both the Protestant Reformation and the Age of Enlightenment. Speaking about this kind of radical change in the field of theology, Küng described it this way:

> In theology ... from time to time, there are drastic changes... As in the change from the geocentric to the heliocentric theory, from phlogiston to oxygen chemistry, from corpuscular to wave theory, so also in the change from one theology to another: Fixed and familiar concepts are changed; laws and criteria controlling the admissibility of certain problems and solutions are shifted; theories and models are upset.
>
> In a word, the paradigm, or model of understanding, is changed, together with the whole complex of different methods, fields of problems, and attempted solutions as had previously been recognized by the theological community. The theologians get used to a different way of seeing things, to see them in the context of a new model. Some things are now perceived that were not seen formerly, and possibly some things are overlooked that were formerly noticed. A new view of man, world, and God begins to prevail in the theological community, where the whole and its details appear in a different light.[266]

From this, it also follows that for a paradigm shift to occur there must be a considerable accumulation of information and experience to elicit such a change, all of which, as one can imagine, can only occur through the coordinated efforts of committed individuals over the span of several decades. In rare cases, the onset of a paradigm shift can be noted with a fair amount of accuracy, as with the Reformation, which is dated from 1520, and is widely attributed to the influence of one man, Martin Luther, and one document, his Ninety-Five Theses, which he nailed to the church door in Wittenberg. More often than not, though, there is little consensus as to when this shift occurs, as with the Enlightenment, which is said to have begun as early as the middle of the seventeenth century and as late as the beginning of the eighteenth century. And whereas one man looms above all others in the case of the Reformation, numerous names stand out in regard to the inception of the Age of Enlightenment. In philosophy, there were Rene Descartes, Immanuel Kant, and Voltaire; in politics, John Locke, Jean-Jacques Rousseau, and Thomas Hobbes.

---

266 *Paradigm Change in Theology: A Symposium for the Future*, Hans Küng, David Tracy (Editors), p. 21

On With the Struggle

CONSIDERING THE facts of history, then, one can feel quite intimidated by an awareness of all that it takes to stem the tide of the status quo. Moreover, this work can only be truly grasped upon reading it more than once. This is because one's frame of reference always determines his or her ability to assimilate any new philosophy, and because of this basic human reality, each reading will provide a new depth of understanding not possible until after being confronted with the ideas here. Even more important, persuasive words alone do not initiate the next paradigm shift in any given field, as Küng went on to explain.

> Not only in theology, but in natural science, a new model of understanding demands something like a *conversion*, which cannot be extorted in a rational way. I speak less of the initiator—the person who, because of a sudden intuitive experience or a long and arduous ripening, has suggested a new model—than of the recipients, those who have to decide for or against. The defenders of the old and of the new model—something that must not be underestimated—live in "different worlds," different worlds of ideas and of language; often they can scarcely understand each other. Translation from the old to the new language is necessary, but at the same time there must be a new conviction, a conversion.[267]

This is why I have chosen to convey the message of this work in, dare I say, sublimely poetic terms rather than purely "rational" ones, to echo the words of Küng. In approaching the material this way, I have, of course, taken my cue from what I have come to detect in God's own mode of communication, in terms of the dramas that transcend interpretation—a point I hope I have already adequately expressed—so hopefully you will not think that I am claiming any priority in such an approach.

In all of this, however, I am encouraged in light of what the Nobel Prize-winning German physicist Max Planck said about the improbability of affecting change in one's lifetime, and the fact that Küng insisted that what is applicable to the physicist is even more so in regard to the theologian. I am inspired to carry on with the struggle when I hear Planck say, "New scientific ideas never spring from a communal body, however organized, but rather from the head of an individually-inspired researcher who struggles with his problems in lonely thought, and unites all his thought on one single point, which is his whole world for the moment."[268] But however much I take heart

---

267 *Paradigm Change in Theology: A Symposium for the Future*, Hans Küng, David Tracy (Editors), p. 25

268 *Surviving the Swastika: Scientific Research in Nazi Germany*, Kristie Macrakis, p. 97

from hearing that statement by Planck, I am equally discouraged by another: "A new scientific truth does not triumph by convincing its opponents and making them see the light, but rather because its opponents eventually die, and a new generation grows up familiar with it."[269] Such is the bitter irony of the paradigm pioneers, or as Küng calls them, "model-testers" and "new-thinkers."[270]

Notwithstanding Küng's attitude that as physicists go so do theologians, I would also like to parenthetically point out something to anyone who might be put off by the idea that what Planck said about scientific truth has any bearing in regard to theological truth. And to this objection, I admit I, too, might feel obliged to recant my potentially tenuous position; if not for one small detail, that is. Because as it turns out, Planck himself, whose own work paved the way for the shift from special relativity to quantum physics, firmly believed otherwise. Said Planck: "Both religion and science require a belief in God. For believers, God is the beginning, and for physicists, He is the goal of every thought process. To the former, He is the foundation; to the latter, the crown of the edifice of every generalized worldview."[271] And in no uncertain terms, Planck further insisted:

> No matter where and how far we look, nowhere do we find a contradiction between religion and science. On the contrary, we find a complete concordance in the very points of decisive importance. Religion and science do not exclude each other, as many contemporaries of ours believe or fear. They mutually supplement and condition each other. The most immediate proof of the compatibility of religion and science, even under the most thoroughly critical scrutiny, is the historical fact that the very greatest scientists of all time — men such as Kepler, Newton, Leibniz — were permeated by a most profound religious attitude.[272]

So, even though Planck was realistic enough to acknowledge the forces that resist every advancement toward the next shift in human awareness, he never lost faith in the indivisible nature of theological and scientific truth. Therefore, I can expect nothing less of myself in attempting to elicit a "conversion" by way of my discourse concerning the connectivity of things that have themselves been seen as so many disconnected points on the frontier of a new paradigm that lies just beyond the next horizon. And as I already mentioned in an opening chapter of this work:

---

269 *Scientific Autobiography and Other Papers*, Max Planck, pp. 33-34
270 *Paradigm Change in Theology: A Symposium for the Future*, Hans Küng, David Tracy (Editors), p. 20
271 *Scientific Autobiography and Other Papers*, Max Planck, p. 184
272 Ibid. p. 186

Although there are many pitfalls along the way, the God of *The Bible* does not hesitate to beckon us onward in this journey of discovery. Therefore, if one can appreciate that it is God Himself Who is guiding our quest, then it should come as no surprise that He is also the One Who has provided sufficient signposts to help us along the way.

The End

Rising from the Ashes

TO ANYONE who is still wrestling with the notion of whether or not such extra-biblical literature constitutes genuine biblical truth, the story of Enoch presents yet another reason to take a fresh look at these remarkable narratives. It is time at last to tear down the walls of prejudice and disinformation that one might retain in light of everything offered in this work, particularly because of the way such narratives have provided the ultimate linchpin in connecting the various lost truths presented here.

Without works like *The Book*, a knowledge of the prophecy of The Great Five and a Half Days is at risk of being forgotten yet again. Without an awareness of this promise of "days," there would be no reason to believe that there was any more truth to the 5,500-year chronology from Adam to Christ in *The Septuagint Bible* than the 4,000-year version found in *The Hebrew Bible*. Without an awareness of the importance of the *Septuagint* chronology, there would be nothing to point to the prophetic significance encrypted in the dimensions of The Ark and The Pyramid, or the symbolic message conveyed in The Spear and The Shroud. And without an awareness of this promise of "days," there would be no knowledge of how the fulfillment of this prophecy confirms the faithfulness of a God, Who "in the fullness of time," sent forth His Son to make good on His promise to "rescue Adam and his descendants after *five and a half* 'days.'"

Having said all that, I am, of course, willing to concede that there are diehard skeptics out there who still cling to the possibility that this entire work is merely an exercise in wishful thinking; and for them, I am just as willing — being the eternal optimist that I am — to offer one last argument on their behalf. This argument is presented in the form of an allegory, one in which Enoch's life story reveals a special truth concerning the literature that has virtually become synonymous with his name. As such, the allegory that I will attempt to describe, just like that of Hippolytus' allegory of The Ark of the Covenant, will be couched in the same terms that we have seen throughout this work, that is to say, that of death and resurrection. But whereas Hippolytus' allegory of The Ark pertained to the resurrection of Christ, this allegory of Enoch points not to a bodily resurrection but to a resurrection of the hidden wisdom of the ages penned by him and others like him.

And the reason I am doing this is to address the main objection made by anyone who still insists that any talk of extra-biblical literature is meaningless because, in their view, there was a perfectly good reason these books were left out of Scripture, not to mention, there is nothing in history to account for the restoration of such books once they were excised. Simply put, there is no precedence to be had in all of history for such things as the "death and resurrection" of *wisdom*. And this, they would further insist, is made all the more evident by the fact that the only thing God has ever seen fit to resurrect is His beloved Son, Jesus.

Sure Enoch walked and talked with the Lord. Sure they must have had a very interesting conversation, but if God never saw fit to make sure that that conversation was inserted into the accepted Canon, then all the conjecture about this literature being providentially lost and restored simply has no precedence in history — biblically or culturally speaking. In short, if it is not in our *Bible* of today, then that is that: The End.

Or is it? Does the death of wisdom, especially that kind of wisdom associated with *The Bible*, really spell the end? Or, as we have so often seen in the remarkable world of the supernatural, does this end simply lead, instead, to a new beginning?

We now come to the point where I can present the aforementioned allegory, an allegory that reveals how a central truth of Enoch's life story illuminates God's intention toward humanity by way of His concealing and revealing His most precious truths. I would now like to remind the reader of one of the most enduring mythic figures known to mankind. It is the age-old story of a remarkable bird found throughout much of the world's history, despite cultural differences across the globe. I am referring to that remarkable creature known as the Phoenix, which to the modern mind doubtlessly seems like just another fairy tale. Yet for the greater part of history and the world, it has clearly been nothing of the sort. In fact, the cultural traces of this legendary bird are so pervasive that it calls to mind the notion set forth by Giambattista Vico, who insisted that "uniform ideas originating from entire peoples unknown to each other must have a common ground of truth."[273] Strange as it may seem, then, the story of the Phoenix appears to be one of those traditions that is just as resilient as the bird itself, as the following litany of believers would indicate.

According to ancient writers such as Herodotus, Tacitus, Pliny, and Ovid, the Phoenix resembled an eagle, with its vivid golden and scarlet feathers, and was said to perish in a burst of flames every five hundred years, only to be reborn, having risen from its own ashes. Because of this ability to rise again from the ashes, its legend has permutated the world over, becoming ever after associated with immortality and resurrection. To the Hebrews, it was connected with the eternal cycle of life; to the Egyptians, it symbolized rebirth; to the Persians, it was the bird of Paradise; to the Greeks and Romans, it conveyed the power of regeneration; and to the

---

273 *New Science*, Giambattista Vico, Book 1, Establishment of Principles: XIII, 144

Chinese, it denoted completeness, harmoniously combining both *yin* and *yang*. It was this association with rebirth that naturally lent itself to the advent of Christianity, as a direct influence of either Hebrew or Greco-Roman thought. States *The New World Encyclopedia*:

> The ideology of the Phoenix fit perfectly with the story of Christ. The Phoenix's resurrection from death as new and pure can be viewed as a metaphor for Christ's resurrection, central to Christian belief... Most of the Christian-based Phoenix symbolism appears within works of literature, especially in medieval and Renaissance Christian literature that combined classical and regional myth and folklore with more mainstream doctrine.[274]

Even Leonardo da Vinci wrote about the famed bird, saying, "For constancy, the Phoenix serves as a type; for understanding by nature its renewal, it is steadfast to endure the burning flames which consume it, and then it is reborn anew."[275]

This was not only the case for Christian theology, however, but included Jewish eschatological thought as well. According to Louis Ginzberg, "The Church Fathers, as well as the rabbis, refer to the Phoenix as a proof of the resurrection."[276] Concerning this association of the Phoenix with both Christian and Jewish theology, Roelof van den Broek, of Utrecht University in the Netherlands, wrote extensively in his book *The Myth of the Phoenix*. In it, he cited a fifth-century Coptic manuscript called *The Sermon on Mary*, which describes a series of appearances of the creature in connection with three pivotal biblical events.

> The first of these appearances took place when Abel made the sacrifice that found more favor in the sight of God than that of Cain... According to the Coptic text, thus, the Phoenix was consumed together with Abel's sacrifice by the heavenly fire ... as a type of Christ. According to the Coptic text, at the first sacrifice mentioned in *The Bible*, the bolt of fire was accompanied by an appearance of the Phoenix... The fire from Heaven is a sign that the event had divine approval; it legitimizes the sacrifice. The appearance of the Phoenix indicates that the event in question is, by God's will, the beginning of a new time, of a new era in the history of salvation...
>
> The second appearance of the Phoenix ... mentioned in the Coptic sermon: "When God brought the Children of Israel out of Egypt

---

274 *New World Encyclopedia*

275 *Leonardo's Notebooks: Writing and Art of the Great Master*, Leonardo da Vinci, p. 404

276 *The Legends of the Jews, From the Creation to Exodus: Notes for Volumes 1 and 2*, Louis Ginzberg, p. 51

by the hand of Moses, the Phoenix showed itself on the Temple of On, the city of the Sun..." Here again its manifestation marks the beginning of a new era in the history of salvation. Before the meaning of this can be elucidated, we must take up the third appearance of the Phoenix mentioned in the Coptic sermon.

In the year of Christ's birth, the Phoenix is supposed to have burned itself on a pinnacle of the Temple at Jerusalem... The report of this burning begins with a sentence that at first seems rather puzzling: "According to the number of its years, it was its tenth time since its genesis after Abel's sacrifice that it had sacrificed itself: In this year now the Son of God was born in Bethlehem." The intention here is to fix the year of the birth of Christ, chronologically, by means of the Phoenix's appearance every 500 years: 500 years must have preceded Abel's sacrifice, and since there were ten more such periods after it, the birth of Christ must have taken place in the year 5,500 after the creation of the world. This is a concept we encounter frequently in early Christian literature...

In his *Chronographia*, Julius Africanus has divided the history of the world according to this scheme of six periods, each lasting one thousand years, in which he put the birth of Christ in the year 5,500. This had already been done previously by Hippolytus in his commentary on *The Book of Daniel*, the date having been derived from the dimensions of ... The Ark [of the Covenant]...

The author of the Coptic sermon, therefore, drew on a familiar conception when he placed the birth of Christ in the year of the eleventh appearance of the Phoenix, i.e., in the year 5,500 after the creation of the world.[277]

The Light of a New Day

NOTWITHSTANDING the fact that the previous narrative further substantiates the validity of the all-important period of the *five and a half* "days" from Adam to Christ, what could possibly account for such parallels in both Jewish and Christian thought? Considering the intractable antagonism between the two camps at the time, what could have united such disparate groups? One answer, I believe, not only explains this riddle but also provides an answer to a question alluded to previously in this chapter, which was: What historical evidence is there to suggest that the story of Enoch's life could in any way reveal a hidden truth regarding the so-called "death and resurrection" of apocryphal literature? In this instance, the answer is

---

277 *The Myth of the Phoenix: According to Classical and Early Christian Traditions*, Roelof van den Broek, pp. 119, 121-25

one that should connect Jewish and Christian theology, and one that, in doing so, must predate them both in order for it to influence them equally. In short, what could tie together the mystery of the Phoenix with the Jewish and Christian doctrines of the resurrection of the dead? One word: Enoch.

Of utmost importance here is that one notices I said, "word," because it is to the etymological connection between the words "Phoenix" and "Enoch" to which we will next turn, and thus "end" our story with the new beginning that I spoke of earlier. As it turns out, the Greek word for "Phoenix" is said to have been derived from the Egyptian word *Pa-Hanok*, which means "The House of Enoch." Should one doubt such a possibility, simply examine the etymological aspects of our English word "Enoch," which comes to us straight from the Latin, while in Hebrew it is rendered *Hanokh*. So from the Hebrew *Hanokh*, we get the Egyptian word *Pa-Hanok*, which, in Greek, becomes "Phoenix." Considering, then—a fact we spent considerable time establishing in our chapter entitled *A Capstone to Time*—that Enoch undoubtedly left an indelible impact on the history of Egypt, it is not at all surprising that his very name would become a rich source for all sorts of legend and lore.

With this etymological connection in mind, next consider the common characteristics that the two share: Both Enoch and the Phoenix are associated with rebirth, renewal, and resurrection. Implicit in this also is that they are both associated with the transition from a previous state of existence, or awareness, to a new one. In other words, they are both said to inaugurate new beginnings. We are particularly concerned here with this notion, because above all it has been my intention to verify that the God of *The Bible* has never been embarrassed that the forgotten wisdom contained in books like Enoch's have been, "for a time," stigmatized and marginalized by an indifferent world. In fact, it has been His predetermined plan of the ages to have this timeless pattern built into the very tapestry of the greater dramas that only God's hidden hand in history could have orchestrated.

So, just as these lost books, lost chronologies, and lost truths that demonstrate the Lord's control and faithfulness were destined to temporarily fade from the horizon of human consciousness, the legend of the Phoenix conveys this same idea of periodic death and resurrection. And just as that legendary bird was said to make an appearance to mark the turning points in the history of salvation, we should expect nothing less when, in the unfolding of God's revelation, these hidden gems of wisdom have similarly risen from the ashes of oblivion and thus taken wing in the hearts and minds of those reborn into the light of a new day.

A Parting Shot

THE HERO SLAYS the monster, once … twice … but still, as any fan of the cinema knows all too well, the monster will not stay dead. Like the dying-and-rising hero so integral to the great tales, the monster, too, can and will rise again as it resorts to every nasty trick in its relentless pursuit of vanquishing the hero. In movie parlance, it is known as the Law of Triple Endings. In line with this classic principle, then, I would like to provide a parting shot before we finally ride off into the sunset and fade to black.

Throughout this work, we have sought a variety of ways to offset the three most dreaded archenemies of not only a book like this but, dare I say, of mankind itself. They are doubt, skepticism, and cynicism, because doubt is the ultimate adversary of faith and hope; skepticism, of truth and certainty; and cynicism, of beauty and grace. So, just when we think doubt has been conquered by meticulously comparing our non-canonical sources with the more familiar canonical texts and found them compatible beyond question, our old nemesis, skepticism, rears its ugly head. Then, just when we think skepticism has been overcome by painstakingly confirming the existence of the multitudinous ways that the broader landscape of human existence substantiates the truths contained in them, our final enemy, cynicism, seeks to undermine all our previous efforts.

Sure, you may say, I have answered the question of whether there is sufficient evidence to demonstrate the reliability of the texts in question and that wherever we look there is corroborating evidence that my conclusions are sound, but that still does nothing to answer the question that has plagued mankind since the dawn of time. And that is, just because it can be demonstrated that God is faithful and that our Universe speaks of His control: How does this adequately explain why He allowed evil to enter our world in the first place? In short: Just because God is in control and is faithful still does not make up for the fact that He personally unleashed the ultimate monster — evil — upon an unsuspecting humanity. Whether that monster is seen in terms of death, Hell, and the grave, or darkness, sadness, and pain, the fact that God is clearly to blame for the dire predicament we are in — quite apart from Adam's guilt in the whole debacle — undermines any of our bold pronouncements of "God is in control" and "God is faithful." Such is the power of that dreaded archenemy of humanity, such is its power that no vision of divine beauty and grace can withstand its corrosive sting, such is the power of cynicism.

Therefore, it is with the utmost urgency that I turn to delivering the final deathblow to such a one as cynicism, an enemy of such magnitude that it alone can single-handedly undermine every valiant effort that I have made to this point. How, then, does one answer the ultimate question on the lips of anyone who has ever asked such an obvious question? Why, in fact, would a loving and compassionate God allow evil to enter a world with such potential for hope, truth, and beauty? As anyone who has ever pondered why the Fall was allowed to occur in the first place, this is the great conundrum of human existence.

And the answer I will offer, like so many that have been offered throughout this work, will be a multi-faceted one; that is to say, it will be an answer that comes in the form of both word and image. Simply put, just like the universal truths conveyed in the numerological significance contained in the sacred dimensions depicted herein, this answer will be the same regardless of what language it is conveyed in, and as such will hopefully be understood by everyone the world over, be they young or old, simple or wise, literate or illiterate. Furthermore, this answer addresses the one thing that is so often overlooked by anyone who insists on putting God on trial by asking such questions, as if He would actually be embarrassed that His own creatures have discovered a flaw that He Himself has overlooked.

The answer comes in the form of the image seen on the next page. Like so much of this work, which aims at unveiling the hidden truth in the sacred dimensions around us, this image—called *The Beginning of Days*—is full of symbolic meaning just waiting to make itself known. On the surface, it is a depiction of the most tragic event in human history, known ever since as the Fall of Mankind. The hand of Eve places the deadly orb into Adam's hand, after having already taken a bite from that Forbidden Fruit, in the hopes that he will follow in her willing descent, thereby plunging them and their descendants into endless disaster, despair, and death. But as tragic as this scenario appears at first glance, there is another aspect to it—albeit hidden in plain sight—that is not so obvious; that is, not until it is pointed out, and then, like the proverbial snake that would have bitten you, it literally leaps out and grabs you.

And although it is clearly a picture of the Fall, it is of the utmost importance that you understand it is not, as one would assume, a portrait of unmitigated doom. Again—on the surface—it might look that way; but hidden within its imagery is a simple but overriding dimension, something that becomes apparent upon my asking a few questions: Is this really just an image of Eve handing over the Forbidden Fruit to Adam? What else does one see upon closer inspection? In fact, it is a depiction of that Fruit being handed over while at the same time "eclipsing," as it were, the rising Sun behind it. Why is that important? Well, as it turns out, by portraying the lethal orb of the Fruit this way, in relation to the celestial orb of the Sun, one is actually

looking at an allegory for the way in which the consequences of the Fall
have been nullified by the inconspicuous actions of that solar timepiece.

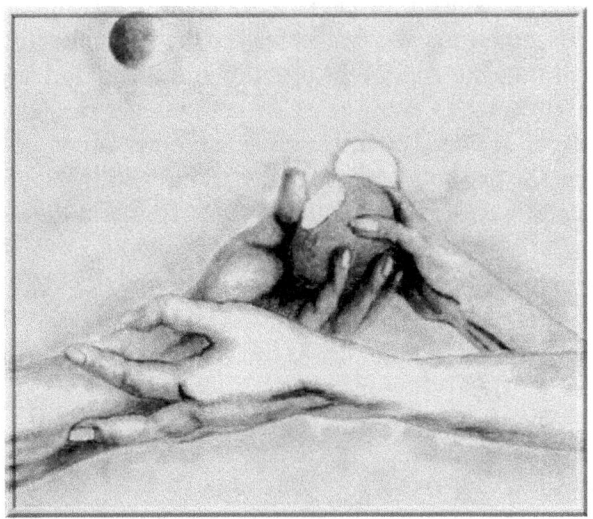

The end of innocence; the beginning of "days."

This image, then, which is nothing less than an allegory for the promise
of "days" given to Adam and his descendants by God Himself, constitutes
the answer to the question posed by anyone who seeks to penetrate the mystery of "the fly of evil" in the otherwise perfect ointment of creation. Because
springing from the mind of God Who knew in creating divinely-constituted
beings like ourselves, the one thing He could not create — as a function of the
God-like spark of free will — was both innocence *and* maturity at the same
time in those created beings *from the start*. The only way to know what it
means to be truly human, to be our "selves" in every sense of that word, as
opposed to the Great Other Who created us, we must first experience, in our
own finiteness, the duality of God's Universe. But in order to do that — and
herein lies the rub — one cannot remain blissfully innocent forever. In other words, without being "cast out" of the womb of Eden, we would never
have known darkness, sadness, or pain, but ironically, without knowing
any of these things, we would never be able to realize our full potential as
individuals made in the image of God. Because without knowing darkness,
we could never appreciate light; without knowing sadness, we could never experience happiness; without knowing pain, we could never embrace
pleasure. Simply put, to go through life without experiencing such dualities
would be like never living at all.

Therefore, armed with this awareness of what God knew, even before we did, the significant thing to realize about the Fall — illustrated by the Fruit against the backdrop of the Sun, from which we derive our experience of time — is that two concomitant events are being represented here and not just one. In this superimposed image, we see the beginning of not only humanity's fallen state but also God's unfolding drama of redemptive history so that we might come to know what we could never have known had we remained forever in Eden. What we have is the beginning not only of our own mortality — with all its potential for darkness, sadness, and pain — but also the days and weeks and years that were to count off the ages-long procession of God's set times that eventually culminated in our redemption obtained at Calvary — and with it, the ultimate attainment of light, happiness, and pleasure.

It was the end of innocence; it was the beginning of "days."

THIS CONCLUDES *The Book of Days: In Search of the 5,500-year Prophecy Given to Adam About the Coming of Christ*. To read further, please refer to the companion text, entitled *The Book of Tales: Stories That Confirm the 5,500-year Prophecy Given to Adam About the Coming of Christ*.

For those of you who are so inclined, it would be greatly appreciated if you could post a positive review of this book on such websites as Amazon Books so that others might become aware of its valuable contents. Because this book was not published by a conglomerate-style publishing house, we rely more heavily on word-of-mouth to advertise its importance to others who, like yourself, are searching for books like this. Thank you for your support.

THE CREDITS

*If this present work has anything to add in the way
of enlightening the world, it is only because I have
been afforded the tremendous honor to "stand
upon the shoulders of giants."*

W. Kent Smith, *The Book of Days*

Selected Biographies

WITHOUT THE groundbreaking work of an intrepid band of discoverers, translators, and scholars, this book would never have been possible. For that reason, the following group must be acknowledged for their achievements, without whose contributions this planet would be a much sadder and bleaker place. Therefore, if this present work has anything to add in the way of enriching, enlightening, or educating the world, it is only because I have been afforded the rare and tremendous honor to, for a moment in time, "stand upon the shoulders of giants."

The Discoverers

Johann Grynaeus (1540-1617) was a Swiss Protestant divine, professor of *The New Testament*, and collector of biblical manuscripts. For more than twenty-five years, Grynaeus exerted tremendous influence on both church and state affairs, acquiring quite a reputation as a skillful theologian of the school of Huldrych Zwingli. His many works include commentaries on various books of *The Old Testament* and *The New Testament* as well as an exhaustive collection of patristic literature entitled *Orthodoxographa* (1569), from which we get the present-day version of *The Gospel of Nicodemus*.

Giuseppe Assemani (1687-1768) was a Lebanese Orientalist and Vatican librarian. Serving as a scribe of Oriental manuscripts, Assemani was sent, in 1715, to Egypt and Syria in search of valuable parchments. Two years later, he returned with one hundred and fifty choice documents, which then became part of the Vatican Library. This success eventually induced Pope Clement XII to send him east again, some twenty years later, and this time Assemani returned with a collection that was even more ancient and more valuable than his first trip. It was among this cache of manuscripts that he discovered a work attributed to Ephrem the Syrian, entitled *The Cave of Treasures: The Book of the Succession of the Generations* (c. 350), which later scholars determined bore an uncanny similarity to *The First Book of Adam and Eve*.

James Bruce (1730-1794) was a Scottish explorer and travel writer. Having spent more than a dozen years in North Africa and Ethiopia, Bruce, among other things, traced the origins of the Blue Nile. An examination of Oriental manuscripts at an early age led him to the study of Arabic and Geez, and eventually would determine his future career. Apart from his travels up the Nile River, Bruce also brought back a collection of rare Ethiopian manuscripts, which, according to British historian Edward Ullendorff, "opened up new vistas for the study of Ethiopian languages and placed this branch of Oriental scholarship on a much more secure basis."[278] Among this collection of at least twenty-six manuscripts were the Ethiopic versions of *The First Book of Enoch*, *The Book of Jubilees*, and *The First Book* and *Second Book of Adam and Eve*.

E.A. Wallis Budge (1857-1934) was a British Egyptologist, Orientalist, philologist, and author. Working for the British Museum, Budge made numerous trips to Egypt and the Sudan, where he was able to procure a great many objects of antiquity, which in turn helped to build up the museum's collection of cuneiform tablets, manuscripts, and papyri. His various publications on Egyptology helped bring a knowledge of these discoveries to a much larger audience. In 1920 he was knighted for his services to Egyptology and the British Museum. Perhaps his best-known work, which also incorporated his skills as a translator, was *The Egyptian Book of the Dead* (1895), while one of his lesser-known, though no less significant, was his translation of *The Book of the Cave of Treasures* (1927).

The Translators

William Wake (1657-1737) was a British clergyman, dean at Exeter, bishop at Lincoln, and archbishop of Canterbury. According to biographer Joseph Hirst Lipton, Wake was said to be "a man of wide reading, immense industry, and liberal and tolerant spirit."[279] Of his numerous writings, his most important work was an anthology entitled *The Genuine Epistles of the Apostolic Fathers* (1693), which includes the first English translation of *The Gospel of Nicodemus*.

Richard Laurence (1760-1838) was a British Hebraist and Anglican churchman. He was made regius professor of Hebrew and canon of Christ Church at Oxford, in 1814, and archbishop of Cashel, Ireland, in 1822. According to biographer Gordon Goodwin, Laurence's "writings are a model of exactness and judicious moderation. His erudition is well illustrated by the three volumes in which he printed, with Latin and English translations, Ethiopic versions of apocryphal books of *The Bible*, which include *The First Book of Enoch* (1821) from the manuscript Scottish explorer James Bruce brought from Abyssinia and presented to the Bodleian Library."[280]

Moses Samuel (1795-1860) was a British author and translator of Hebrew works. According to *The Jewish Encyclopedia*, Samuel "acquired a consid-

278 *James Bruce*, Edward Ullendorff, p. 133
279 *Dictionary of National Biography*, Joseph Hirst Lipton, 1885-1900, Volume 58
280 *Dictionary of National Biography*, Gordon Goodwin, 1885-1900, Volume 32

erable reputation as a Hebrew scholar and an authority on rabbinical literature."[281] From an early age, Samuel had a talent for mathematics and languages, speaking twelve languages in all. He is best known for having been the originally anonymous translator of a 1625 Hebrew edition of *The Book of Jasher* (1838) into English, printed in Venice, after becoming convinced by the core of the work that it was the same book referenced in Scripture.

S.C. Malan (1812-1894) was a British biblical scholar and linguist of Oriental languages. Malan was greatly occupied with theological controversy, and published some of his most valuable work illustrative of the Christian East, especially translations from the Syriac, Coptic, Ethiopic, Armenian, and Georgian literatures. According to biographer Cecil Bendall, "In practical knowledge of Oriental languages, Malan had no equal in England, and probably none in the world."[282] Among his more than fifty publications was his English translation of the Ethiopic works of *The First Book* and *Second Book of Adam and Eve* (1882).

William Wright (1830-1889) was a British Orientalist and professor of Arabic at Cambridge. He early developed a fondness for Oriental languages, devoting his main efforts to Syriac, but also acquiring a knowledge of all the Semitic languages together with Sanskrit. Many of Wright's works on Syriac literature are still in print and of considerable scholarly value. As a result of his extensive scholarship, he produced such works as *Contributions to the Apocryphal Literature of The New Testament* (1865), from which we have the first English translation of *The Letters of Herod and Pila*te.

B. Harris Cowper (1822-1904) was a British archeologist, historian, and translator. As an archeologist, Cowper is credited with having discovered Loughton Camp, an Iron Age hill fort in England, dating from around 500 B.C. As a translator, his work appears in *Apocryphal Gospels and Other Documents relating to the History of Christ* (1865), which gave us English versions of *The Epistles of Pilate to Tiberius Caesar*, *The Trial and Condemnation of Pilate*, and *The Death of Pilate, who Condemned Jesus*.

W.R. Morfill (1834-1909) was a British professor of Slavonic languages at Oxford. He also became curator of the Taylor Institution and was appointed a Fellow of the British Academy in 1903. Writing in his obituary, Sir James Murray said, "We lose in him a unique scholar, whose knowledge of the Slavonic languages was greater than that of any other Englishman, so far as I know." Besides Morfill's various books on Slavonic grammar, he provided,

281 *The Jewish Encyclopedia: Samson-Talmid Hakam*, Isidore Singer, Cyrus Adler (Editors), Funk and Wagnalls, 1860, p. 24

282 *Dictionary of National Biography*, Cecil Bendall, 1901 Supplement

at the behest of R.H. Charles, the English translation of *The Secrets of Enoch* (1896), sometimes designated *The Slavonic Enoch* or *The Second Book of Enoch*.

R.H. Charles (1855-1931) was an Irish biblical scholar and theologian. He gained a Doctor of Divinity and was professor of biblical Greek at Trinity College. Charles is known particularly for English translations of apocryphal and pseudepigraphal works, which includes both *The Book of Jubilees* (1895) and *The Testaments of the Twelve Patriarchs* (1908).

The Scholars

Theophilus of Antioch (c. 120-181) was a Syrian theologian, apologist, author, and chronologist. The seventh bishop of Antioch, Theophilus was a prolific writer whom Eusebius, Jerome, Lactantius, and others mention in reference to his numerous works against the prevailing heresies of the time, of which only his three-volume *Defense of Christianity* (c. 175) survives to this day. Cited as the founder of the science of biblical chronology, he calculated the period from Adam to Christ at about 5,500 years, using a dating system derived from *The Septuagint*.

Julius Africanus (c. 160-240) was a Libyan historian and traveler. He is important primarily because of his influence on Eusebius, all the later writers of biblical history among the Church Fathers, and the entire Greek school of Christian chronologists. He wrote a history of the world entitled *Chronographia* (c. 222) in which he calculated the period from Creation to Christ as 5,500 years. This reckoning of time led to numerous creation eras being used in the Greek Eastern Mediterranean that placed Creation within one decade of 5,500 B.C. Although his history is no longer extant, copious extracts from it can found in the works of Eusebius, Georgius Syncellus, Georgius Cedrenus, and others.

Hippolytus of Rome (c. 170-235) was a Greek theologian, apologist, and chronologist. Hippolytus' voluminous writings embrace the spheres of exegesis, homiletics, apologetics, polemics, and chronography. As an important figure in the development in Christian eschatology, his *Commentary on the Prophet Daniel* is the oldest extant treatise on Scripture. In it, Hippolytus stated that, based on an interpretation on Moses' construction of The Ark of the Covenant it could be determined that the Christ was predicted to arrive on the Earth 5,500 years after the Fall of Adam.

Ephrem the Syrian (c. 306-373) was a theologian, deacon, and hymn writer. His works are hailed by Christians throughout the world, and many denominations venerate him as a saint. Ephrem has been declared a Doctor of the Church by Roman Catholics and is especially beloved in the Syriac

Orthodox Church. His hymns, poems, sermons in verse, and prose biblical exegesis were works of practical theology for the edification of a church in troubled times. He is considered the most significant Church Father of the Syriac tradition.

Giambattista Vico (1668-1744) was an Italian historian, political philosopher, and apologist of classical antiquity. Recognized as one of the greatest Enlightenment thinkers, Vico famously criticized the development of modern rationalism. Best known for his *magnum opus* entitled *New Science* (1725), he is generally regarded as the father of social science, having inaugurated the modern school of the philosophy of history.

George Smith (1800-1868) was a British historian, theologian, and author. According to biographer William Prideaux Courtney: "All his life he was a diligent student, and he was famed throughout Cornwall for his powers in speaking and lecturing. In 1823 he became a local preacher among the Wesleyan Methodists, and for many years before his death was one of the leading laypersons in that society."[283] A member of the Royal Asiatic Society, the Society of Antiquaries of London, and the Royal Society of Literature, he wrote, among other titles, *An Attempt to Ascertain the True Chronology of the Book of Genesis* (1842) and *The Patriarchal Age* (1854).

Joseph A. Seiss (1823-1904) was an American theologian, Lutheran minister, and author. Among his more than one hundred published works, perhaps his best-known are *The Great Pyramid of Egypt: Miracle in Stone* (1877) and *The Gospel in the Stars* (1882). In addition to pyramidology, Seiss was a Christian dispensationalist, a nineteenth-century millennialist school of thought, which viewed history as a series of covenants with God and which became the basis for beliefs widely held by contemporary evangelical Christians.

E.W. Bullinger (1837-1913) was a British clergyman and theologian. Educated at King's College, London, he was a recognized scholar in the field of biblical languages, and in 1881 the archbishop of Canterbury Archibald Tate granted him an honorary Doctor of Divinity in recognition of his scholarship. As an outspoken theologian, Bullinger's views were often unique and sometimes controversial. Among his numerous publications the most noteworthy are *The Witness of the Stars* (1893) and *Number in Scripture: Its Supernatural Design and Spiritual Significance* (1921).

Louis Ginzberg (1873-1953) was a Lithuanian professor of Judaism, a Talmudist, and a leading figure in conservative Judaism. As a result of his

---

283 *Dictionary of National Biography*, William Prideaux Courtney, 1885-1900, Volume 53

impressive scholarship in Jewish studies, Ginzberg was one of sixty scholars honored with a doctorate by Harvard University. The author of a number of scholarly works, he is probably best known for his four volume work, *The Legends of the Jews* (1913), which is an original synthesis of classical rabbinical, apocryphal, pseudepigraphal, and early Christian literature.

Edgar J. Goodspeed (1871-1962) was an American theologian and scholar of Greek and *The New Testament*. For many years, Goodspeed taught at the University of Chicago, and is best remembered for his various modern translations of *The Bible*, such as *The Apocrypha: An American Translation* (1938), all of which stressed an emphasis on updating the archaic language of the original texts into the present-day vernacular English.

Cyrus H. Gordon (1908-2001), was an American biblical scholar and professor of ancient Near East culture and languages. Best known for his key role in the decipherment of Ugaritic, an ancient Semitic language of fourteenth-century B.C., Gordon's contribution has been called "the greatest literary discovery from antiquity since the deciphering of hieroglyphics and cuneiform."[284] With his textbooks in hand, later scholars have since been able to penetrate the meaning of numerous biblical Hebrew texts and discover striking parallels between the culture of ancient Israel and its neighbors. Prior to Gordon's pioneering work of synthesizing biblical and ancient Near East studies, most scholarship assumed that early civilizations such as Israel and Greece existed as entirely segregated entities, but that basic assumption completely changed with Gordon's publication of *The Common Background of Greek and Hebrew Civilizations* (1965), which boldly challenged the prevailing theories of the day.

---

284 *The Ancient Near East*, Cyrus H. Gordon, p. 99

Source Material

THE FOLLOWING titles represent a list of the various sources from which this present work is derived. They include written sources as well as audio and visual ones; while written sources range from the apocryphal to the scholarly and the Internet, audio visual sources range from art to film.

Apocryphal

The First Book of Adam and Eve, also called *The Conflict of Adam and Eve with Satan*, and *The Second Book of Adam and Eve*, translated by S.C. Malan, 1882

The Book of Enoch, also called *The First Book of Enoch*, translated by Richard Laurence, 1821

The Secrets of Enoch, also called *The Slavonic Enoch* or *The Second Book of Enoch*, translated by W.R. Morfill, 1896

The Book of Jasher, also called *The Book of the Upright*, translated by Moses Samuel, 1838

The Book of Jubilees and *The Testaments of the Twelve Patriarchs*, translated by R.H. Charles, 1895 and 1908, respectively

The Gospel of Nicodemus, formerly called *The Acts of Pontius Pilate*, translated by William Wake, 1693

The Letters of Herod and Pilate, translated by William Wright, 1865

The Epistles of Pilate to Tiberius Caesar, The Trial and Condemnation of Pilate, and *The Death of Pilate, who Condemned Jesus*, translated by B. Harris Cowper, 1867

Art

The Expulsion of Adam and Eve from Paradise, Benjamin West, 1791

Scholarly

New Science, Giambattista Vico, 1725

The Common Background of Greek and Hebrew Civilizations, Cyrus H. Gordon; W.W. Norton and Company, Inc., 1965

Edgar Johnson Goodspeed: Articulate Scholar, James I. Cook; Scholars Press, 1981

The Apocrypha: An American Translation, Edgar J. Goodspeed; The University of Chicago, 1938

The Criswell Study Bible, W.A. Criswell (Editor); Criswell Center for Biblical Studies, 1979

The Apocrypha and Pseudepigrapha of The Old Testament, Volume 2, R.H. Charles; Clarendon Press, 1913

A Dissertation on Sacred Chronology, Nathan Rouse; Longman, Brown, Green and Longmans, 1856

Dictionary of the Middle Ages, Volume 1: Aachen to Augustinism, Stephen A. Barney (Contributor), Joseph R. Strayer (Editor); Charles Scribner's Sons, 1982

The Epistle to Can Grande, Dante Alighieri, 1319

Icons of the Middle Ages: Rulers, Writers, Rebels, and Saints: Volume 1, Elizabeth K. Haller (Contributor), Lister M. Matheson (Editor); Greenwood Publishing, 2012

Spiritual Gems: The Mystical Koran Commentary, Jafar al-Sadiq; Louisville: Fons Vitae, 2011

The Legends of the Jews, Volume 2, From Joseph to the Exodus, Louis Ginzberg; The Jewish Publication Society of America, 1913

The Witness of the Stars, E.W. Bullinger; Kregel Publications, 1893

Profiles of the Future, Arthur C. Clarke; Bantam Books, Inc., 1961

Screening Out the Past: The Birth of Mass Culture and the Motion Picture Industry, Lary May; The University of Chicago Press Books, 1983

Seventy Years at the Movies: From Silent Films to Today's Screen Hits, David Robinson (Consulting Editor); Crescent Books, 1988

The Many Faces of Christ: The Thousand-Year Story of the Survival and Influence of the Lost Gospels, Philip Jenkins; Basic Books, 2015

The Making of the English New Testament, Edgar J. Goodspeed; The University of Chicago Press, 1925

Romantic Quest and Modern Query: A History of the Modern Theater, Tom F. Driver; Delacorte Press, 1970

The Ancient Near East, Cyrus H. Gordon; W.W. Norton and Company, Inc., 1965

Cast of Characters

A

Abel. *See* Adam and Eve, children of
Abraham 23, 37, 38, 105, 161
  Abram 104
  father of faith 34
  father of many nations 105
    father of faith 105
  great-great-grandson of Reu 36
  type of God 34
Abraham Lincoln 12, 167
Abraham, sons of 34–36, 38–40
  Isaac 34–36, 38–40, 161
    son of Abraham and Sarah 34
      faithful son of Abraham 39
    son of faith 34
    type of Christ 34, 35, 37, 39, 47
  Ishmael 36
Absalom 89
Adam i, 1, 8, 9, 24, 25, 27, 28, 30, 32, 50,
  55, 57, 66, 92, 97, 101, 129, 134,
  136, 145, 158, 164, 167, 176, 186,
  192
  father of mankind 89, 90, 108, 128, 177
  father of Seth 66, 82
  father of the *Nephilim* 90
  husband of Eve 92
  type of Christ 91
Adam and Eve, children of 66, 82, 92, 162
  Abel 92, 188, 189
    brother of Seth 92
    twin brother of Aklia 162
  Aklia, twin sister of Abel 162
  Cain 92
    brother of Seth 92
    slayer of Abel 92
    twin brother of Luluwa 162
  Luluwa, twin sister of Cain 162
  Seth 66, 92, 112
    brother of Cain and Abel 92

father of Enos 97
  grandfather of Cainan 97
  great-grandfather of Mahalaleel 97
  third son of Adam 66, 82, 91, 96, 114
  type of Christ 92
Adam Rutherford 58, 70, 73, 74, 76, 101,
  102, 104, 110, 112, 129, 137, 138
  British biblical chronologist 57, 107, 111
  pyramidologist 73, 136
Adolf Hitler 149–155
  Supreme Commander of the Nazis 157
  Supreme Leader of the Holy Roman
    Empire 153
  ultimate would-be world conqueror 155
Agatha Christie 142
Alaric the Bold 148
Amos 159
Annas 28, 32, 66, 100, 103, 114, 116
  chief priest at Jerusalem 66, 114–116
Ann Nyland 82
Anti-Christ, substance of Nimrod 155
Archibald Tate, archbishop of Canterbury
  201
Arthur C. Clarke, English physicist and sci-
  ence fiction writer 166, 167
Arthur C. Custance 110
Asahel 89
Attila the Hun 148
August Dillmann, 19th-century German
  Orientalist 122

B

Barakiel, father of Dinah the wife of Maha-
  laleel 91
Benjamin. *See* Jacob, sons of
B. Harris Cowper 15, 199
  British archeologist 15, 199
  historian 15, 199

205

H

Z

About the Author

SINCE 1976, W. KENT SMITH has been an avid student of all things *Bible*, when he began at the tender age of sixteen to read every book on the subject in his father's private collection. By age nineteen, having digested the works of William Barclay, Werner Keller, and C.S. Lewis, Kent embarked upon a lifelong effort that provided the foundation for everything that followed—a biblical timeline that chronicles the history of God's dealing with mankind. As a result of this endeavor, Kent came to the realization that the traditional view of biblical history was fraught with contradictions and inconsistencies, and so required a radically original approach to reconcile such discrepancies.

Then, sometime during the mid-1980s, he was introduced to a body of ancient wisdom literature that unexpectedly steered him in a new direction that provided him with the missing pieces of a puzzle that is nothing less than the epic tale of God's control throughout the long ages of history. This wisdom literature—parabiblical literature, to be more precise—is known as *pseudepigraphal* literature, often called apocryphal literature. As it turned out, this fresh literary infusion opened up a brand-new chapter of biblical history for Kent, and more importantly, provided him with the framework for this very work, *The Book of Days: In Search of the 5,500-year Prophecy Given to Adam About the Coming of Christ*.

Kent lives in West Covina, California, an eastern suburb of Los Angeles. He can be contacted at wkent@loststorieschannel.com or lodestarcinema@msn.com.